THE

REYKJAVIK
CONFESSIONS

THE
REYKJAVIK
CONFESSIONS

The Incredible True Story
of Iceland's Most Notorious
Murder Case

SIMON COX

1 3 5 7 9 10 8 6 4 2

BBC Books, an imprint of Ebury Publishing
20 Vauxhall Bridge Road,
London SW1V 2SA

BBC Books is part of the Penguin Random House group
of companies whose addresses can be found at
global.penguinrandomhouse.com

First published by BBC Books in 2018

www.penguin.co.uk

A CIP catalogue record for this book is available from the
British Library

ISBN 9781785942884

Printed and bound in Great Britain by Clays Ltd, St Ives PLC

Penguin Random House is committed to a sustainable future
for our business, our readers and our planet. This book is
made from Forest Stewardship Council® certified paper.

Front and back cover images are used with the kind
permission of the National Archives of Iceland.

For Jo, Luli and Biba

Author's note

From the moment I came across this case, it struck me as one of the highest public interest, exposing as it does the many failings of the Icelandic justice system. In order to write this book I interviewed many people, including some of the key players in the story. I also contacted all of the main investigators who were involved in the case and conducted extensive research on the material that had been revealed through the two official enquiries into the case. These enquiries and the interview testimonies showed repeated mistreatment of the suspects during their time in Sidumuli. Despite repeated attempts to speak to the investigators involved in the case, they did not want to talk generally about the case, nor did they answer specific allegations that had emerged from the official reports and interview testimonies about how the suspects had been treated while they were held in Sidumuli prison.

Dramatis Personae

The victims

Gudmundur Einarsson. The 18-year-old went missing in January 1974 after leaving a nightclub in Hafnarfjordur. He was assumed to have been killed. His body has never been found.

Geirfinnur Einarsson. The 32-year-old disappeared after going to a meeting at a café in Keflavik in November 1974. He was assumed to have been killed. His body has never been found.

The suspects

Saevar Marino Cieselski. The first suspect to be arrested and supposed ringleader of the gang. He spent 741 days in solitary confinement and was questioned at least 180 times. He was sentenced to 17 years in prison for the murders of Gudmundur Einarsson and Geirfinnur Einarsson. He died in 2011.

Erla Bolladottir. Saevar's girlfriend. She spent 241 days in solitary confinement and was questioned at least 105 times. She was sentenced to 3 years in prison for making false accusations and obstructing the investigation.

Kristjan Vidar Vidarsson. Childhood friend of Saevar's. He was questioned over 160 times and spent 682 days in solitary confinement. He was found guilty of the murders of Gudmundur and Geirfinnur Einarsson and jailed for 16 years.

Gudjon Skarphedinsson. Saevar's former teacher who tried to import drugs into Iceland with him. He spent 412 days in solitary confinement and was questioned at least 75 times. He was jailed for 10 years for the murder of Geirfinnur Einarsson.

Tryggvi Runar Leifsson. Teenage friend of Kristjan and Saevar. He spent 627 days in solitary confinement and was questioned at least 95 times. He was jailed for 13 years for the murder of Gudmundur Einarsson. He died in 2009.

Albert Klahn Skaftason. Childhood friend of Saevar. He was in solitary confinement for 88 days and questioned 26 times. He was convicted of obstructing the investigation into Gudmundur Einarsson and jailed for 12 months.

Magnus Leopoldsson. Manager of Klubburin. Arrested in January 1976 over the murder of Geirfinnur Einarsson and held for 105 days in solitary confinement before being released without charge.

Einar Bollason. Erla's half brother. Arrested in January 1976 over the murder of Geirfinnur Einarsson and held for 105 days in solitary confinement before being released without charge.

Valdimar Olsen. Friend of Erla's half brother Einar. Arrested in January 1976 over the murder of Geirfinnur Einarsson and held for 105 days before being released without charge.

Sigurbjorn Eriksson. Owner of Klubburin. Arrested in February 1976 over the murder of Geirfinnur Einarsson and held for 90 days before being released without charge.

The investigators

Njordur Snaeholm. Veteran detective who investigated the disappearance of Gudmundur Einarsson in Hafnarfjordur in January 1974.

Valtyr Sigurdsson. A magistrate who investigated the disappearance of Geirfinnur Einarsson from November 1974 until June 1975.

Haukur Gudmundsson. A detective who investigated the disappearance of Geirfinnur Einarsson from November 1974 until June 1975.

Orn Hoskuldsson. The Reykjavik magistrate who investigated the murders of Gudmundur and Geirfinnur Einarsson in 1975 until 1977.

Karl Schutz. A German detective hired by the Icelandic government in July 1976 until January 1977 to help solve the murder of Geirfinnur Einarsson.

Sigurbjorn Eggertsson. Detective who investigated the murders of Gudmundur and Geirfinnur Einarsson.

Eggert Bjarnasson. Detective who investigated the murders of Gudmundur and Geirfinnur Einarsson.

Gretar Saemundsson. Detective who investigated the murders of Gudmundur and Geirfinnur Einarsson.

Gisli Gudmundsson. Detective who investigated the murders of Gudmundur and Geirfinnur Einarsson.

Hallvardur Einvardsson. Deputy prosecutor who prepared the cases to bring to court.

Gunnlaugur Briem. Judge who investigated and passed judgement on the cases in 1977.

Gisli Gudjonsson. Former detective who became renowned forensic psychologist.

At the prison

Gunnar Gudmundsson. Chief prison warden at Sidumuli jail.

Hlynur Thor Magnussson. Warden who worked at Sidumuli jail and befriended Erla Bolladottir.

Gudmundur Gudbjarnarson. Warden who worked at Sidumuli jail.

Rev Jon Bjarman. Prison chaplain who regularly visited the suspects in Sidumuli jail.

Introduction

A dark Arctic wind howled along Skolavordustigur, funnelling the icy cold of the Atlantic in an unrelenting wave, until at the Hegningarhusid – Reykjavik's old prison – it met an immovable force. The squat, black basalt building had withstood the buffeting of Iceland's harsh tundra climate for over a century. The jail normally housed a mixture of drunkards and petty thieves but in one part, isolated from the others, was a special prisoner: Iceland's most notorious female inmate.

Erla Bolladottir didn't look scary or dangerous. She was a 20-year-old elfin figure, her big rimmed glasses framing her deep brown eyes and hair, which was burnt orange in colour. Erla sat in the interrogation room at the back of the jail. Occasionally voices would float up from the prisoners below, having a smoke and stretching their legs in the tiny black asphalt yard, but there was little to distract her in the stark and functional white room, with its few hard chairs and barred window. The room was dominated by the big wooden desk, its fine grain stained black with smoke and grime and the occasional light circle left by a scalding cup. Erla had created many of these rings, with the coffee and cigarettes she had been living on during her time in isolation.

Sitting across from her was the detective she thought of as a friend, Sigurbjorn Eggertsson – a young inexperienced cop, he had been assigned to befriend Erla and extract information from her. He was part of the biggest police task force Iceland had ever assembled, charged with cracking a complex murder case that the country's small, fledgling force was struggling to solve.

Erla had been arrested in May as the summer was approaching, a time of long white nights when the azure blue skies only dim. That was months ago, and she had lost count of the number of times she had been brought in for interviews – again and again, for hours on end, facing the same set of interrogators. Time started to become fuzzy, blurred around the edges, which was not helped when the perpetual nighttime of Iceland's winter began to descend. She hadn't been charged with any crime but every 30 days, the big, imposing investigating magistrate, Orn Hoskuldsson, would extend her detention by another month. For five months she had been held in solitary confinement, alone in a tiny cell with a bed, a desk and a stool bolted to the floor. Hazy light came in through the windows at the top of the cell.

Erla was not allowed any communication with family and friends; the detectives and prison wardens were her only human contact. Their incessant and interminable interviews became her sole connection with the outside world. For Erla, 'These were the only people I ever spoke to. A lot of the time they were very friendly and I was in such a desperate need for human contact they were never the monsters – just guys I knew well.'

On this particular day, as Erla sat in the stale smoke-filled air, Sigurbjorn sat forward, a smile softening his features. 'We are close to finishing the case and you will soon be released,' he told her. This was what she had been waiting to hear; finally she could be reunited with her baby daughter, Julia, who she had not seen for months. There were just a few things to clear up first. All he needed was for Erla to tell him how she had helped dispose of the body.

The police believed that on a freezing November night, when the temperature dipped down to minus 7 degrees, Erla had driven this body out of Reykjavik to the Raudholar, the red lava landscape the colour of dried blood. Formed five thousand years ago, the area was a network of red volcanic hills and deep craters filled with dark, icy water. The police thought Erla had watched her accomplices put the body in a shallow grave, pour petrol on it and burn it.

Sigurbjorn leaned back in his chair, watching this sink in and gauging Erla's reaction. Erla felt trapped, she couldn't understand how a man she thought understood her could actually believe that she was capable of such a callous act. She knew from her previous encounters with the detective running the investigation, Karl Schutz, that he couldn't decide if she was 'an innocent country girl or a hardened and devious criminal'. Her denials were of no use; the statement had been prepared for her. Erla was told if she signed it, 'your testimony is complete. Then there is nothing to keep you here'. She would be free to return to her baby.

Erla did as she was told but the police didn't keep their promise, she wasn't to be released. She flew into a rage, lashing out, throwing ashtrays, coffee cups, anything, until the police officers held her down.

Erla was returned to her tiny cell. She realised that no matter what she said, she would never be released. She tried to search back through her mind – but reality and fantasy had merged so she was no longer certain which of her memories were real. She needed to piece together how she had ended up here, in this hell that would never end.

PART 1

PART 1

1

27 January 1974

In the early hours of the morning, 18-year-old Gudmundur Einarsson stumbled out of the one nightclub in Hafnarfjordur into a taut, flinty gale that drove fat snow-flakes onto his long, wavy, dark hair. The weather was so bad even the town's taxi drivers had decided to call it a night, convinced they wouldn't get very far on the roads.

The club wasn't much to talk about – 'a crummy hill-billy place' was the glowing description from one regular – but nightlife was in short supply in Iceland. Party goers would drive long distances, sometimes hundreds of kilometres from Reykjavik, to a dance in the countryside, just to have a different experience.

The night had started out well for Gudmundur. First it was a party in the Reykjavik suburbs with his friend Gretar Haraldsson, who had known Gudmundur since they were seven years old. He remembered, 'He liked to fish, play football; he liked the Beatles and he liked to go bowling.' Gudmundur also liked mischief, stealing copper with his friends to melt it down, using the money to buy booze. Gudmundur and his friends would head into Reykjavik to watch bands or try and pick up girls at one of the nightclubs. When they were in town, Gretar said his friend would never be pushed around: 'He was a good fighter, he was strong, he would stand up for himself.'

On this night, Gudmundur was going further afield to Hafnarfjordur, a fishing town six miles outside of Reykjavik. The club was on the main street, across from the harbour, where the hulking fishing boats prepared to venture out into the turbulent Atlantic to harvest the cod and haddock that were the lifeblood of the town.

Gudmundur had a bottle of brandy to get through with his friends before hitting the club's sweaty mosh pit, filled with other drunken teenagers. One of the barmaids, Kristrun Steindorsdottir, had noticed how Gudmundur stood out. In his drunken haze, Gudmundur had been separated from his buddies, who were off chasing girls, but it didn't matter, he picked up another companion. The barmaid remembered later how Gudmundur's tall frame had to be supported by a shorter, older friend.

When the club closed, Gudmundur faced a three hour walk back to his home in Blesugrof, on the outskirts of Reykjavik. The safest way was along the long and winding Reykjavikvegur, while the more perilous route was across the lava fields of the Reykjanes peninsula. Only a crazy person or a young drunk one would dare to think of this. In the daytime you could spot the potential dangers in this sullen, blasted landscape of charcoal, grey and brown, but the snow had turned the lava fields into a soft cotton-wool pixie land, a place of beauty but also menace. Lurking beneath the snow were gaping fissures, big enough to swallow a man whole. Gudmundur and his companion thought they would chance their luck and thumb a lift home to escape the gnawing, raw wind that bit into their chafed hands.

Elinborg Rafnsdottir was driving through Hafnarfjordur with her friend Sigridur when she spotted Gudmundur.

Sigridur had a crush on the boy with deep set eyes and long dark hair, so Elinborg slowed down to offer him a lift. As she stopped, Gudmundur's companion threw himself onto the bonnet of her car. 'We got scared when we saw how drunk he was,' Elinborg later recalled, and so they decided to let the drunken boys find another way home. She drove on, leaving Gudmundur with his angry friend.

Several hours later, Gudmundur was seen again, this time alone, walking out of Hafnarfjordur on the main road to Reykjavik. He wasn't very steady on his feet and almost fell in front of a car, but once the driver saw he hadn't hurt the swaying young man, he left him on the road, dismissing him as another foolish drunk. As the snow fell thick and fast, turning the brightly painted roofs a soft white, silence fell on the town.

By Monday morning, Gudmundur hadn't returned home from his weekend revelry. His friends assumed he had hooked up with a girl but his father, Einar, knew something was wrong, so he reported his son missing. The case was assigned to Njordur Snaeholm, a veteran detective, and on 29 January the police and rescue organisation, the Life Saving Association mobilised an extensive search for the young man. His friends gathered at his family's house, one of a group on a stretch by the river, and Gudmundur's brother, Baldur organised 200 people into teams to scour the lava fields around Hafnarfjordur, while overhead a coast guard helicopter looked for any trace. Gudmundur's disappearance had become front-page news in the island's main newspaper, *Morgunbladid*.

Iceland's treacherous winter was doing the search teams no favours: 60cm of snow had fallen in the area in a few days and Arctic gusts had blown it into drifts, so in some places volunteers had to wade waist deep through the snow. The police thought Gudmundur may have tried to make it to a friend's house, so they asked for the teams to search in sheds and outhouses where he might have taken shelter. There were appeals for people to keep an eye out for the handsome teenager in a polka dot jacket, green pants and brown shoes.

For several days, his parents and three brothers waited anxiously for any news, but less than a week after he went missing, on 3 February, the search was wound down. His disappearance drew a phlegmatic response from Icelanders. In this volcanic, muscular land, people disappear all the time. Some are consumed by the dark, thrashing waves of the Atlantic while others perish falling from cliffs or, like Gudmundur, it was thought, are hidden somewhere deep in the lava.

There were no tearful, emotional appeals from his dad Einar or brother Baldur, indeed there was no public comment from his family at all. They were left to grieve in peace. It wasn't the practice of Icelandic journalists to intrude upon families who had suffered such a tragedy.

Gudmundur's body was never found; the most likely assumption was that he had been swallowed beneath the lava, forever in the long shadows, where the Huldufolk dwell, the mythical hidden elves of Icelandic folklore.

Erla Bolladottir would never forget the events of that long January night. She had reluctantly agreed to go into Reykjavik with her friend Hulda, to the throbbing excess of Klubburin, Iceland's prime nightspot. She had been spending a lot of time by herself lately and feeling very depressed, and hadn't felt up to socialising. Plus it wasn't really Erla's scene – way too straight, more disco than the hippy vibe she liked. At least there were three floors in the club, so when the pulsing beats became too much she could head up the spiral staircase to the banging rock floor at the top. There wasn't much choice; there were only a handful of nightclubs to cater for the young who were increasingly keen to kick back against the Lutheran shackles of their parents' generation. Erla drank a little but wasn't in the mood to party and succumb to the sweet, mellow aroma of hash wafting through the club. By the time she left, she had missed the last bus but managed to hitch a lift back to her apartment in Hafnarfjordur with some boys she knew.

As she walked up to her apartment at number 11 Hamarsbraut, Erla was enveloped by the thick, dark folds of night. It was still hours before the thinning of the darkness, signalling morning during this beginning of winter. The tiny apartment was pitch black. As her boyfriend, Saevar, had the only key Erla had to get in by crawling through the basement window of the laundry room. Exhausted she crashed out in bed.

Later she woke, hearing something outside her window. It took her a moment to figure out that it was men's voices, whispering in low, hushed tones. They sounded menacing and conspiratorial and Erla was alone in the apartment. Saevar was nowhere to be seen.

As she listened, not daring to breathe, she could hear that the men were checking whether she was awake or asleep. The apartment was so small that if these men could have reached in through the window they could almost touch Erla who was frozen with fear on her bed. She heard the group walk around to the front of the apartment, their footsteps cushioned by the generous carpet of snow that covered the town. The men seemed intent on getting inside, but why did they want to come into her home in the dead of night, when she was alone and vulnerable?

She recognised their voices, they were friends of Saevar's: Kristjan, Tryggvi and Albert. Saevar had warned her that he didn't want Erla ever to be alone with them.

Albert was laid back and harmless but Tryggvi and Kristjan could turn nasty when they were drunk. They were part of the petty crime scene in Reykjavik, making money from doing whatever manual jobs they could, so that they could buy booze or hash. They had appeared at the apartment a week before. Erla remembered, 'I was watching *The Late Late Show* and I turned and saw the three of them standing in the hall and I thought, "Why are they inside?"' Saevar had been annoyed; he didn't want them there, as, Erla said, 'If they got drunk they could make trouble.'

Here they were, back again and she knew that she didn't want them in her home.

Then she woke up, hot and confused, her hair slick with sweat. It was still dark and she sat up to listen to see if the men were still outside. There was no sound, just the numbing silence of winter. She realised it must have been a dream, purging her troubled thoughts of the day.

She felt marooned in Hafnarfjordur, hemmed in by the lava fields of the Reykjanes peninsula. She could guess where Saevar was, probably with another woman. He had cheated on her in the past and she was sure he was up to it again.

Last winter had been a rough time for her. Her Dad, Bolli, had suffered a stroke and was in rehabilitation in hospital. Much of the time she was alone in her little apartment. During the day she worked at the Icelandic Post and Telephone company and she would return home for interminable evenings with coal black star-filled skies.

She looked at the packet of Viceroy cigarettes next to her bed. She only had to reach across and light a cigarette and, as the smoke filled her lungs, it would calm her down. But she couldn't rouse herself, she thought, 'What difference does it make whether I smoke a cigarette or not?' A cigarette couldn't alter her miserable life. She would have to move though as she needed the toilet. It was hardly far, but she just didn't have the energy to do it. She could feel her bowels loosening, she knew she had to leave the bed but she had no will for this most basic human task. The bed would become her toilet. How had she ended up living like this, in a tiny flat with Saevar, her boyfriend who cheated on her, was never here and yet tried to control her life?

As the Douglas DC-8 banked, climbing through the clouds, away from Keflavik airport out across the swirling grey Atlantic, Erla sat back in her seat, excited. She was on a Loftleider flight, Iceland's self-proclaimed 'hippy airline', cheap, cheerful and taking her away from the, murky, bleak Icelandic winter for the crisp, winter skies of New York state. For the 18-year-old Erla, America offered freedom; a chance to escape from the conservative constraints of Iceland and enjoy the freewheeling counter-culture vibe.

It was December 1973, and Erla would have almost a month away in the country where she had spent the first seven years of her life. There was just one problem and he was sitting in the seat next to her: Saevar Cieselski. Erla was not a fan of the slight, cocky young man with his straight black hair and the dark complexion that made him stand out among the Icelandic Celts. She said later, 'He always had an air about him that he knew everything.' She had seen him around town when he would flash his winning smile. He had boasted that he knew about Erla and her family; so much so that she wondered if he was stalking her. The answer was far more straightforward. With a population then of just over 200,000, there are often only a few degrees of separation between people in Iceland. That was the case with Erla and Saevar, who had first met many years before.

Erla's brother Arthur had spent summers working at a farm owned by Saevar's grandparents. Arthur shared a room with the young Saevar and liked his manner. Erla remembered the sweet ten-year-old Saevar who didn't say much to Erla and her sisters when they visited the farm, but smiled a lot and took them to the barn where he showed them how to jump into the hay.

The sweet boy had grown into a troublesome teenager with a reputation for pilfering and petty drug dealing. He was sleeping with Erla's good friend, Hulda, and she was bemused: 'I couldn't understand her choice, I really didn't like him.' Erla was supposed to be making the trip to the United States with Hulda but when she pulled out at the last minute, Saevar took her place.

At least they wouldn't have to spend long together as the plan was for them to part as soon as they reached JFK airport in New York. Saevar was heading to his family in Massachusetts to sort out an inheritance from his estranged father, Michael, who had been killed in a car crash. Saevar had a complicated relationship with his father who'd believed in the old school parenting of 'my way or the belt'. And yet his death was a massive blow to Saevar who was adrift with no strong role model to draw him back.

As they chatted on the flight, cocooned alone above the clouds, miles above the real world, Saevar started to work his magic on her, persuading Erla to let him come and stay with her in Buffalo, New York where she was staying with friends.

Buffalo was a city dominated by steel and grain mills, the General Motors car factory and the football stadium where tens of thousands of people would gather in freezing conditions to watch the Buffalo Bills and their star running back OJ Simpson. To Erla, it was beautiful; a welcome respite from Iceland. She had a strong affection for America from her time there as a child when her dad worked as a manager for Icelandair at JFK and the family lived in Long Island. She had fond memories of days at the beach playing with her siblings.

Erla had missed the sprawling American suburbs with their wide, tree-lined streets, full of detached houses with clipped lawns and expansive back gardens. Saevar was not the ideal house guest, though; he had nightmares and would wake, shouting in his sleep. These were the dreams he never discussed with anyone, remnants from a dark chapter in his childhood. This disturbed Erla's friends and after a few days she decided his behaviour was too much to take. She dispatched her awkward travelling companion to his relatives in Massachusetts while she stayed on in Buffalo, soaking up opportunities she would never get in her provincial hometown.

Buffalo was on the touring circuit so the city's football stadium would often shake with a different roar, as mega bands like Led Zeppelin and Pink Floyd played there. There was also the chance to hang out with musicians, who Erla would never get to see in Iceland, like famous jazz pianist, Chick Corea, who she chatted to at a friend's college gig.

There was more fun to be had in Washington DC where she stayed with her friend, Steve, whose father was a professor in Icelandic literature. Steve had a mane of black curly hair and a penchant for high leather boots. Saevar had soon tired of his family in Massachusetts, though, and he called Erla every day until she agreed to let him stay with her. It was an early indication of his persistence and growing obsession with Erla.

The three of them would hang out at Georgetown University, lying on the grass smoking joints and planning how to change the world. Saevar never joined in with the smoking or drinking. He had started indulging at a young age; he was 9 years old when he gave up drinking, 16 when he stopped taking hard drugs like

LSD – the drug of choice in Iceland at this time, along with cannabis. For Erla, though, this was the life; she could happily stay here forever. She had hitch-hiked from Providence to Maine that summer and was already planning her next trip. America held endless possibilities.

When Steve threw a leaving party for Erla, it seemed like the whole neighbourhood turned up. It was the biggest party she had ever been to, there were people everywhere and the booze was flowing. Erla stuck to Coca-Cola, but after a while and a long, particularly dull chat with a Vietnam vet, she began to feel trippy, in a way she hadn't experienced before and didn't like. She had tried LSD and thought she might be having a flashback.

She needed to be alone, somewhere quiet. She made her way upstairs looking for a place to lie down and get herself together. She stumbled into an empty bedroom, pitch black except for a tiny red light in the corner. Fumbling her way towards the light, she tripped over Saevar. He was in a mess too, and suspected someone had slipped LSD into his drink. They lay down side by side, listening to Frank Zappa and Pink Floyd and talked for most of the night. 'We opened our hearts about everything,' Erla remembered, 'it was the most we ever talked, he told me everything.'

There was a lot to tell about Saevar's first 18 years. He had grown up in the east of Reykjavik, in one of the capital's poorer neighbourhoods. His dad, Michael, was an American who worked at the air base at Keflavik as a meteorologist. He had fallen for Sigurbjorg, a beautiful blonde Icelandic girl who was the opposite of the swarthy Polish-American.

The couple moved to America but it was short lived and they returned to Iceland several years later where Saevar was born. His sister, Anna, remembers a fun-loving, happy child who loved playing with his siblings and friends. As theirs was the only house on their street with a television there was a constant throng of children who would come to the Cieselskis' house to watch the TV and Saevar's father, Michael, would make popcorn and brownies. The Cieselski children would create home-made theatres and put on elaborate shows for their friends with costumes and magic tricks. But behind this happy front, there was a darkness. Saevar's father believed in firm punishment, that the best way to instil discipline was to use his belt, and he handed out this treatment to Saevar on a regular basis. It was a well-known secret among his friends who grew up alongside him in the narrow warren of streets and anodyne apartment blocks.

Away from the US base at Keflavik foreigners were a rarity – strange beings from other more exotic or scary worlds. Saevar's surname, Cieselski, a mixture of Jewish and Polish, stood out in the ethnically homogeneous Iceland of the 1960s. Combined with his short stature and slight build it made Saevar an easy target for bullies at school. He began to truant, and then found a protector – a big, beefy kid named Kristjan Vidar Vidarsson. This worried his older sister, Anna, who thought his friends were 'very intimidating and had a bad reputation among the other students'. Saevar also befriended Albert Klahn Skaftason, who was small, quiet and well-liked because he didn't cause trouble. The network of streets in east Reykjavik, crammed with pebble-dashed apartment blocks and houses clad in corrugated iron to protect from the never-ending wind, became their playground.

Sigurdor Stefansson, who grew up in the same neighbourhood and would later become a close friend of Saevar, said, 'There were very many young guys like them in that neighbourhood who were sort of alley cats – stealing from shops and so on.'

Michael had never truly settled in Iceland. After leaving the airbase at Keflavik he worked as an accountant at a supermarket but he couldn't speak Icelandic so remained an outsider. His drinking and temper got worse and, unable to cope any longer, Sigurbjorg decided they should split. With Saevar increasingly out of control, she turned to social services for help. Aged just 14, Saevar was sent away to Breidavik, a boarding school for 'troubled youngsters'.

Breidavik was out in the Westfjords, 300 miles and a day's drive from the capital. It was a sprawling residential school and farm, set in total isolation 28 miles from the nearest town. When the winter weather closed in it was totally cut off. The only company was the migrating birds who flocked to the dramatic Latrabjarg cliffs and the stunning beach with soft golden sand. The school's remoteness was a deliberate attempt to return its students to a simpler, rural lifestyle, intended to end their offending behaviour.

Breidavik had been opened by the government in the 1950s under pressure from people in Reykjavik to do something about the surge in anti-social behaviour amoung young boys who were under the age of 15 and so couldn't be prosecuted. The school was run as a family unit with a housemaster, cook and teacher to look after the seven or so boys who lived there. In the summer, the children helped on the farm, looking after the sheep and cows and preparing hay bales for the winter. The troubled young boys were expected to stay there for up to two years to curb their problem behaviour. It was seen as a huge success story with many boys sent there supposedly cured of their delinquency. When Saevar returned from Breidavik his family were pleased with his academic progress, as his school work had significantly improved.

Breidavik, however, had a dark secret: it was a brutal and horrific place where boys were sexually and physically abused by the staff and other pupils, far away from any prying eyes of family and friends. It would be many years and many scarred lives before this horrific abuse was exposed. Saevar never revealed the indignity and humiliation meted out by the sadistic teachers and older pupils to his family or friends.

Now, years later, Saevar was lying on the floor of a bedroom in America with Erla next to him and something felt different. In his altered, vulnerable state, Saevar opened up to Erla about the gruesome years he spent at Breidavik. It was during his time there that his brutal yet still beloved father was killed in a car crash. His pain and hurt was compounded when Saevar wasn't allowed to attend the funeral. Erla would never tell anyone exactly what Saevar revealed to her in that room ('He would turn in his grave'), but it's clear he was violently abused by the staff and older boys. As the bright moon melted into a watery sun, Erla began to warm to the difficult, vulnerable young man. They had 'bonded to the point I could never leave him after that, no matter how hard I tried'.

Saevar and Erla returned to Keflavik airport in time for Christmas 1973. It wasn't like other airports; it was a huge US naval airbase where fighter planes would be lined up in the hangars waiting to fly off to guard the Atlantic from Soviet warplanes. In the arrivals lounge, Erla's relatives were waiting to welcome her sister who was visiting from her home in Hawaii.

Erla and Saevar had a less pleasant reception party, lead by the pugnacious head of customs, Kristjan Petursson. A thick-set former policeman built like a rugby player, Petursson was fixated with Saevar. He had been looking for an opportunity to collar the cock-sure young man who he was certain was a key figure in the local drugs trade. Petursson believed drugs were swamping Iceland and had successfully lobbied the government to set up a special drugs court. Petursson's obsession wasn't shared by the small detective force in Reykjavik, though. Arnprudur Karlsdottir, a no-nonsense, chain smoking detective – and one of the first women to enter this macho world – thought Petursson was on a wild goose chase, and that he had 'an agenda to find drugs everywhere. It was very strange to me and we would talk a lot about it, why is he always after Saevar?' Petursson seemed convinced if he could get Saevar he would punch a hole in the growing market for cannabis and LSD. He would also make a name for himself.

At the airport, Petursson made sure Erla and Saevar faced the indignity of being strip searched, but while Erla was released, Saevar was taken away for further questioning. Back home, Erla called everywhere trying to find Saevar but he had been swallowed up by the criminal justice system. A week later she was at a party with friends when Saevar showed up. He took hold of her hand and said, 'Let's get out of here.' They went straight to her apartment and Saevar told her about his week in custody.

Petursson had accused Saevar of having a kilo of morphine stashed away somewhere in Reykjavik. He had been placed in solitary confinement in the basic facilities of Sidumuli prison. This was common practice in Iceland at the time, a way of making suspects more amenable during the interrogation. Saevar maintained his innocence, but this only served to further antagonise the customs chief and Saevar was knocked about a bit, to soften him up. After a week of getting nowhere, Saevar had been released. Although free from custody he was a marked man. The police were biding their time, waiting for the opportunity to catch him and take him off the streets for a long, long time.

Erla had been living with her dad, Bolli, in his apartment in Hafnarfjordur. There wasn't much to it, two interconnecting living/bedrooms, a bathroom and a laundry room. Erla asked her dad if Saevar could stay with them, which would mean Saevar sharing Erla's single bed. Her Dad agreed but had one condition, 'that Saevar needed to do some honest work and get a proper job'. Saevar did occasionally try to enter the world of normal work but it never lasted. He did a stint in the fishing trade out in the Westfjords, but he couldn't stick it. Saevar was not going to follow a conventional path.

In February 1974 Saevar was arrested again by Kristjan Petursson. Rather than taking him to the police station or prison, Petursson brought him to his home where he offered him a drink. He wanted Saevar to confess to the biggest jewellery robbery that had ever been committed in Iceland. Saevar said he knew nothing about it but Erla said he later told her, 'He was frustrated that someone else had gotten away with it. It was a crime he would have liked to get away with, he was always very curious who had done it.' When this soft approach didn't work Saevar was taken to Sidumuli for another stint in solitary confinement, this time for a month. Saevar got out of trouble by informing on his fellow small-time dealer and friend, Sigurbor Stefansson, who surprisingly stood by him. ('I told him I would never do any business with him but I would be his friend.')

In the 1970s Iceland was still a land of prohibition. There were only three government-run off licences in Reykjavik where you could get expensive spirits but no beer, which was banned, and remained illegal until 1989. This created the ideal environment for cheap smuggled booze and for petty criminals like Saevar to make some money.

Saevar had the gift of the gab and a charm that enabled him to enlist his friends in his criminal schemes. One of these involved exploiting a friend working at the docks where the legal alcohol was shipped in. Saevar would visit him for a chat to distract him so his friends Kristjan and Albert could steal whatever alcohol they could get their hands on. It was hardly a master criminal enterprise but it worked. Over several trips they built up a hoard of whisky, cognac and vodka. Erla was their 'fence' who would sell it to her co-workers at the Icelandic Post and Telephone company. As Friday approached, she became popular for being able to get alcohol to get the weekend started.

Saevar needed a longer term regular source of income, however, and he went for the other big vice in 1970s Iceland, drugs. Kristjan Vidar was always at his side; after all, it didn't hurt to have a well built, tall friend with a reputation for violence to look out for you. Saevar didn't fit in with the prevailing hippy vibe of the drug dealing community. 'He was a stranger when he came into the hash business,' his friend Sigurdor observed, 'and not many people liked him or Kristjan because they were from the other side, they were not hippies.'

Saevar's drug dealing meant leaving Erla alone for days whilst he went overseas to buy hashish. Erla was the only one working and bringing in a regular wage and by July 1974 she had had enough of her wayward boyfriend. Erla found out he was cheating on her. It was the final straw and she told him it was over, this time for good. Saevar could see she was serious and he lashed out, kicking her in the stomach with his steel toe-capped boots. The blow meant Erla couldn't walk properly for several days.

With Saevar out of her life, Erla had a new freedom. She headed to the Westmann islands for their annual music festival. There she met a new man. He was French and, unlike Saevar, he respected her. She could see a future without the chaos and instability of Saevar, but her time apart from him wasn't to last very long.

Erla's relationship with Saevar had created a rift with her family. In her early life she hadn't known her half brother Einar, but after her parents split she got to know him. She was in awe of the basketball legend and the two became close. But Einar couldn't stand Saevar and had persuaded her dad to sell the apartment in Hafnarfjordur, forcing Erla to move. With no one else to turn to, she had to ask Saevar to help her. He used his forceful charm to manoeuvre himself back into her life, promising her this time things would be different. He had developed in interest in filmmaking and he told her he would direct a film and transform their lives, but he needed money to finance his project. He had no intention of working to earn it, instead he came up with a scheme to steal it from Erla's employers, the Icelandic Post and Telephone company. It was this scam that would be his undoing.

Saevar and Erla had found a flaw in the system for wiring money. Erla used her insider knowledge of the post office codes to pretend they were wiring money from abroad and then Erla would go and collect it using a fake identity. On their first attempt they got away with almost half a million kronor, but for Erla it wasn't about cash: 'I never really thought about what I would do with the money. It was to piss off the system and show them they were stupid.' Although she had a false ID and forged a signature, Erla was nervous that as an employee of the phone and telegraph company she would be spotted.

In total they embezzled a million kronor – around $10,000 – a sizeable sum at the time, enough to put down a deposit on a house. Saevar wanted to pull off the perfect crime, one that couldn't be solved. It would be his way to get back at the authorities who he felt had bullied and harassed him since he was a child. Erla was also driven by a similar desire to hit back at the establishment: 'It was all about getting away with it and laughing at them, to get back at all of them. All who were stupid and mean and unjust and all these rich people were assholes. I was really angry.'

Saevar gave 300,000 kronor to his friend Vilhjalmur Knudsen who was a filmmaker, who in return let Saevar borrow his film equipment. That still left hundreds of thousands of kronor spare. Erla splashed out on a sporty white 1968 Mustang with green stripes down the sides. They weren't sure what else to do with the money. They couldn't suddenly buy a property as that would attract too much attention. There was nothing else they particularly desired, so they stashed it away in a wardrobe, raiding it when they needed money for food. Their only extravagance was a night in the upmarket Icelandair hotel complete with room service.

As the months rolled on, Saevar thought he had got away with the crime, that he had fooled the police. But Iceland is a small place and Saevar had a big mouth. The police were watching and listening waiting to make their move. Then, in November 1974, the police had a new case land on their desk, one which would dominate the work of the small detective force for years.

2

19 November 1974

Geirfinnur Einarsson lived an ordinary life but his name would be remembered for decades in Iceland. He lived in the industrial town of Keflavik, 30 miles from the capital. As well as being home to the sprawling US airbase, Keflavik is a port from where fishing boats set out to harvest cod from the cold waters of the Atlantic, processing them in the plants surrounding the harbour. Geirfinnur made his living doing manual labour and often had to work away from home, leaving his wife Gudni and young children, Sigridur and Anna Birgitta.

Geirfinnur was a man of simple pleasures and didn't go out much. His life revolved around work and his family and the occasional evening out with friends. On the evening of 19 November, he was planning to relax after a hard day at work by seeing a movie with a friend, Thordur Ingimarsson. But when Thordur arrived at the wide, grey, pebble-dashed house on Brekkubraut, his friend had some bad news, he had to cancel their evening out. Geirfinnur had been called to a meeting with some men in the Hafnarbudin, the simple cafe in Keflavik harbour where fishermen would gather for a smoke, a decent cup of coffee and bearable food. Thordur offered his friend a lift to his rendezvous.

It was a short drive through the quiet roads towards the Hafnarbudin, looking out over a jetty to the thrashing Atlantic Ocean. Geirfinnur told his friend about the strange nature of the meeting, that he had been asked to come alone and on foot. Geirfinnur was not his usual self; he seemed edgy, even suggesting he should be armed, which was so out of keeping with his friend's usual character that Thordur was sure he was joking – or at least he hoped he was. As they drove towards the harbour, Geirfinnur speculated that the meeting might be a hoax, a cheap joke played by one of his workmates. Thordur had no idea who his friend was meeting or why.

Sure enough, when Geirfinnur reached the cafe there was no mysterious person there to meet him. Gudlaug Jonssdottir had worked at the harbour cafe long enough to know her regulars and immediately recognised the quietly spoken and unassuming Geirfinnur, as he would often stop by late in the evening and buy some cigarettes. He did the same this night and, frustrated at what he thought was a prank, he returned home.

Shortly after walking in his front door, the phone rang at Geirfinnur's house. During the short conversation his wife overheard Geirfinnur clearly say, annoyed, 'I've already been there'. It sounded like the person Geirfinnur was supposed to meet at Hafnarbudin was summoning him back there. Although it was now after ten, he headed out once again, this time driving there himself in his red Ford Cortina. He parked it 200 metres from the cafe with the keys still in the ignition, traipsing across the muddy ground and the narrow road to the cafe, one of a group of sturdy low rise buildings facing out to sea.

When he hadn't returned home the next morning his wife, Gudni was in a panic. This was out of character for Geirfinnur and she phoned the police to check if there had been accidents reported overnight. A friend came over to keep Gudni company while she waited, but still

Geirfinnur failed to show up or phone her. A day later Geirfinnur's boss reported him missing.

Valtyr Sigurdsson was in his cramped office in Keflavik trying to get through the usual mountain of paperwork when detective Haukur Gudmundsson walked in and told him, 'Boss, we have a strange case.'

The two couldn't have looked more different; Haukur was every inch the bull-headed cop while Valtyr, with his long dark hair, suede jacket and white cheesecloth shirt, looked more like the manager of a rock band than an investigating magistrate. Valtyr had only been in the job for three years and was used to boring fare: thefts, drink driving or fines.

Valtyr was ambitious, though, and maybe this could be the case that would get him out of this backwater and into Reykjavik, where everything happened. He decided early on he wasn't going to rely on a pack of beagles roaming around the harbour and the lava fields. The Gudmundur Einarsson disappearance at the beginning of the year had been discussed a lot within police ranks. The force had been criticised for their decision to close down the investigation after less than a week, based on the assumption that Gudmundur had been lost in the carpet of lava.

Valtyr felt this new case was different: 'This was something special, I didn't know if it was criminal, just strange.'

He moved down to the Keflavik police station from his office, just him and two detectives – Haukur and another officer, John Hill – in an office not much bigger than a broom cupboard, with a sofa and a low desk. Valtyr told his small team, 'This time we will do some real investigating.'

A few days later, the first story appeared in the daily tabloid newspaper, *Visir*. There was a picture of the

Hafnarbudin cafe and another of Geirfinnur, looking like a fifties throwback with a fine quiff. Geirfinnur looked nothing like this now but it was better than nothing.

Valtyr thought the key to solving the case was to find the man who had phoned Geirfinnur and summoned him to his final meeting. They were convinced this call had been made from the Hafnarbudin just before Geirfinnur left his home. The police appealed for the man to come forward. They also had two important witnesses in the women who were in the cafe. The younger of the two, Elin Gretarsdottir, didn't remember much, but Gudlaug Jonssdottir had a much clearer recollection of the caller that the police were trying to trace. Valtyr said they were 'very different women, the young one was totally blank and the older one was the talk of the town, she couldn't close her mouth'.

Gudlaug remembered how a man came in ten minutes after Geirfinnur had left. When she asked if he wanted any help he seemed a bit agitated and replied that he was going to wait there. He asked if he could make a phone call. She didn't hear what he said, but he left the money for the call afterwards and headed out of the cafe.

She gave a clear description of him: slim about 1.80 metres tall with dark hair, wearing a fake leather jacket with a belt and light coloured pants. He smiled or grinned when he spoke. He seemed healthy; he wasn't a junkie or a drunk. Elin didn't get as good a view of him and her description of his face and hair was significantly different to Gudlaug's. Valtyr commissioned an artist to do a drawing of the man but the two women couldn't agree.

The team's inexperience in dealing with such cases started to show. They failed to check with the telephone company that the call from the cafe had indeed been to

Geirfinnur's house. By the time they thought of doing this, the information was no longer available. There is also an unwritten rule in a missing person investigation that the first suspect to be eliminated from the inquiry is the partner, who is also often the last person to see the missing person alive. It took Valtyr and Haukur a week to visit Geirfinnur's wife, Gudni, despite the fact she lived in a house opposite their office. They didn't interview her in their office but in her house. Gudni explained that it had been an odd evening. Geirfinnur had come home from work while she was washing up, rushing in asking what was wrong. 'Weren't you screaming? I heard a scream like you were being killed?' he asked. Neither the TV or radio was on in the apartment and when they both went and checked where this sound could have come from, they found nothing. Later he had gone out with his friend Thordur but was back 20 minutes later. He was hardly in the house when he received a phone call and then was gone again, never to return.

Valtyr and Haukur wanted to know more about Gudni's husband, but Geirfinnur was a man of few words, even with his wife. He was calm and his wife had only ever seen him really angry once, when he was drunk. And yet it was not a happy marriage; Geirfinnur was always tired after work and showed little interest in their children or his wife. This indifference to her lead to months of bickering and she even suggested getting a divorce. Scared at the thought of losing his wife and family, his behaviour dramatically changed. He started helping around the house, doing the dishes, helping the children with their homework. Gudni was surprised at the transformation; he even bought her flowers, something he had never done before.

His lack of interest in her until then, though, led to Gudni suggesting she might need 'to look for love somewhere else'. Geirfinnur didn't ask about this and the next day she asked if he would forgive her if she had an affair and he said he would. She had already embarked on a series of affairs that she had kept secret from Geirfinnur, but sitting on the couch in her living room, she revealed them to the police. These men were important potential leads – maybe they had a grudge against Geirfinnur or perhaps he had found out about their relationships with his wife? But Valtyr Sigurdsson chose not to pursue this: 'I didn't judge, it was a private matter.'

The Keflavik investigators were under enormous pressure and out of their depth. When he arrived in 1971, Valtyr Sigurdsson had found the magistrate's office was a mess. He had started to organise it, but this case was still beyond them. 'The office was incapable of dealing with it, I had no experience, nothing, no jurisdiction,' he admitted. He wanted the better equipped and more experienced Reykjavik office to take on the case but they wouldn't bite. 'They didn't want it, everyone was scared of the publicity and that Geirfinnur would appear and we would be a laughing stock. I had that feeling.' He was stuck with the case.[*]

Soon phone calls started coming in from members of the public. There were strange ones, such as a witness who had seen two men fighting and one repeatedly telling the other, 'You killed a man in Keflavik.' He gave a description of the man which probably covered half the young male population. Despite Valtyr's feeling that he could just show up, there was an extensive search for Geirfinnur: divers plunged into Keflavik harbour, and teams scoured the rugged coastline and the lava fields

---

[*] The detectives in Reykjavik saw their Keflavik cousins as rural inferiors dealing with nickel and dime problems, while they investigated the more serious crimes from their office in Borgutun 7, in the centre of the capital.

of Reykjanes, but, like Gudmundur Einarsson earlier that year, he had vanished without a trace.

Journalists were eager for any titbits about the investigation. A week after he went missing, stories began appearing in the newspapers about Geirfinnur Einarsson. One carried the headline 'The Crimes Behind the Disappearance of Keflavik Man', alluding to a theory that he could have been caught up in smuggling. Haukur and Valtyr gave an interview to *Morgunbladid* newspaper where they revealed the case was being treated as a murder enquiry. Valtyr said they had a very good description of a man who had phoned Geirfinnur from the Hafnarbudin cafe. Publicly he may have put on a brave face, but Valtyr knew he didn't have a clear idea what the mystery caller looked like as the witnesses couldn't agree on a description.

The investigation had limited resources, so the Keflavik team gratefully accepted an offer from an artist, who was the wife of a police officer, to make a clay head of the mystery caller. The witnesses could then look at it and make any modifications before it was unveiled. Gudlaug Jonssdottir, the cafe worker who'd had a clear view of the man, had been shown various photographs to see if they matched the caller. One of those photos was of Magnus Leopoldsson, the manager of Klubburin, Reykjavik's main nightclub. The police had been after Leopoldsson for a while. In 1972 they had closed down Klubburin as they suspected it was selling smuggled alcohol. The club's owner appealed to the Justice Minister, Olafur Johanesson, who said the closure was unlawful and ordered the club re-opened. But Gudlaug was adamant he wasn't the man in the cafe.

On 26 November, exactly a week after Geirfinnur went missing, Gudlaug was in her apartment in Keflavik watching the evening news when she saw the clay head for the first time. Valtyr had agreed to let the reporters photograph and film the head with a promise not to publish it, as he still had doubts that the bust indeed represented the mystery caller and it had not yet been shown to the two witnesses. His lack of experience showed, as the press ignored any supposed deal they had, and the bust was shown on TV and in newspapers and dubbed 'Leirfinnur' or 'Clayfinnur'.

The detectives in Reykjavik were watching, aghast at what was unfolding. 'It was terrible as everyone was a bit afraid as it was TV,' recalled Arnprudur Karlsdottir. 'If it was on TV you had to believe it – it put pressure to find someone.' Haukur added to this pressure when he confidently told journalists, 'It's just a matter of time until we find the man. It could be the next few hours or it could take weeks.' But his boss, Valtyr, sounded more circumspect when interviewed by Icelandic television: 'We believe this, we hope this accurately represents the man,' he said, before predicting, 'We'll find this man, there's no doubt about it.'

Watching at home, and seeing it for the first time on television, Gudlaug thought the bust was better than the drawings that had been made. But it looked identical to the photos she had been shown of Magnus Leopoldsson, who was not the man she had seen come into the cafe that night.

The next day, the Keflavik office was inundated with phone calls giving hundreds of names of potential suspects. Valtyr and Haukur were manning the phones and typing up a list. Not surprisingly, Magnus Leopoldsson's name cropped up a few times. He was a well-known face in Reykjavik, but Valtyr's jurisdiction didn't go beyond Keflavik, so he couldn't question anyone who lived outside of his area. He sent Magnus' name to the police in Reykjavik, along with dozens of others. Valtyr then took the lonely road from Keflavik to Reykjavik, slicing through the gloomy lava plains which flowed down to the ocean. He was heading to Borgutun 7, to see the veteran detective Njordur Snaeholm.

When he arrived, Valtyr noticed files in Snaeholm's office with the names he had phoned through. But the Reykjavik team still didn't seem that interested in the case. They had better things to do than chase up a list of random people. The view in Reykjavik was that Geirfinnur had most likely committed suicide. Valtyr's sense from his visit and from Njordur was that, 'When people went missing they jump in the sea or hang themselves.' As Valtyr headed back to Keflavik, he concluded, 'It was one of these cases, nobody wants to come near it.' The fiasco over the clay head and the inexperience of the Keflavik team meant that picking up the case could be a poisoned chalice, with the embarrassing prospect of Gierfinnur suddenly reappearing at any time.

The police in Reykjavik may not have been interested in the case but the media couldn't get enough of it. This was a country with very little violent crime – only one or two murders on average each year – which were normally pretty straightforward cases and quickly solved, so-called 'domestic crimes'.

In a small town, indeed in a small country, rumours take on a life of their own. The resemblance of the clay head, 'Leirfinnur', to Klubburin's manager, Magnus Leopoldsson, led to rumours about his suspected links to the case. Erla was at Saevar's mother's house in Reykjavik where they were discussing the rumours. Saevar listened for a while to their conversation, barely concealing his annoyance at the women he thought were being so stupid. 'Come on,' he said, 'it's so obvious this guy was shooting his mouth off at the wrong moment in the wrong place, he only has himself to blame.' This was typical Saevar, trying to sound like he knew it all, even when he didn't.

Erla and Saevar had been feeling the heat after their post office caper. Erla had heard there was a warrant out for their arrest, so in December 1974 they fled to Copenhagen. Saevar went first, with Erla to follow later. She took the dwindling stash from the post office embezzlement, changed it into 100 kronor bills and smuggled it out of the country by stuffing it in her boots.

When she arrived in Copenhagen, Erla was given strict instructions by Saevar to stay with Icelanders he knew and wait for him to contact her. Erla did as she was told and headed to the address he had given her. She became good friends with the Icelandic girl who rented the apartment, a young student with a baby that Erla would look after. Saevar showed up weeks later and within a few months their post office loot had run out. They were scared to return to Iceland as they thought they would be arrested for the embezzlement, so they stayed in Copenhagen into the spring with little money. They stole a fox fur coat so they could sell it, but they never got around to it.

To add to her woes, Erla found out she was pregnant. She was throwing up all the time and, with no cash, resorted to stealing tomatoes as it was the only food she could hold down. They were living a miserable existence and Saevar decided to call an acquaintance of his in Iceland, Gudjon Skarphedinsson, to check the lay of the land back home.

Gudjon couldn't have been more different from Saevar and his friends. Ten years older than them, he was educated and a former teacher. But the past year of his life had been a mess. He had dropped out of university and a few months later his father, a Lutheran minister, had been killed in a car crash. This plunged Gudjon into a depression which, combined with increasing financial troubles, had taken a toll on his marriage. He didn't care about work, drifting in and out of professions and having trouble sticking to anything. Gudjon was a country boy at heart, brought up in the Westfjords by his grandparents. It was a rural idyll; Gudjon would ride to school on horseback, surrounded by mountains and the cold blue waters that turned burnished silver when the sun shone. He hated Reykjavik from the moment he arrived in the early sixties, after he had been expelled from his grammar school in Akureyi, in Northern Iceland. Gudjon found the capital, 'the ugliest, sickest little town I've ever seen in my life'. He found the weather far more depressing than up north and the food even worse. He couldn't wait to leave and he relished the opportunity to become a teacher back in the Icelandic wilderness where there were more cows and horses than people.

It was here that he would meet a pupil who would change his life forever. One morning as he called out names in the big green register, one name stood out: Saevar Cieselski, a Polish/Jewish name rare among the Celts. There was something in Gudjon's laconic manner that separated him from the other teachers so that when the young Cieselski was threatened with expulsion for making alcohol, it was Gudjon he turned to. He accosted him one day after school, grabbing the teacher and asking if he could stop the expulsion. But there was nothing Gudjon could do and he thought no more of the boy until years later when Saevar introduced himself again at a party in Reykjavik.

By then, Gudjon had returned to the capital to study theology at the University of Iceland. He eventually switched his studies to Icelandic, which he found 'boring', then medicine for which he admitted he 'didn't have the energy', before dropping out. It wasn't hard to bump into an acquaintance; there weren't many places where you could hang out. Mokka was one of the favourite haunts, a 1950s style, low-lit cafe where artists, musicians and wannabe revolutionaries would squeeze into booths for a coffee and a smoke. They would discuss how they'd take over the country from the controlling, stodgy politicians in their dark suits with their binary view of the world.

Gudjon and Saevar had mutual friends and Gudjon was soon drawn into the network of people Saevar would call upon. They weren't close, however, as Gudjon knew Saevar had a reputation around town as a petty thief 'who would take your money if you weren't looking'. Gudjon thought of the boy as nothing more than a passing acquaintance, albeit a very persistent one who would show up at his work or house unannounced.

Gudjon was at home with his young daughter in March 1975 when he received a collect call from Copenhagen. 'I didn't know who was calling and I thought it was a friend in trouble,' he recalled. When he accepted the call, it was Saevar. They didn't speak for long, 'He was asking about news from Iceland. I said there was nothing new, nothing more to add,' Gudjon recalled.

Saevar was checking if it was safe to return to Iceland, but Erla had already decided she had tired of their listless existence in Copenhagen and was going home. Saevar couldn't bear the thought of her leaving and flew into a rage and the black mood Erla had experienced once before. He tried to kick her. 'He aimed for my stomach and I was pregnant and he missed,' Erla recalled, 'but I said I know what you tried to do, you're dangerous.' She didn't want to be anywhere near him so she packed and left. Pregnant and vulnerable and having burned her bridges with her family she had to stay with Saevar's mother, Sigurbjorg. She was delighted to take her in and excited about the baby.

THE REYKJAVIK CONFESSIONS

The police were already on to the embezzlement. It hadn't taken them long to figure it out, but they didn't arrest Erla when she returned. They would wait and bide their time.

3

Inside the pokey office that served as the hub of the Keflavik investigation, they were getting nowhere fast. Within weeks of starting the enquiry, Valtyr Sigurdsson was already sick of it. At Christmas he went on a skiing holiday, handing over the day-to-day running to his detective, Haukur Gudmundsson, and the ever-present customs chief, Kristjan Petursson. Petursson had helped out by going through all of the passenger lists to find out who had left the country at the time of Geirfinnur's disappearance. He now saw his brief as beyond merely policing the customs unit at the airport. He wanted to be part of the action.

Initially the inquiry had focused on going through Geirfinnur's background and the search for the mystery caller. In January 1975 they changed tack. Haukur and Kristjan investigated the smuggling of alcohol from the merchant ships that docked at Keflavik. Valtyr is clear: 'It was not connected to the case though we tried to make it look that way.' The idea was that it paid for Haukur's time and stopped him being pulled onto other work.

Haukur, however, viewed things slightly differently to his boss, always looking to see if he could identify a link between Geirfinnur and smuggling, and early in 1975 he received a tip that Geirfinnur Einarsson had been asked if he knew anyone who could smuggle alcohol into the country. On its own this wasn't that significant, but it was out of character for Geirfinnur who kept his head down and never caused a fuss. More significant to Haukur was the fact that a few days before he went missing, Geirfinnur had gone to Klubburin with some friends. He wasn't a regular visitor to Klubburin or clubs generally. Inside, helped by some overpriced alcohol, it seemed that Geirfinnur got chatting to some men. The suspicion was that these men were involved in smuggling and wanted to get Geirfinnur involved. The Keflavik investigators had to find them, but they didn't know who they were. The police couldn't find these men or anything to substantiate the tip-off that Geirfinnur was a smuggler but Haukur still had a hunch he was. It was these 'hunches' and 'gut feelings' that would be the fuel that drove this inquiry to its doomed conclusion.

By February, after a month investigating Geirfinnur's possible involvement in smuggling, Haukur Gudmundsson told journalists they hadn't excluded the fact that it could be related to him going missing. 'We're checking it now as this is the only possible motive we've come across yet,' he said. His boss Valtyr Sigurdsson, however, was emphatic: 'Yes, he tried to make alcohol at home, but there was no evidence he was involved in smuggling.'

Without any further indication that Geirfinnur was a smuggler, the main focus of the Keflavik team returned to tracking down the man who had phoned him. By now there were only a few names left on the list of possible suspects. One of them was Magnus Leopoldsson. A drip feed of allegations had continued about the Klubburin nightclub and its boss. Magnus had hoped these rumours would fade away but they only got louder. The gossip about him became so persistent that eventually he wrote to the Ministry of Justice asking officials to put up or shut up – arrest him or issue a statement quashing these rumours. This was particularly tricky for Olafur Johannesson, the Justice Minister. Johannesson was a giant of Icelandic politics, a former prime minister who had fought off the troublesome British in the 'Cod War' dispute over rights to fish in Iceland's bountiful waters. For Olafur's ruling Progressive party, Klubburin was no ordinary venue: its premises were rented from the Progressive party. This supposedly gave Klubburin some political clout as it gave them direct contact with the ruling party machinery. However, it was also potentially embarrassing for a conservative right-of-centre party that had been founded to represent Iceland's farmers and drew much of its support from less liberal rural areas. It was impossible to totally quash the gossip but the rumours about Magnus died down and he assumed the police had moved on to other leads.

By June 1975 the Ministry of Justice's patience had run out with the Keflavik investigators. Haukur Gudmundsson was pulled off the case and the investigation was put on the shelf. Geirfinnur's body hadn't been found and there were still no suspects – just gossip and hunches. Haukur and Valtyr's confident assertions about the case now looked a little foolish. They knew almost as little about Geirfinnur and what had happened to him as the day he went missing.

The anniversary of Geirfinnur's disappearance in November 1975 passed with no new developments in the case. However, it did provide a chance for the press to return to the story. Haukur Gudmundsson told *Morgunbladid* that he was convinced it would be solved in time, though not by him as he was back to the daily grind in Keflavik.

Haukur may have been off the investigation, but that didn't stop him trying to find answers, and in the most unconventional places. Shortly before the case was shut down a man got in touch with the police with an intriguing but bizarre proposal: a psychic based in Jordan said he might be able to help find Geirfinnur. With no other leads, Haukur thought it might be worth a shot. Valtyr Sigurdsson agreed. 'There were all sorts of possibilities, lots of people thought he had committed suicide, and we would try anything.' They sent the psychic a tape with information about the case but this clearly wasn't enough, he needed to see a relative of Geirfinnur's, in person, so he could feel Geirfinnur's psyche. The news leaked to the press that Haukur had taken Geirfinnur's wife, Gudni, to Jordan to see the psychic at the Icelandic taxpayer's expense. *Dagbladid* reported that Haukur had spent a week with Gudni on their trip to the psychic but it had been an expensive waste of time. The psychic had not been able to shed light on the whereabouts of Geirfinnur Einarsson and the caller who had summoned Geirfinnur to his last meeting at the cafe in Keflavik harbour remained unidentified. In the nightclubs and among the ranks of the petty criminals the rumours and speculation continued.

Saevar Cieselski had returned to Iceland from Copenhagen and was continually trying to play the big shot. He was always painfully aware that he was different, that his foreign name and looks meant he stood out and made him an easy target. To compensate for this, he would boast to try to look important. One former policeman who knew him said he was seen as 'a clever dick' with a big mouth. 'He would boast about things; people who bullshit, they talk big and want to look big. He would try to make himself more important – he would say "I know something about Geirfinnur". People like him, they want others to think they know all the answers to compensate for their own inadequacies. He was a bit like that, so he was his own worst enemy.'

Gudjon Skarphedinsson knew all about Saevar's foibles. His former pupil liked to call in at Gudjon's home or his office at the Cultural Fund in Reykjavik. Gudjon suspected he came to see 'if he could pick pockets or use anything' and joked to his colleagues that they were in the presence of a drug dealer and killer. Gudjon said, 'I didn't know what he wanted, he was somehow all over the old part of Reykjavik, dropping in wherever he wanted.'

That summer, Gudjon had separated from his wife, though they were still on good terms. So much so that in November 1975 he went away with her and his daughter to escape the driving horizontal rain and unrelenting wind for a road trip through southern Europe. After his family had returned home, Gudjon carried on alone to the south of France, working in the fields, drifting, as he had been for the past decade. He ended up in Paris and found even there he couldn't escape from Saevar, who was on a trip to buy hash. Knowing that the police and the customs chief were keeping tabs on him, Saevar needed a way to get the drugs back into Iceland and Gudjon was the ideal foil. Saevar had come up with a plan that, like all of his schemes, seemed smart but was bound to fail. He wanted to stash the drugs in Gudjon's car, which would then be shipped back to Iceland from Rotterdam. Saevar never liked taking no for an answer, Gudjon had no money and wasn't much of a businessman so he agreed. Saevar ended up buying poor quality hash, which they discovered when they tested the product.

While Gudjon and Saevar flew back to Iceland, the car made its slow passage 1,500 miles through the crowded North Sea and then through the convulsing Atlantic Ocean to Reykjavik. As soon as the car arrived, it was immediately impounded. 'The police knew all about it,' Gudjon said, 'who had sold Saevar the hash and how it was put in the car.' They arrested Saevar and Gudjon and brought them to Sidumuli.

As a former garage, the makeshift jail was housed in a non-threatening, low-slung building with a thick wooden door and a clanking barred one behind. It was a soulless, desperate place to keep prisoners for a few days. After five days they were released, while the police looked for evidence to strengthen the case, but Gudjon, isolated and alone with his thoughts, left even more depressed and frightened. For Saevar, the net was closing in.

It was now almost two years since Gudmundur Einarsson had disappeared in a blizzard of thick snow. The surfeit of decent leads provided a potentially valuable opening amongst Reykjavik's small criminal community. Erla said that Sigurd Stefan Almarsson knew Saevar's sidekick Kristjan. They were both inmates in Litla Hraun prison, Iceland's newer purpose-built jail, located down on the south coast at the end of a single-track road, hours from Reykjavik. The prison looked out over the flat, dark landscape and was bordered by the ocean, which made escape an almost impossible prospect. Sigurd told the police that Kristjan had told him about Erla and Saevar's embezzlement scheme.

On 11 December detectives spent four hours questioning Kristjan. Neither the police nor the prison kept a detailed record of what was said, but he was asked about his friendship with Erla and Saevar when the embezzlement took place. Kristjan told them Saevar had mentioned that his girlfriend Erla had talked about how to carry out fraud at the post and telephone company.

The next day Sigurd was released from prison and flown to the east of the country for Christmas with his family. The police now had enough to get to Saevar.

4

December 1975

It was early in the morning. Erla hadn't long finished feeding her baby daughter, Julia, when the police arrived in force at her apartment in Kopavagur, in one of the tower blocks that had sprung up around Reykjavik. She lived here with Saevar, who had been taken in the previous day for questioning. So Erla knew it was only a matter of time before they came for her too.

Erla frantically called her sister to take her baby before she was driven to Sidumuli prison. The police let Erla stew for days in her cell and she tried to play the hardened criminal, determined she wouldn't give in, sticking two fingers up at people she thought of as 'assholes'. The chief asshole was the investigating magistrate, Orn Hoskuldsson. He looked like he had walked straight out of a TV crime drama, with his leather jacket, thatch of curly hair, thick moustache and imposing, forceful manner. Those who knew him said he was taciturn, rarely cracking a smile. Rookie cop Sigurbjorn Eggertsson was his sidekick. He had only been in the service a few years but was a smooth-talking communicator who could get suspects to open up and was predicted to go far.

The police had collected plenty of incriminating evidence, including eyewitnesses who had seen Erla signing for money with a forged ID, but for some reason they had sat on this evidence for months. It was only after Sigurd Almarsson's prison tip off that they acted. Erla wasn't going to give in easily. She may have been small but she was feisty too. If anything, she was proud of her crime. 'I never felt shame about it,' she admitted, 'It's mischief that you get up to when you're younger to show those assholes, we had all this stuff against the system and it really pissed off a lot of people.'

In the early 1970s, Iceland had become consumed with fear about drugs and what they might do to the tiny nation. A special drugs police and drugs court had been set up, mostly handing out fines. This was a time when policing was like the Wild West. Iceland had tried to curb this with strict rules and procedures on how suspects should be questioned. Detectives were supposed to have an open mind, not to ask leading questions and to make sure suspects weren't interrogated for longer than six hours. But the investigators questioned Erla repeatedly about the post office embezzlement. She was interrogated seven times in two days for over 25 hours in total. They were slowly grinding her down. What worried her most was that if she confessed she would be sent to prison and taken away from Julia. For Erla her baby daughter was 'the best thing that had ever happened to me, the only thing that had meaning in my life'. Saevar paled in comparison to the tiny being she was still breastfeeding. Julia was an affirming, empowering force that gave her the strength to stand up to Saevar. When he had threatened to hit Erla she had flipped, grabbed him and slammed him against the wall. She could feel she had more strength than Saevar, when he fell to the floor. He lay there and gave Erla the smile that always melted her heart and sheepishly conceded, 'now my woman can beat me'.

Erla was from a successful, high-profile family. Her dad, Bolli was working for Icelandair at JFK airport when her mum, also named Erla, fell for the older handsome man in his airline uniform. Bolli already had two children, Einar and his namesake Bolli from a previous marriage, who had been raised by his sister. Erla was only 18 at the time and was soon pregnant with Bolli's child. Days before the baby was due, Bolli was on a Loftleider flight from Luxembourg to the US which was scheduled to make a refuelling stop in Reykjavik. An hour before the plane was due to land it flew into a snowstorm and all contact with the crew was lost. A search was launched but it was assumed the plane had crashed into the sea and the six crew had perished. Their obituaries appeared in the newspapers and Erla was heartbroken; barely an adult, she was facing life as a widow with a new baby.

Four days after the plane went missing, though, when all hope seemed lost, a coastguard vessel picked up a faint radio signal: 'Location unknown – all alive'. It was the aeroplane crew; they had survived and were transmitting from a life raft. They were on Bardarbunga, high on the Vatnajokull glacier, a vast expanse of ice 8,000-kilometre square reaching up to Iceland's highest peak, Hvannadalshnjukur. A perilous rescue mission brought the entire crew back home, in time for the birth of Bolli and Erla's son Arthur.

Baby Erla arrived five years later. She was one of her father's seven children and they were high achievers. Her half-brother Einar was the most famous, becoming a huge basketball star in Iceland, inducted into the nation's basketball hall of fame. Her brother Arthur would follow his dad into the airline industry, working for Icelandair in Germany while her other brother, Bolli, worked for the Icelandic government. One of her sisters married into one of Iceland's wealthiest families, and another emigrated to Hawaii. But from a young age Erla felt different to her siblings. 'I had nothing in common with them, I started stealing and smoking cigarettes and always looking for my own space.' She felt so alienated from her family that she had a fantasy she dreamed up: 'a doorbell would ring and a husband and wife with the same age kids say "you were swapped accidentally and you have our daughter" and I would go with them.'

Saevar was the ultimate embodiment of this rebellious nature and her choice hadn't gone down well. A rift developed long before her arrest which led her mother to vow never to have Saevar under her roof again. Erla had chosen her young boyfriend over her family. The wound was so deep that when Julia was born in September 1975, Erla told the nurses not to let her mum visit and see the young baby. 'I didn't want to talk to my mum, she hurt me so much,' Erla recalled, 'she started calling me after I had given birth I said leave me alone, stay away from me.' Her mum persuaded the nurses to let her sneak in and see her granddaughter without Erla's permission. When Erla found out, she threw a fit.

It seemed they would remain estranged but they were brought together again in unusual circumstances on a sunny day in the autumn of 1975. Iceland was still firmly stuck in the macho, sexist culture of the 1970s: men did all the hard jobs – politics, business, teaching – while a woman's place was in the kitchen and the bed. The country's nascent feminist movement decided to fight back, and on 24 October they organised a day of protest. Thousands of women went on strike for the day, refusing to work, cook or clean. Banks, schools, nurseries and factories all had to close. Men were forced to bring their children to work while 25,000 women, over a tenth of the population, gathered in Reykjavik to listen to speeches, sing and discuss their place in society. Erla was among them with Julia, now a month old, in her arms. Erla was not part of the feminist movement in Iceland – groups like the Red Stockings who had helped organise the protest – but she loved what they had achieved. 'I was such an outsider,' she remembered, 'I liked the feeling in the air of female empowerment and the comments of men indicated they were scared and I liked that.' As she worked her way through the crowd she bumped into her mother. There amidst the crowds, banners, speeches, singing and air of rebellion they had an emotional reunion. Erla agreed her mum could come and visit and see her new granddaughter.

Erla had hoped the birth of Julia would change Saevar's behaviour but he was incapable of living a normal life. In the two years Erla had been with Saevar, he was always dodging the police. When Saevar was arrested for smuggling three kilos of hash from Rotterdam hidden in Gudjon Skarphinsson's car, it was only two months after Julia's birth. Erla's patience had been exhausted: 'We can't live like this anymore, we have to hide away, we can't even have our name on the doorbell.' Saevar had tried to reassure her that he would make some money and they could move to South America and start afresh. Erla knew it was a hollow promise that would never happen.

A few days after this conversation, Saevar arrived home in shock, dripping wet. On his way back to their apartment in Kopavagur, on the outskirts of Reykjavik, he had been walking through a valley when something whizzed past him. He realised it was a bullet, meant for him. He fell into the water and scrambled up a bank, running away as fast as he could. He was highly agitated. 'Someone tried to shoot me,' he told Erla as they stood in their tiny kitchen. He threw off his sodden clothes into the wash room, blocking a tap, managing to flood the apartment. It had all become too much for Erla. She told him, 'That's it, it's over, I can't live like this.' She felt Saevar finally understood her unhappiness. Erla was emphatic, she was going to leave him and take everything, as she had bought all of the possessions they had. She didn't want any misunderstandings later so she drew up a note stating this, which she got him to sign.

When Erla was arrested a month later, the police found this note and used it to drive a wedge further between Erla and Saevar. 'Look at this guy,' Orn Hoskuldsson told her, 'he's selling drugs and you have a new born baby. He doesn't care about this baby and it's always going to be trouble.' Orn told Erla stories about her boyfriend and his links to crime, which she had not heard before and added to her doubts about him.

During questioning, the police repeatedly raised her absence from her daughter, tugging at the guilt of her being away from a young baby, barely three months old. She said Orn Hoskuldsson told her, 'The child will grow up to respect the mother who co-operated, but if you do not co-operate, you will never see your baby until it's an adult.' Erla believed that if she owned up to the fraud she would be released and be re-united with her daughter, able to hold her close and breathe in the milky scent of her skin.

Erla was alone, a young mother barely out of her teens, with no one to lean on and ask for help. Although she hated the idea of giving in to the police, she said 'motherhood got the better of me'.

After days of intensive questioning, she told her interrogators, 'I'm gonna come clean, so whatever I tell you now will be the last thing I say and I'll walk out of here, I'm finished.' She confessed to the embezzlement and signed a statement admitting the crime. She felt relieved; at last she would be released and could see her baby. After a week in solitary confinement she was emotionally drained and ready to go home.

As she got up to leave, Orn Hoskuldsson pulled out a photo of a handsome young man with long dark hair. 'Do you know this guy?' he asked. Erla recognised him straightaway as Gudmundur Einarsson. She had met him four years earlier at a school disco, when she was sixteen, and had seen his picture in the paper after he disappeared. 'I remembered him as he liked me that evening,' she told the police, 'he was good looking. We had a pleasant chat, I was flattered and I had seen him one more time downtown.'

Orn couldn't remember why he chose this point to ask her about this, but the police had heard rumours thought to be from Sigurd Almarsson, the prisoner who had informed on Saevar, that Saevar might know something about the unsolved disappearance of Gudmundur Einarsson.

Now Erla had to face a whole new set of questions from Orn Hoskuldsson: 'What were you doing in January 1974? Where was Saevar?' As soon as he starting pursuing this, Erla felt extremely uncomfortable. 'This was a time in my life that I didn't want to discuss with anyone,' she recalled, 'It had been a really bad time.' It was unlikely anyone could remember the specifics of one evening two years later, but Erla knew exactly what happened that night. She remembered the nightmare, the one involving Saevar's friends outside the window trying to get into the apartment. It was the incident after this that had scarred her and that she did not want to revisit.

When she had woken the morning after her nightmare, Erla was covered in excrement, having soiled herself. She couldn't believe she had been so depressed, with so little self-esteem that she could let this happen. Her immediate response was to dispose of the evidence before anyone else saw it. She yanked the sheet from her bed and took it outside to the rubbish bin, but to her dismay there was nothing else in there to cover it. She panicked, 'I thought the neighbours are going to see this and that was my biggest shame at the age of 18.' She put the sheet in anyway, and then hurried back to her apartment, hoping no one noticed her. The ignominy was overwhelming. She had tried to bury it so deep that she was scared to acknowledge it, even to herself.

In the interrogation room filled with a cloudy fug of smoke, Erla felt the investigators were getting close to her shame. She told them about the dream and that when she had woken she had gone outside to the rubbish bin where she saw a sheet that had been thrown in at the bottom of it. Orn pushed further, asking Erla to tell him more about the nightmare. Why she had gone to the bin and why was the sheet there? Erla didn't have a plausible answer and she sounded evasive. The police began to pull at this thread. Erla recalled, 'Everything became about this bed sheet.' The questioning went on and on for hours. But still Erla held on to her secret. 'I never told them. I was never going to tell a living soul,' she said. Her shame and embarrassment would cost her dearly.

The detectives read Erla's reticence as guilt. They told her they thought she had experienced something very traumatic. They explained to her, 'We can see something terrible has happened to you, don't worry, we're going to help you remember, we know exactly how to do that.' The imposing Orn Hoskuldsson came right up to Erla, 'We will help you,' he said, 'but one thing is for certain: you are not leaving here until we have found out what happened to Gudmundur Einarsson.'

Under the Icelandic system, as the investigating magistrate, Orn Hoskuldsson had immense power.

Iceland had an inquisitorial system, where the magistrate was in charge of the investigation. When cases came to trial there was no jury – district judges would hear the evidence from the prosecution and defence and then pass judgement. If found guilty, the accused could appeal to the Supreme Court where the five Supreme Court judges would pass final jugement. They could quash the original district court verdict or reduce the length of sentences.

Under this system, the detectives Eggert Bjarnasson and Sigurbjorn Eggertsson worked for the courts not the police, so in this case they answered to Orn. If suspects weren't willing to play ball the magistrate could remand them for months at a time, until they admitted their guilt. Orn remanded Erla for a further 30 days and said he would be back for another interview the next day.

Erla was left in no doubt how serious the situation was. She was frightened that they would hold her indefinitely. She wasn't going to be reunited with her baby. Instead she was sent her back to her cell with a desk, a thin mattress on the hard bed and a slim row of glass bricks instead of a window. She went 'from being on the way to seeing my baby into a darkness that was indefinite. It was a complete shock.'

Alone in her cell, Erla couldn't sleep. Outside the murky Icelandic winter had taken hold; a doleful darkness enveloped the island for months only allowing the anaemic winter sun a brief appearance. For a week she had held out against the police and denied her part in the embezzlement, scared that if she confessed, she would go to prison and be taken away from her baby. She had given in because they had promised she would be released, but now the police saw her as a deceiver and a liar. If she had lied about the fraud, she was probably lying about Gudmundur too. Her spirit was broken; she was vulnerable and knew they were not going to let her go until she told them exactly what they wanted to hear. Still in shock, she began replaying her memories from the night Gudmundur went missing.

The police's questioning had started to get to Erla. Alone in the darkness, curled up on her thin mattress, she began to doubt her own memory as she relived the nightmare over and over again. 'I had heard something in passing about how you can forget something if it is too painful. It sounded like they knew about that sort of stuff. But still at this point in time it was very clear to me that nothing had happened because I remembered that night.' She started to wonder if you could commit a crime and not remember it, even one as heinous as a murder. Was your mind powerful enough to suppress such a terrible memory? In the interview, the police had convinced Erla that it was possible. They said that they would help her to remember, to unlock those toxic memories – no matter how long it took. She was told to recall everything she could about that January night in 1974. She would help them, or she would never be freed.

Knowing that she had to offer the detectives something the next day, Erla went through, step by step, all of the memories she could dredge up from that time. Erla wondered, 'Is it possible they killed someone in the apartment and I saw the whole thing and I can't remember?' Her apartment in Hafnarfjordur was extremely small and she wondered where a fight could have taken place without anything breaking or the neighbours upstairs being disturbed. She tried to imagine different scenarios, which she replayed in her mind over and over. By the time she was interrogated again the next morning she felt, 'Half of me was trying to decide, "Oh, just tell them a story and get out of here". The other half was saying, I can't make something up, because innocent people could go to prison.'

The investigators were subtly leading Erla, asking if certain things were possible, if she could recall certain events. They kept returning to the nightmare of the men outside her apartment. 'Was it possible Saevar's friends were outside the window?' they asked. 'Do you remember anyone coming in?' Erla tried to be helpful but her replies were vague: of course it was *possible*, they might really have been there and trying to get in, she couldn't say for sure. Orn, Eggert and Sigurbjorn kept hammering home the fact that Saevar had brought these men to the house.

Over many hours she began telling a very different version of events that took place on the night in January 1974 when Gudmundur Einarsson disappeared:

Erla returned to the apartment from a night at a disco and party, no one was there. She went to bed but woke later when she heard voices in the apartment. She got up and made her way to the storage room where she saw Saevar, Kristjan and a third man with something heavy between them, covered in a sheet. Kristjan and Saevar tied each end of the sheet with a knot. Erla hadn't seen what was inside but she thought it was a body. There was also a foul smell in the room and a strange wet patch on the floor. By this point Kristjan had noticed her in the doorway and angrily asked what was she doing there. Erla was rooted to the spot and freezing, despite the fact that her hair was covered in sweat. The three men picked up the body, pushing past her in the doorway, knocking her over. She lay there a while unable to move until Saevar reappeared, picked her up and put her into bed. When he asked if she had seen anything she didn't reply, what could she say? He told her never to say a word about it if she was ever asked. Saevar left and she somehow managed to fall asleep until the morning.

When she woke, she went to the garbage bins, she wasn't sure why. Out there in the frosty morning, she found a bed sheet covered in human faeces which she hurriedly put back into the bin. She had tried as hard as possible not to think about this and had felt ill for days after. When she saw the reports about the disappearance of Gudmundur Einarsson, she hadn't put this together with the body in the sheet. She never talked to Saevar about the events of that night again.

It had taken many hours to construct the details of this story. It was a patchwork with many holes but it managed to implicate her lover and his friend Kristjan in a murder. All the time the police were encouraging her, telling her she was doing the right thing by solving this mystery and not to worry about it. They knew that she had several weaknesses; her relationship with Saevar was crumbling and she was making the smart move by separating from him, they told her. Just as they had in the embezzlement case, the detectives also played on her separation from her baby.

Erla had told a long and elaborate story. When she was stuck for details, she said, 'They would explain that we needed to get it done or I was risking that I would lose my child and they didn't want to see that happen.' However, 'somewhere I always knew it didn't happen. So I really needed to believe that it had happened and they kept throwing me something to help me believe it.' If she faltered the detectives would remind her of the trouble she would be in that they couldn't prevent, if she did not co-operate.

After going through the story for six hours she signed a statement which she desperately needed to believe. 'The entire communication between me and police was about it having happened,' she said. 'By the time I'm signing some sort of incrimination, someone else is not in the picture. It's all about how did it happen.' She signed her statement and was released; finally she could see Julia. The police told her she had 'contributed to justice and should now be able to sleep peacefully'. But Erla knew that was a lie. Afterwards, she said, 'It was my soul that went. They didn't have to be very technical, I was very vulnerable. By cracking me, which was so easy, they could sweep up the others.'

5

December 1975

Like Erla, Saevar was already in custody for the post office embezzlement scheme. After years of petty crime, stretching back to his early teens, Saevar was used to dealing with the police. He didn't fear them and hated them for harassing him over the years.

The detectives knew he was guilty of the embezzlement but he had lied about it. The die was cast. If he had lied once, he could do it again, and for an even more serious crime. The tactics the investigators used on Erla wouldn't work on her boyfriend. He had previously been held in solitary confinement for a month, accused of a drugs offence he hadn't committed.

They needed a different approach. Orn Hoskuldsson, the smooth talking Sigurbjorn and the solid, tougher Eggert Bjarnasson all questioned Saevar throughout the day and into the early morning for over ten hours in total. It was tough going, but Saevar didn't crack.

The next day Saevar was interrogated again, and in the afternoon the investigators had a surprise for him. They told him about Erla's testimony and the body in the sheet. Saevar denied any knowledge of it. As the police confronted him with more of Erla's statement, though, his tone changed. He was used to tough questioning but he knew Erla was vulnerable; he had exploited this himself repeatedly to get her back into his life. He worried how she would cope after a week of intensive questioning. Presented with Erla's statement in full, Saevar conceded he knew something about Gudmundur's fate, but didn't want to say any more. His lawyer, Jon Oddsson, was called and Saevar was read Erla's statement. Saevar was now faced with the mother of his child implicating him in a murder.

During a five-hour interrogation, Saevar told the police his version of what had happened. On the night of 26 January 1974 he had just returned from a trip to buy cannabis abroad. He was with his sidekick, Kristjan, a friend named Tryggvi Runar Leifsson and Gudmundur Einarsson at the apartment in Hamarsbraut. They wanted alcohol and started arguing with Gudmundur, asking him to pay for it. A fight broke out. It soon turned into three against one and in the melee Gudmundur was hit and killed. They didn't call the police or a doctor but instead phoned another of Saevar's friends, Albert Klahn Skaftason. Albert had one thing none of them possessed, access to a car. When Albert arrived they shifted the body out of the apartment, put it in the boot and drove out to the lava fields south of Hafnarfjordur. There, amid the crepuscular darkness with squally winds blowing snow into their faces, they dumped Gudmundur into a crevasse.

The apartment in Hamarsbraut was more a bedsit – two rooms for Saevar and Erla in a peaceful cul-de-sac. At night the only sounds were the incessant wind driving the soft snow falling onto the brightly coloured roofs. There were neighbours upstairs, so close it felt like they were sharing an apartment with them. What did they see or hear? The police never asked them. The mystery surrounding Gudmundur's disappearance was finally being solved.

Soon a whole set of suspects would be in custody accused of his murder.

Armed with Erla and Saevar's testimony the police moved swiftly. On 23 December 1975 they arrested Albert Klahn and Tryggvi Runar. Kristjan Vidar was brought to Sidumuli jail from the bigger Litla Hraun prison where he was serving a sentence for theft. The questioning of Kristjan didn't take very long. He had been at school with Gudmundur Einarsson in Austurbaejar, but he didn't have a clue how he went missing or what had happened to him. He refused to sign any statement without his lawyer being present. Despite Kristjan's denials, the damning testimony from Erla and Saevar led the court to decide he could be held for 90 days and that he should have a psychiatric evaluation.

Tryggvi Runar was in a daze as he was led into the prison, and it wasn't just the drugs. Tryggvi was stocky and pugnacious, with long wavy ginger hair and a cropped beard and moustache. At 24, he was older than the other suspects and had a two-year-old son with his girlfriend. He was a well known to the police and had been in trouble from the age of 16. He recalled how at that age, 'I met a group of kids that I found exciting to be with... when I was in their company it was as if something was pushing me.' It drove him towards trouble; drinking, stealing and faking cheques. He was always caught and had been in and out of prison since his late teens for theft and fighting.

One of the young prison guards, Gudmundur Gudbjarnarson, knew Tryggvi well as they had grown up near each other in the centre of Reykjavik near Hallgrimskirkja, the towering Lutheran church. The streets that fanned out from the church were filled with functional apartment blocks and terraced houses clad in corrugated iron to protect them from the wind and rain. He knew Tryggvi as a fighter: 'He liked to hit people but when I met him he was always fine, he was no trouble.' That could change, however, after a few drinks.

Tryggvi had been in trouble with the police before so wasn't easily intimidated by them. The older generation that had lived through the Second World War and the threat of the Nazis were worried and afraid for this new generation of young Icelanders. Tryggvi started drinking when he was 14, did badly at school and when he got into his twenties began to hit the bottle and pills hard. He had been hospitalised three times because of drugs. The last time had been a year before when he was brought in unconscious having taken sleeping tablets. The doctors were worried he was in imminent danger because of drug toxicity and he was put on an infusion in the intensive care unit.

When Tryggvi arrived at Sidumuli, Gudbjarnason said he had not fully grasped what was happening. 'He was quite confused, he was saying "They are accusing me of having something to do with Gudmundur".' Such denials were pretty common among new inmates, but the young guard found Tryggvi's convincing. Tryggvi was brought before the court where he continued to deny any involvement in Gudmundur's disappearance and was held for 90 days and placed in solitary confinement.

Albert Klahn was a different matter; he was a quiet, laidback pothead who kept out of trouble. He had been friends with Saevar since they were young kids and spent a great deal of time with him. Albert Klahn was different to the rest of Saevar's group of friends. His background had been more cultured than the others'; his father had played with the Icelandic Symphony Orchestra. Albert went to Austerburbaejar school in east Reykjavik where he started hanging out with the 'alley cats', Saevar and Kristjan. He was a smoker not a fighter, always on the look out for drugs. When he was arrested he was clearly stoned; in one mug shot he stares half-dazed into the camera with a tag hung around his neck.

Under scrutiny in the interrogation room the investigators could see Albert was the weak link. He was easily intimidated and willing to co-operate. He began telling them his version of events of the night Gudmundur went missing:

> Saevar had phoned Albert really late at night, sometime between midnight and five in the morning. (It was a wide time frame but he couldn't be more precise.) Saevar asked him if he would drive over to Hafnarfjordur in his dad's yellow Toyota. Albert did as he was told and made his way through the compacting snow that crunched softly under the wheels as he drove out of Reykjavik. When he arrived, Saevar emerged from his apartment and asked Albert to open the boot. Albert couldn't see much as there was poor street lighting; he could only really see through his rearview mirror.
>
> After a while, Saevar, Kristjan and Tryggvi emerged with a big bag. The car 'was rocking a bit and it seemed they were putting something heavy in the boot'. All this had happened in the dead of night in a narrow street where homes stood cheek by jowl.
>
> Kristjan and Tryggvi got in the back seat while Saevar sat in the front and directed Albert out of Hafnarfjordur. He wasn't sure how far they had got but he noticed they went past the aluminium plant at Straumsvik with its distinctive red and white towers. They then pulled off the main road into the silent opacity of the lava fields.[*]

---

[*] He didn't tell them how he managed to do this during a heavy snow storm which had been so bad that taxi drivers had gone home.

> *While Albert waited in the driver's seat, Saevar,*
> *Tryggvi and Kristjan took the heavy bag out of the car*
> *past the glare of the headlights, the only lights for miles*
> *around. They returned after about half an hour without*
> *the bag. Albert drove them back – he wasn't sure where,*
> *probably to Kristjan's apartment in Reykjavik. He asked*
> *Saevar what was in the bag. Saevar told him it was a*
> *body.*

The case was starting to take shape. Albert's account tallied with Saevar's and they had Erla's story of what happened inside the apartment. The detectives decided to strike while they could. Albert had not seen a lawyer and in the few hours he had been questioned he had already told detectives that he helped dispose of a body. Before he had to chance to speak to anyone else, he was taken out of Sidumuli for a drive to see if he could locate the burial spot. This went against normal rules and protocols but the police were sure that by acting swiftly they could find Gudmundur's body and clear up the mystery of his disappearance.

The detectives spent hours driving Albert around the Reykjanes peninsula through the craggy, ashen wasteland trying to locate the spot where Gudmundur had been dumped. It was wishful thinking that Albert could pinpoint, within the hundreds of square miles of lava fields, the place where almost two years before they had left Gudmundur. It was early evening and dark when Albert returned to the prison. He had been helpful but Orn Hoskuldsson had heard enough to detain him for 45 days; plenty of time for the detectives to keep probing him about the case.

Christmas 1975 was one that Albert Klahn would never forget. On Christmas Day his treat was a second drive out to the desolate lava fields with Orn Hoskuldsson to look for the body of Gudmundur. Each time he went he chose a different location where he thought the body might be. He was stranded, hopelessly lost, trying to restore his fractured memory of that night. After three hours they returned with no success. The detectives had told Albert he would get a lighter sentence if he incriminated the others and warned that if he didn't help and kept quiet about what he had witnessed, he would never see the light of day.

By 27 December, after four days in custody, Albert and the others began to unravel. Fifteen minutes into Sigurbjorn and Eggert's questioning in the interrogation room, Albert had smashed up a chair in a rage. Placed in leg irons and handcuffs, he was taken back to his cell.

Tryggvi Runar may have been physically far stronger than Albert but he was struggling too with the enforced isolation. His only human interaction was with the prison wardens and the police and being stuck in the three by two metre cell was crushing his spirit. Tryggvi was fit and loved being outdoors, but he was also used to a regular supply of drink and drugs and deprived of this he couldn't sleep. His insomnia went on for four days, making him more anxious and agitated. He started hearing voices in his head; fragments of conversations. On 27 December at two o'clock in the morning, the prison guards heard Tryggvi talking to himself. They called the prison doctor Gudsteinn who injected him with Diazepam to help him sleep. It didn't work and he was back several hours later to give Tryggvi another sedative. These drugs were the first of a cocktail of medication that would be prescribed to Tryggvi while he was in solitary confinement. Yet, despite his agitated state, Orn Hoskuldsson paid him a private visit in his cell. What he said remained a secret between him and Tryggvi; a pattern that would be repeated again and again by the police and prison wardens.

The sensational arrests were splashed across the front page of the *Morgunbladid* newspaper on 30 December. It said four men were in custody suspected of the murder of Gudmundur Einarsson and the case was being investigated by Orn Hoskuldsson, Eggert Bjarnasson and Sigurbjorn Eggertsson. It was reported that the suspects were being interrogated every day and sometimes late into the night, and that there had been confessions which were being used in the investigation.

A follow-up story the next day reported that the questioning of the four men had strengthened their connection to Gudmundur's disappearance. Before the men had even been charged, there were leaks fed to journalists which implied that Saevar, Kristjan, Tryggvi and Albert were guilty. The trial would be just a formality.

At the beginning of January, inside the offices of Borgutun 7, Orn Hoskuldsson and his team gathered to go over the statements they now had. The investigators needed to fill in the many blanks they had from the initial statements. They needed the suspects' testimonies to be as detailed as possible; after all, this might be the only evidence the police had.

Saevar faced almost daily interrogations, each one stretching for hours on end. After two weeks of this, on 6 January 1976, Saevar told them another more vivid version of that night:

Saevar had returned to the apartment in Hamarsbraut to find Kristjan and Tryggvi waiting for him with a third man he didn't know, someone named Gudmundur Einarsson. He was annoyed with his friends, he didn't like them being at his apartment, his sanctuary with Erla. They followed him into the apartment. He couldn't remember whether Erla was there or even how he had got in, as they only had one key between them. When he went to check if Erla was there, the others followed him. He tried to complain about them being in the apartment, but they told him to keep quiet if he knew what was good for him. There was little he could do stand up to Kristjan and Tryggvi, both bigger and stronger than him.

Kristjan attacked Gudmundur, punching him in the face, and Gudmundur ended up lying on the floor. Tryggvi and Kristjan shook Gudmundur but he didn't respond. Saevar clearly heard Kristjan say the man was dead. He was scared that Kristjan was going to attack him too and Tryggvi warned him not to say anything about what he had seen.

Kristjan and Tryggvi went into panic mode, pacing the floor and discussing what to do. Saevar stood in the living room, traumatised by what he had just witnessed – a young man being killed. He was really scared and went into the toilet to pull himself together and think what he should do next.

He heard a strange sound, something dragged from the bedroom along the corridor and into the storage room. Kristjan was the dominant, driving force. He told Saevar to phone Albert and tell him to come over on the pretence he was going to give him some hash. That would get the pot head over straight away. Saevar did as he was told and Albert took the bait. Saevar could hear Kristjan and Tryggvi in the storage room through the thin walls of the apartment.

Albert arrived in his dad's Volkswagen*. They left the body in the apartment and went for a drive south out of

---

* This was a different car to the yellow Toyota that Albert said he had driven. It was late and dark and Saevar did not drive so his knowledge of cars was probably limited. This contradiction would become more important later on.

*Hafnarfjordur on the road to Keflavik, their headlights
cutting through the blackness around them, illuminating
the strange rocky shapes. The only other light was the
twinkling of the airport far in the distance and the red
from the towers at Straumsvik. They pulled over to smoke
some weed. They then returned to Hamarsbraut and the
apartment, and by this time they were all high. Saevar
heard Erla arrive home and she saw them covering
Gudmundur's body in a sheet. Saevar could see from her
expression she was clearly upset at what she saw. She
was rooted to the spot in the doorway so Kristjan pushed
her aside as they carried the body out. Saevar couldn't
remember exactly what was said to her, but Kristjan had
warned her not to tell anyone what she had seen or heard.
Distraught, Erla retreated to her bedroom while the men
went out.*

*Several days later, Saevar heard about a man who was
supposed to have disappeared in Hafnarfjordur on the
night he was describing. Saevar didn't have the nerve to
tell anybody about that night, because he was scared
what Kristjan and Tryggvi might do to him.*

In Saevar's updated account he was now the observer,
scared of retribution from his violent friends. But his
statement didn't make sense. Kristjan had always been
seen as his sidekick and very much in Saevar's shadow.
It seemed improbable that he was the driving force. The
police were not having the same success getting Tryggvi
to open up and confess. He had been questioned for over
22 hours since he had been arrested and had stuck to his
story, that he knew nothing. Then on 9 January 1976, he
finally cracked.

It was morning and Sigurbjorn Eggertsson was trying
again to get Tryggvi to come clean about his involvement.
Alone in his cell with only his ragged thoughts for
company, Tryggvi told the detectives he had 'thought a

lot about this issue' and now he was ready to explain what really happened. Indeed, Tryggvi had thought of little else in the time he had spent in solitary confinement. He had replayed the events of that night again and again as he lay on his bed, paced the cell or sat on the stool bolted to the floor:

Tryggvi was in the apartment with Saevar, Kristjan Vidar and an unknown man, who Kristjan seemed to know. This was Gudmundur Einarsson. He couldn't remember where the apartment was or who it belonged to, but he could recall some of the layout and that there was a storage room. An argument had started between Gudmundur and Kristjan. They were shouting at first and then it ended up in a fight. Saevar came to help and when he was hit Tryggvi joined in too. Gudmundur fell to the floor but he wasn't knocked out. He tried to get up but was swaying and was hit again. This time he didn't get up. To make sure, Saevar kicked him in the head while he was down. It was a swift and brutal attack, over in seconds. He didn't look like he had any major injuries, just some blood in his mouth. He remembered that Saevar had checked and said the man was dead. Tryggvi tried Gudmundur's pulse and found no signs of life.

These petty criminals had crossed a line, moving into darker territory, but the police accounts of these confessions contain no sense of the shock, remorse or panic. In Tryggvi's account there is a brief mention of panic as they realised they had a dead man on their hands, but it was a fleeting reference. Tryggvi said they knew they had to get rid of the dead man, but he could not remember how they carried him out.

Tryggvi was the last of the suspects to fall. Days earlier Kristjan had given detectives a vivid account that seemed to tally with the others' statements. In his account it had been Tryggvi and Saevar who had attacked Gudmundur, but Kristjan admitted he was very drunk so the events were a bit hazy. He described the drive into the lava fields and going past the plant at Straumsvik too. Kristjan appeared in court and confirmed the statement he had given to detectives that Gudmundur had been killed in Saevar and Erla's apartment and they had brought him to the lava fields and dumped him in a pit and put a big stone over the spot.

The detectives needed the confessions as eyewitness testimony was in short supply, despite the fact that Hamarsbraut was a peaceful road, the kind of place where the neighbours would hear any disturbances. Regardless, the detectives now had detailed accounts of Gudmundur's final hours from all of the suspects – even if they were not 'clean' confessions. The accounts were filled with imprecision and vagueness about certain key details. The motive seemed to be that Gudmundur had been killed in an argument over who should pay for alcohol, with each of the suspects blaming the others for Gudmundur's death. But confessions they were, from the killers and their accomplices. In Iceland, where 90 per cent of convictions were secured with confessions, this was vital. Among the police and investigating magistrates, getting a confession was valued above all else.

Saevar had developed a reputation as a player, particularly in the mind of the customs chief, Kristjan Petursson, who had questioned Saevar on several occasions in the preceeding years for potential drugs offences and even for a major robbery. The Reykjavik detective Arnprudur Karlsdottir knew of Saevar as a small-time drug dealer and never understood Petursson's obsession with him as a one-man crime wave, 'It was very strange in my mind and we would talk a lot about it – why is Kristjan Petursson always after Saevar?' The police could see that

Petursson was frustrated by his customs role and wanted to expand his empire and get involved in investigations rather than just seizing goods at the airport.

Petursson had made his suspicions about Saevar clear to the detectives. Through their questioning over the post office embezzlement, the team saw Saevar as a devious liar who had tried to fool them. His role in the Gudmundur case now made him a serious criminal. If Saevar was capable of one killing, were there other unsolved crimes he might be responsible for, too?

6

January 1976

For six months, the manila folders containing the 70-odd typed statements and evidence on Geirfinnur Einarsson's disappearance had been gathering dust in the office of Keflavik magistrate, Valtyr Sigurdsson. On 30 December 1975, a week after the arrests for Gudmundur's murder, Valtyr had been asked to send over all the Geirfinnur files to the state prosecutor's office.

A week later, Valtyr drove along the Reykjavikvegur through the lava fields to the capital. Here, according to the suspects, underneath the bracken and moss, was where Gudmundur lay – and perhaps Geirfinnur too. When Valtyr reached Reykjavik, he handed over all of the documents to the office of the chief prosecutor: the files about Geirfinnur's finances; the statements from his wife, Gudni, from her lover, and from Geirfinnur's boss; even the clay head. There were problems with the documents; many of the statements had not been signed, for instance, making them useless as pieces of evidence. Valtyr was glad to finally get the case off his plate.

On the same day as Valtyr's visit, an article appeared on the front page of the left-wing newspaper *Althydubladid* with the headline: 'Is Gudmundur's disappearance linked to the Geirfinnur case?' The report said four people were already in custody for Gudmundur's disappearance, which now looked like a murder case.

It seemed like mischief making and speculation from the press, but the story didn't come out of nowhere. The idea of a link between the two cases had been taking root in the detectives' minds for a while. They now had the Geirfinnur case files and were trying to find any links between him and the suspects in custody. They just needed someone to help them flesh it out. And they knew exactly who to turn to.

Having been released from custody, Erla Bolladottir thought it was only a matter of time before the police realised her story was not true and the others in Sidumuli joined her. Although she was no longer in a cell staring at the flat, smeared walls, she was in a different kind of prison, racked with guilt. It was her statement about the body in the sheet that led to the arrest of Saevar and his friends. She still thought the detectives would see that her statement had been constructed with their help and prompting and that, as they investigated the case further, her tale would unravel. The reverse was true; the police wanted more from her.

Sigurbjorn Eggertsson had started calling Erla as soon as she was released. It seemed to her like a genuinely kind gesture, an effort to see if she was coping and needed any help. After a few days, though, he phoned with some startling news. 'You can rest easy now,' he reassured her, 'because Saevar, Kristjan and Albert have confessed.' He told her their stories matched Erla's one hundred per cent, down to the last detail. For Erla this was seismic. 'That was the point in time,' she recalled, 'where I lost all sense of what was real and what wasn't, what was true and what wasn't.'

Her already shaky hold on what happened that night in January 1974 started to waiver further. She had been sure the voices at the window had been a nightmare, that what she had told the police was a fiction. She recalled, 'I didn't have one memory of any of it and I still remembered clearly the real night that happened.' But when three other people had told the police the same story, she was filled with new doubts – 'Maybe the police had a technique I didn't understand and they had managed to get the whole truth out of me even without me being able to connect with it in my own mind.' Perhaps the dream that had haunted her for so long was real, and maybe she had witnessed the aftermath of a murder in her apartment after all. How could she have locked this away for so long without it bubbling up to the surface?

With Saevar in prison and estranged from most of her family, she had moved in with her mother. During her relationship with Saevar, he had controlled her access to her friends and now she had few visitors. But there was one regular caller: Sigurbjorn Eggertsson, who would make unannounced visits. Erla lapped up this warmth and attention. For her it was 'water in a desert, someone listening to me and caring for me'. Sigurbjorn was empathetic and a great listener. She responded to this warmth: 'I would pour my heart our and he would be really nice.'

There was nothing left for Erla in Iceland. She wanted a new life, to get away from Saevar, her family, the hateful case and the lies she had spread. In January 1976 she decided to move to her beloved United States, to the warmer volcanic haven of Hawaii where her sister lived. She discussed this plan when she called on Saevar's acquaintance, the former teacher Gudjon Skarphedinsson, in mid January.

Gudjon was surprised when Erla showed up at his home, but she clearly needed help. He felt she was 'very nervous and very out of control'. As they chatted over tea, she told him about the threatening phone calls she had received at her mum's house. The caller wouldn't say much but had mentioned something that suggested he knew about Erla's intention to go to Hawaii. They were trying to send a message that they knew her and her plans. The only people she had told were her mum and sister, who had told other relatives including her half-brother, Einar. This suggested the caller was someone close, someone who knew one of her relatives.

Gudjon could see she was terrified. He tried to reassure her, although he knew her plans to live in Hawaii were pure fantasy, as with the case active 'there was no way she would be allowed to leave the country'. He didn't dismiss everything she said, though, as he had received his own threatening phone call about the case. A man had rung asking if Gudjon knew where Geirfinnur was and asked to meet him at the bus station in Reykjavik to discuss it. Gudjon dismissed it as nonsense and hung up, but it was more significant than he realised. Whether he liked it or not, his name had started to figure in the rumours about Geirfinnur too.

If she stayed in Iceland, Erla needed someone to protect her, to fill the role that Saevar had assiduously guarded since she had become his girlfriend. With so few family and friends for Erla to rely upon, Sigurbjorn was only too willing to step in. Erla no longer saw him as a policeman investigating her partner, but as a friend. She told him about the threatening calls and he immediately arranged for armed police to protect her. Later Erla would wonder if the calls had been a ruse thought up by the police to draw her closer to them. But at the time, it confirmed her belief that Sigurbjorn was on her side, looking out for her, and that there were others who were intent on hurting her. She knew she didn't want to let him down or offend him in any way.

The start of the new Geirfinnur investigation was not in a police station or in Borgutun 7 but in Erla's old apartment. In January 1976 it was still sealed off by the police as a crime scene. Sigurbjorn had offered to help Erla get some clothes for herself and her baby from the apartment – just the kind of gesture that helped endear him to her. As she searched through the bedroom, Sigurbjorn asked her a question: 'Is it possible that Saevar was involved in the disappearance of Geirfinnur Einarsson in November 1974?' Erla was caught off guard. Where had this come from? She had been sure Saevar wasn't involved in the Gudmundur case, but then he had confessed and her doubts had started. Now she was being asked about this totally new case. Sigurbjorn continued to chat, asking her what Saevar had said about Geirfinnur Einarsson. There was nothing that she could easily recall. As she sorted through the clothes she was still relaxed, telling herself this was just a chat between friends.

When Geirfinnur went missing in November 1974 it was big news, leading to much speculation and gossip. Erla recalled the clear ideas Saevar seemed to have had about the case, and the conversation she'd had with Saevar about the gossip linking the disappearance to the people who owned and ran Klubburin. Saevar had made barbed comments about Geirfinnur's fate, 'This guy was shooting his mouth off at the wrong moment in the wrong place, he only has himself to blame.'

This was enough of an opening for Sigurbjorn and standing inside her small bedroom, he probed further. What exactly did Saevar know about it? Erla was emphatic: 'He didn't know anything but he liked to look like he knew.' She said Saevar always had 'this Al Capone dream about getting away with the perfect crime that could not be solved'.

As they drove back through town, Sigurbjorn returned to the topic of Geirfinnur. When they pulled up outside her mum's apartment he looked at her and said, 'Do you know if Saevar knows something about what happened to Geirfinnur?' Erla realised he was asking as a detective not a friend. This was turning into a police interview. Erla said, 'My heart just dropped, all of a sudden this wasn't just a chat.' She hesitated, she was 'afraid to upset him and his colleagues', scared they would start treating her badly. She had come to rely on Sigurbjorn's friendship and company. If she let him down maybe he would stop phoning her and visiting, which Erla didn't want to happen. So she replied that she didn't think Saevar knew anything. She pleaded with Sigurbjorn not to mention this to the head of the investigation, to treat it as just a private conversation between them. He promised it would stay that way, just between them.

The detectives' version of this was very different. In a note in the police records they said that Erla had got in touch with them as she had been receiving threatening phone calls. When they spoke to her about this she said she was scared because of the Geirfinnur case. That was when they began their new inquiry into his disappearance.

The next morning after she had spoken to Sigurbjorn the doorbell rang at Erla's mother's house. She wasn't expecting any visitors and she didn't think Sigurbjorn would be back so soon. When she opened the door he was there, but this time he wasn't alone. Next to him was the tall, leather jacketed figure of Orn Hoskuldsson. They invited themselves in, sat down on the sofa and Orn declared, 'We have reason to believe that you have experienced something traumatic concerning Geirfinnur Einarsson's disappearance and we are going to help you remember.' Erla's new nightmare had begun.

7

January 1976

The investigators were not going to settle for a cosy chat at Erla's house. They needed to apply pressure, so they brought her back to Sidumuli prison, and the interrogation room where she had been broken before. Having got her to confess during the Gudmundur case, Hoskuldsson and Eggertsson knew exactly which buttons to press.

They started by asking what she did when Saevar was away on his 'trips abroad', when he disappeared, sometimes to buy drugs but on other occasions, both of them knew, into the arms of another woman. Erla explained how she spent a lot of time at her friend Hulda's house. Hulda was the girl Saevar had been sleeping with when he first got together with Erla on their US trip. Hulda was quiet, a loner, who loved being with the more extroverted Erla, and Erla liked having a friend who was more grounded and not as angry as she was with the world. Being at Hulda's house was fun; she had an older brother, Valdimar, who moved in a different world to Erla and her stoner friends. Valdimar's friends were on the way up in Icelandic society: they were hotel managers, artists, businessman, and the people running Klubburin. To them, the world was full of possibilities that lay far beyond Iceland. They had the money to do as they pleased would throw parties where the drinks flowed. Erla remembered how one night they decided Iceland's nightlife was too tepid and they would go to England instead. In no time at all they had chartered a flight to England to party. In spite of her hatred of the capitalist system, Erla was impressed by their swagger. Orn and Sigurbjorn listened patiently as Erla talked and talked.

As the police had done with the Gudmundur case, Orn and Sigurbjorn spent hours talking about this time in 1974 when Erla had been extremely depressed. She didn't want to reveal how lonely she was then, with so few friends. Lurking in the back of her mind was her eternal shame, the humiliation of soiling the sheet the night Gudmundur went missing. Erla said the police 'sensed that, asking how I felt when I would get home from work and Saevar wasn't there'. They were like the school bullies deciding to play nice but knowing where her weak points were and that they could hone in on them at any time.

Alone in the interrogation room with no lawyer present, Erla was once again being dominated by forceful men. She felt backed into a corner, giving away information, but she couldn't stop herself. After hours of chipping away looking for an opening, Orn and Sigurbjorn knew Einar was their way in. The police knew Erla's partnership with Saevar had strained her relationship with her big brother. Yet Erla still idolised him, she said in her eyes 'he had a special place, he was like a god'.

She told them about a scheme, more of a prank, that Einar had carried out that had been discussed at some of the parties thrown by Hulda's brother, Valdimar. When he was younger, Einar had set up a chain letter where each person who received it would send a bottle of whisky to the name at the top. Einar and his friends ended up with so much whisky they embarked on what Erla called a '1,000 day party'. For Erla, it was a throwaway remark, but it planted the seed in her interogators' minds that Einar was someone who could get access to illegal alcohol and could therefore be involved in smuggling.

Einar was friends with Valdimar, who in turn knew Magnus Leopoldsson, the manager of Klubburin. This was important information for the police. Magnus was the spitting image of the infamous clay head the police had commissioned in 1975 of the man in the cafe who had supposedly summoned Geirfinnur to his death. The police had long suspected Klubburin of selling smuggled alcohol and, despite his best efforts, the fevered speculation that Magnus was involved in Geirfinnur's disappearance had never quite gone away. Now, a year later, through Erla's conversation about booze and her brother's attempts to get alcohol, Magnus was being drawn back into the police's orbit. At midnight they let Erla go, ready to move on to her boyfriend.

Saevar was the one inmate who wasn't buckling from the strictures of solitary confinement. Although he had confessed to involvement in the Gudmundur case, he would then go for days refusing to answer any more questions, which outraged the detectives. 'It was like a tension in the air every time the investigators entered the cell,' Saevar said. 'It was like they thought I was behind all the major crimes committed in the country.'

One of their tactics was to leave late at night and return the next morning to ask the same questions. If they didn't like Saevar's response the police would resort to tough measures. Saevar said during the first few weeks in custody they had twisted the collar of his shirt to strangle him until he lost consciousness.

When the investigators presented Saevar with Erla's testimony on 22 January he said he knew about the

Geirfinnur disappearance, because everyone did. He had watched the case on the television and read about it. Then, remarkably, he opened up:

A few days before Geirfinnur went missing, Saevar was walking on Laugavegur, the wide road that starts out at the edge of Reykjavik and turns into the city's main shopping street. It was late, between ten and eleven in the evening, when a man in a blue Mercedes called Saevar over. He knew him straight away as Einar Bollason, Erla's half brother. He asked Saevar into his car for a chat. There were two others in the car. Saevar recognised the driver as Magnus Leopoldsson, the manager of Klubburin. The other man he didn't know, but he later found out this was Geirfinnur Einarsson. They took a drive around the city; it was November when the cold and thrusting wind drove people off the streets and into the warmth of home or one of the few bars. The men knew Saevar had connections who knew how to move on illicit goods. They knew he was importing drugs and selling them, and so they had a propostion for him; they wanted to use his skills to sell on smuggled alcohol.

They stopped outside Klubburin, the hub of the city's nightlife, where they told Saevar they were expecting a big shipment of vodka and other spirits. They asked him to explore potential ways to distribute the alcohol without being discovered. Einar and Magnus did the talking while Geirfinnur stayed quiet.

Einar followed this up a few days later by calling at Saevar's mother's house to take him for another late-night drive. As Saevar got into the red Fiat he saw Magnus was there again along with party boy Valdimar Olsen, brother of Saevar's ex-girlfriend, Hulda. As the four men drove around Reykjavik past closed shops, the men wanted to know if Saevar had figured out where he might sell the smuggled alcohol. They were heading to Keflavik and asked Saevar to join them.

They drove along the Reykjavikvegur through the desolate, silent, black lava fields, with the background howl and beat of the wind. The men talked about the alcohol scheme, and Saevar's involvement in the drugs trade.

When the Fiat reached Keflavik they made for the harbour where they were to meet Geirfinnur. They weren't the only ones there; a second group had arrived in another car. The plan was for Valdimar and Magnus to go out to sea in a small boat to retrieve the alcohol which had been dumped from one of the cargo boats that Iceland was dependent upon to bring in almost everything the country needed. Saevar and Einar killed time by driving around Keflavik and Njardvik waiting for the smugglers to return. Saevar talked to Einar about his trips abroad and his disastrous attempt to smuggle drugs from Rotterdam.

When they returned to collect Magnus, he was alone and he had bad news: as they were going to collect the alcohol, there was an accident and Geirfinnur had fallen overboard. He had drowned. Magnus didn't go into detail about how the accident happened or even if they had got Geirfinnur back into the boat. But he warned Saevar not to mention the accident to anyone. The three men drove back towards Reykjavik and dropped Saevar at his mum's house at about three in the morning.

Saevar had found the perfect way to get back at Einar, who he knew despised him and who had thrown him and Erla out of her dad's apartment in Hafnarfjordur.

The detectives started playing the suspects off against one another. Having got Saevar's statement they immediately brought Erla back to the prison so she could hear what he had told them. She couldn't believe it, 'I was aware the whole time this was totally crazy,' she thought. 'It was so far-fetched and absurd it would never fly with anyone.' But it soared with the police. After months of effort and a chaotic and flawed early investigation, they finally had an idea of what had happened to Geirfinnur.

Erla was informed her testimony could affect her closest relatives as they were closing in on her half-brother, Einar. With Gudmundur her mind had been hazy; she thought the events she described at her appartment could have happened. This time she was certain that what Saevar had told the police was fantasy. She was lost, caught up in a world where she said the police were no longer interested in reality. They came up with a theory and found 'facts' to match it.

When Erla had received threatening calls at her mum's house she had contacted the police. The detectives who visited her to investigate had stated that she was afraid of her brother Einar, Sigurbjorn Eriksson (the owner of Klubburin) and one of his friends. There had been tension with Einar over her relationship with Saevar but she had looked up to him. So what had made her fear him? When the detectives asked why was afraid of these men, she answered 'because of the Geirfinnur case'. Having listened to Saevar's account it was Erla's turn to pour out a remarkable and vivid story about the night Geirfinnur went missing and the men she now thought of as friends could barely keep up, filling pages of script:

On the night of 19 November 1974, Erla and Saevar had been at Klubburin and they were not having much fun. They decided to leave, and got into a blue Mercedes with two others, taking off without a planned destination. They headed out of Reykjavik, past the Straumsvik aluminium plant. She remembered that the speedometer of the car was a strange shape. It was square and stood out on the dashboard and as they went faster the speedometer went up vertically.

They drove past her home in Hafnarfjordur, and on towards the airport at Keflavik. Saevar held onto her hand the whole time, even when she tried to release his grip. He spoke to the driver, she couldn't remember the exact conversation, but she knew they were plotting, just like Saevar's friends had at the window in her dream. They were talking about killing someone by taking him out to sea, pretending they were going to get something. It was a last resort, they had tried to offer this man money but he wouldn't listen, they would have to make him disappear. They were on a mission to murder.

When they reached Keflavik they stopped by the foreshore. It was a spooky place at night, littered with battered trawlers propped up on blocks waiting to be repaired before being thrust back into the sea. When they got out of the car Erla saw the face of the driver who had been speaking to Saevar. It was Magnus Leopoldsson from Klubburin. There were other men there and other cars, too. She remembered a red sedan, which could have been her dad's car, and there was a large van that she thought might be a Volkswagen, that stood by the shore. She thought it was a light colour but she couldn't be sure. There was a boat by the pier, a pretty big one, and near it she saw seven men. In front of the car, Magnus and Saevar were talking to someone she didn't know (but would later conclude was Geirfinnur Einarsson). Geirfinnur had promised the men he could get hold of smuggled alcohol being dropped from a boat out at sea.

Erla recognised her half-brother Einar, who was standing to the right of the car, and a bit further away was Saevar's friend and familiar partner in crime,

Kristjan Vidar. Geirfinnur was talking to Saevar and Magnus when a fight broke out. Erla was scared and got out of the car, hoping no one would notice her. The others were preoccupied and didn't see her inching away and then she ran, she wanted to get away and hide. She found an abandoned house which was either still being built or used for storage. She hid there in a corner, she couldn't remember for exactly for how long. As she waited, she felt so bad that she threw up.

Eventually she came out and managed to hitch a lift in an old Moskvitch car. The driver was an elderly man who chatted to her about how he was forced to move from the Westmann islands in 1973 after a violent volcanic eruption engulfed them in ash and boiling lava. She then hitched another lift with a lorry that was on its way to Reykjavik and finally reached Hafnarfjordur. When she got home, Saevar wasn't there.

When he arrived later he never explicitly talked about the trip to Keflavik or what had happened. However, he discussed going to Copenhagen, to get away from the police for the post office fraud. Erla had heard there was a warrant out for her arrest so getting out of Iceland for a while seemed a sensible idea.

Erla had now been talking for three hours. She told them that when she saw the news about Geirfinnur's disappearance she hadn't connected it to the night in Keflavik. She couldn't identify Geirfinnur from the pictures of him she had seen in the media. She said it well may be that Geirfinnur was one of the men there, but it was dark so she couldn't say for sure. Now she thought about it, she concluded that Geirfinnur was the man who the Klubburin men decided should disappear.

Sigurbjorn took Erla home in the afternoon. On the drive to her apartment the detective assured her that she was doing the right thing by helping them. She was now in so deep that she would later forget what she had told them and change her story many times. It didn't matter to the police, what was important was the essential truth that Erla knew about Geirfinnur, just as she had known about Gudmundur. Erla and Saevar had both confessed to being there when Geirfinnur was killed. The only one left in the trio was Kristjan Vidar.

He was stewing in his cell, just metres from Saevar, waiting for his next interrogation. He would spend hours staring at the walls thinking what he should say next. When Kristjan was next brought into the interrogation room, it was the evening of 23 January. The inmates had eaten the food that had to be brought in from outside and a long night stretched out ahead of them. Kristjan began recounting his version of the night in Keflavik:

Initially he thought he hadn't been involved in the disappearance of Geirfinnur, nor did he know about it. He had only been to Keflavik twice in his life. The first time was when he was about 13 years old, but the other time might have been around the time Geirfinnur vanished. At the time he was normally under the influence of various drugs – stimulants (LSD or amphetamines) or more soothing (cannabis). His memory from the second half of 1974 was very unclear at times due to excessive smoking of dope. He remembered at some time that night they went in a big vehicle, the kind used for goods or passengers. It might have been a Mercedes Benz van with windows on the sides and was probably a dark colour. He couldn't remember why he had gone in this car, but he was sure that he knew someone who was in the vehicle otherwise he wouldn't have got into it.

They had driven out of the city to the airport. He was a stranger in Keflavik and couldn't say where they have been driven exactly, but he remembered that the vehicle stopped right next to the sea by the side of a big building which was commercial or office buildings. In front of the building was a concrete dock but the lighting wasn't good there, the only light came from lights on the side of the building. He saw the back of a fairly large boat, he thought it was a steel vessel but he couldn't be sure whether it was in the sea or on the land. There was one other very small boat at the pier. There were at least two other vehicles there, both cars. He wasn't sure what colour they were but he thought they were Volga, Datsun or Mercedes Benz models. There were several men there and one woman. Some of the men were older than him and he recognised Saevar who he knew well and Einar who he had only seen in photos, he didn't know him personally. He had also seen Einar's sister, Erla Bolladottir. The men seemed to be discussing something together. Kristjan didn't remember getting out of the vehicle but he recalled the ground being gravel, there was no concrete or asphalt. He couldn't express himself any more on this, at least not for the time being, but he said he may be able to recall more about the incident later.

It was 1.20am. Kristjan went back to his cell, the three-by-two metres where he spent all day and night, to try to recall more of that night in November 1974. He had told the detectives that his memory of this time was vague as he had been drinking and taking drugs to excess. This was no impediment to the detectives, they would do what they had done in the Gudmundur case, they would help him to remember – and in doing so, would shape his memories.

Kristjan, Saevar, Tryggvi and Albert weren't only in solitary confinement. They were accompanied by guards at all times and never allowed to be alone with the other inmates or to have any visits from friends and family.

Their relations would come with food or clothes, books and magazines but were never allowed to see their loved ones. It was often left to Hlynur Thor Magnusson to provide the empathetic human contact the suspets craved.

A linguist who spoke five languages and loved classical music and quiet contemplation, Hlynur was not your typical prison guard. In the early 1970s he had been a high school teacher and in the summer months during the holidays he would work as a temporary prison guard while the full-time wardens took their holidays. He moved on to be a history researcher at the University of Iceland in 1973, studying abandoned Nordic farms, but after a few years had found it less than inspiring. 'It was absolutely boring,' he recalled. 'I was working on my own and when you are on your own you must have discipline, especially when the work is boring.' He had previously worked with the prison's chief warden, Gunnar Gudmundsson, at the Hegningarhusid prison. After he left to pursue his university studies, Hlynur would drop by every once in a while for a coffee and a chat. The arrival of Saevar and his friends at Sidumuli meant the chief warden needed to recruit more guards to deal with these dangerous young men. When he asked if Hlynur would like a temporary post at the jail, Hlynur jumped at the chance to chuck in his job in academia.

Hlynur found himself as an outlet for the inmates he was guarding. They were desperate to have a normal conversation that didn't involve going over the events of 1974 again and again. The guards were meant to have limited contact with the inmates but Hlynur didn't stick to the rules. He treated Saevar with respect and found that he caused no trouble. They would chat about Saevar's favourite topics of film or literature and Hlynur would smuggle books in for him. Kristjan was less forthcoming but always compliant. For some of these suspects, barely out of their teens and still living at home, he became a kind of surrogate parent.

Tryggvi was out of the picture for Geirfinnur's murder; he had a cast iron alibi as he was away on a trawler at the time which had been logged, so the police couldn't ignore it. But he was firmly implicated in Gudmundur's murder. He had a violent past and a long criminal record so the police weren't letting him go anywhere. The focus on the Geirfinnur case meant Tryggvi was left alone for days and weeks at a time with no one to talk to. He tried to cope with his isolation by exercising and recording his daily progress. Whenever he rang his bell asking for a guard to bring him to the toilet, he would present Hlynur Magnusson with news of his daily routines. 'He was like a son,' Hlynur recalled. 'He showed me how he wrote down how many exercises he had done and he was so proud to show me.' The man with a reputation for violence would recite rhyming couplets to Hlynur ('They were not great poetry but it was very amusing') as well as draw – not figures but decorations and flowers which he would present to the guard. They were 'happy flowers, he was coming to me like a little child with pictures saying, "See this, mummy?".'

Tryggvi was definitely not happy, though. His increasingly fragile mental state was managed with daily doses of medication Hlynur helped to distribute four times a day: Mogadon, Diazepam, and Chlorpromazine were given to Tryggvi and the others to help them sleep and calm them down. The guards had been instructed to make sure all the inmates took their drugs. 'They were crushed up so they couldn't hide it in their mouth,' Hlynur recalled. 'We knew that they would pretend to swallow so we watched them take it and drink the water and if they were capsules we opened them up.'

Some of the guards saw their role as going beyond looking after the inmates – they took it upon themselves to interrogate them. One of the most active was Hogni Einarsson, one of the senior guards at Sidumuli prison. He would question the suspects in their cells at all times of the night and day – an unconventional practice, though no one was going to question such an experienced guard. On 25 January, days after Saevar had given his intitial statement about the Geirfinnur case, Hogni thought he had made a breakthrough. He had an urgent request from Saevar who wanted to talk to the detectives.

It was just after two o'clock on Sunday morning when the phone went at Eggert Bjarnasson's house. In the past he would have been worried it was an emergency, but before he even picked up the receiver he knew it would be about the case. The team were working day and night; interviews that started in the tepid winter daylight would go on and on, ending when the only sound outside was the wind whipping across the flat land and the ocean crashing onto the rocks. A month into the investigation they had the confessions but these were confused and conflicting and there was little other evidence to show for their efforts: two suspected murders, but no bodies or forensic evidence linking the suspects to Gudmundur or Geirfinnur.

Half an hour later, Bjarnasson appeared at Sidumuli. Saevar's lawyer, Jon Oddsson, was not there at this time of the night, but then the suspects' lawyers only made fleeting appearances during the interrogations. Eggert questioned Saevar for almost two hours, finishing at 4.20am. Eggert then spent an hour with Kristjan Vidar and left the prison at 5.20am when the city was starting to wake, the local fishermen already headed out into the unforgiving Atlantic.

The detectives were engaged in a flurry of activity. They spent all of the next day interviewing Kristjan, and

Saevar again. They also took them for trips out of the prison to Keflavik to refresh their memories of the scene.

These interviews with the suspects had solidified the detectives' suspicions about Klubburin and whether the men running the club were involved in some way in Geirfinnur's disappearance. By the evening of Sunday 25 January they now had enough evidence from Erla, Kristjan and Saevar to make their next move.

PART 2

8

On 26 January 1976, the police staged a series of early morning raids and arrested three new suspects. The first to arrive at the prison was Valdimar Olsen, followed by the Klubburin manager, Magnus Leopoldsson, and Erla's brother, Einar Bollason. The three men were in total shock. Unlike the other suspects they had never been in trouble with the police before.

All three had short interviews where they denied any knowledge of Geirfinnur Einarsson. Magnus told them he had previously been interviewed about the case by the Keflavik detective, Haukur Gudmundsson, but didn't know anything. Valdimar said he had heard about Geirfinnur's disappearance but knew nothing about the case and had never met the man. Einar was pretty sure he had been at basketball training when Geirfinnur went missing. Despite their denials they were brought before the court and remanded for 45 days.

With seven prisoners now being held in Sidumuli in connection with the Gudmundur and Geirfinnur cases, the guards made sure there was a strict security regime. The suspects weren't allowed to see their lawyers alone and all messages between them had to be in writing and passed via the police. They were also prevented from having any contact with each other or other prison inmates. They were totally cut off from the outside world.

Guard and former academic Hlynur Magnusson, who now had even more inmates to look after, saw that 'there was one cell that was shorter than the others' and it was decided by the police and chief warden that this was where they would place the tall basketball player, Einar Bollason. 'He was put in that cell so that he could not stretch out. That bed was too short for him and they did that to make his life worse... it was special treatment to be in this cell.' Not only was it smaller than the other cells but the police knew that Einar had rheumatism so this would add to his discomfort and increase the pressure on him.

It didn't take long for the effects of solitary confinement to kick in. Within a week, the prison doctor, Gudsteinn, was being called for Einar and Magnus to give them sedatives to help them sleep. Klubburin's owner Sigurbjorn Eric was also arrested, evidence of the police's determination to prove a link between the club, alcohol smuggling and the disappearances.

The arrest of the owner and manager of Klubburin gave the case a new political impetus. Inside the Althinghusid, home to Iceland's parliament for almost a century, questions were being asked about the links between Klubburin and Justice Minister Olafur Johannesson. In the vaulted debating chamber with its duck egg blue walls and elaborate hanging lights, one MP, Sighvatur Bjorgvinsson, was determined to bring the issue out into the open. He demanded answers about Olafur's links to Klubburin and to the Geirfinnur case. Olafur shifted uncomfortably on his seat. This was the first time he had been personally attacked like this and he didn't like it. Olafur was forced to address Parliament and defend himself: 'I'm being accused of obstructing the investigation of a disappearance, even implying I'm covering up murder.'

Bjorgvinsson reminded the other MPs that the minister's unhealthy links to Klubburin went back to 1972.

Four years earlier, the chief of police in Reykjavik had closed down Klubburin for a variety of misdemeanours. The club had to fight for its survival, and Magnus and Sigurbjorn Eric appealed to the Justice Minister. Johannesson was a former law professor with an unassuming lifestyle for a senior politician, often getting the bus to work rather than using his official car. He studied the evidence supporting the closure and its legal merits. Having reviewed it, he told the chief of police in no uncertain terms that the closure was 'utterly premature and unnecessary and not supported by the proper administration of justice'. He ordered the police to allow the club to re-open.

Olafur's political opponents believed there was another reason for his decision: the links between Klubburin and the Progressive Party. Not only did the club rent their premises from the party, there were rumours the club was even being bankrolled by the party. There was no documentary evidence to support this, but that didn't stop them from taking root.

It was a story Johannesson didn't want to revisit, and he already had enough on his plate as Iceland was again in the middle of a dispute with the United Kingdom over fishing rights. Fishing was the engine that had turned Iceland from a poor agrarian community into a growing, vibrant economy. Each morning, trawlers would set off from ports around the country to face the dangers and collect the riches of the Atlantic Ocean. It was second nature to many families who for generations had looked to the sea for their livelihood. Other nations, however, also wanted to harvest from the Atlantic, hauling in the tonnes of cod and haddock.

Iceland's dispute with the UK had started back in the 1950s when catches of Icelandic cod began to drop from overfishing. Iceland's government felt it had to act to protect its key industry, so they extended their territorial fishing grounds to 12 miles off the coast and set a dead-line for all foreign vessels to fish outside of these limits. This was highly damaging to the British fishing fleet which also wanted the Atlantic cod, haddock and plaice found off Iceland's coast. The UK government objected, backed by European partners, including France, Germany and Spain. So began what quickly became known as the 'Cod Wars'. British trawlers ignored the new limits and were accompanied by warships that were pitted against the handful of vessels in the Icelandic coast guard. After two-and-a-half years of skirmishes and diplomatic manoeuvres, Britain agreed to Iceland's 12-mile limit.

A decade later, with the cod population dropping once more, Iceland extended its fishing territory to 50 miles. This time all Western European countries opposed it. German and British trawlers ignored the new limits but the Icelandic coast guard had a new weapon: net cutters. If foreign trawlers refused to move outside of the 50-mile limit, the Icelandic coast guard cut the trawler's nets, forcing them to return to port empty handed.

Johannesson, who was prime minister at the time, led the negotiations in this second Cod War. Iceland played hard ball, refusing to back down and the dispute led to calls for Iceland to leave NATO, which would have been devastating for the country's economy and its standing in the world. Johannesson tried to get the Americans involved, asking the United States to send jets to monitor British warships protecting the trawlers, to no avail. Eventually an agreement was reached, but this didn't assuage Iceland – they wanted to extend their territory even further.

In 1975 the Icelandic government declared it was extending its fishing grounds to 200 miles from its coast, prompting the hardest fought of all the Cod Wars. There were frequent clashes between British trawlers and the Icelandic coast guard, culminating in an international incident in territiorial waters, when, in December 1975, the Icelandic coastguard vessel *Thor* was involved in a dramatic collision with a Royal Navy frigate, HMS *Andromeda*. *Andromeda*'s hull was dented but *Thor* came off far worse, sustaining a hole in its hull and coming close to being sunk.

With this latest clash proving the most serious of all, the Geirfinnur case was an unwelcome distraction. Having been dragged into an embarrassing session in Parliament, the Justice Minister wanted to make sure it was wrapped up so that he could concentrate on bigger political issues. He needed someone from outside who was more professional and could pull together the disparate threads and get the case to the Prosecutor and the judges.

Inside the investigation offices at Borgutun 7, Orn Hoskuldsson could not have envisaged he would be running such a complex investigation. The arrest of the Klubburin suspects had upped the ante significantly. Magnus, Einar, Valdimar and Sigurbjorn Eriksson were prominent figures in Iceland, well liked and respected. The only evidence the police had linking them to the case were the testimonies of thieves and drug dealers. The police were convinced Kristjan, Saevar and Erla had repeatedly lied to them, but in this instance they chose to believe them, as it suited their purpose: they could finally nail the Klubburin guys, who for years they had suspected of being alcohol smugglers.

The team were now coming under huge pressure from the press and public. Lurid headlines like, 'Geirfinnur, Gudmundur and Drugs: the large crime ring working in Iceland' were appearing with increasing regularity, as were articles complaining about a lack of progress or information from the police. This only added to the political pressure on the Justice Minister, too. Inside the small detective force, Arnprudur Karlsdottir could see the effect first-hand: 'The police were desperate, the nation was desperate, the media were desperate, so they started to pressure the suspects more and more.'

And yet there was still no physical evidence to link any of the seven men being held in Sidmuli to the deaths of Gudmundur and Geirfinnur. If the case was going to stick, all of the suspects had to confess.

There was one witness the detectives could always depend on to help them: Erla Bolladottir. Having implicated her brother Einar she felt even more isolated, alone in her mother's apartment with her baby. She was trapped again, like she had been in Hafnarfjordur when Saevar would leave her alone while he tried to play the big man in town. She was more dependent than ever on the police for support, and particularly her confidante, Sigurbjorn Eggertsson.

Ten days after her first statement about the involvement of the Klubburin suspects, Erla was brought back to Sidumuli for another interview in the room the detectives all referred to as 'the Corner'. Along the corridor were her lover, her brother and the other men she had helped to put into isolation. Erla was caught in a web of her own making and each time she was questioned, she spun new threads. Their patterns became ever more elaborate, expanding and drawing in more people, who became trapped. She would try to remember the shape and structure, but each time she returned she could never make the same web again.

The interview lasted three hours, relatively short for the detectives. The resulting story was broadly similar to the one Erla had given ten days ago, but she changed some important details about the drive to Keflavik. This time, rather than Magnus Leopoldsson driving them straight to the harbour, they had gone around Reykjavik, stopping at a place that sold ammunition. She thought they were going to buy some bullets but that didn't happen. They picked up Kristjan and another passenger on their way to meet Geirfinnur Einarsson. When they arrived at the location, her brother Einar and Valdimar were there and they were all wearing gloves. She couldn't be certain whether Klubburin's owner Sigurbjorn Eriksson was there too.

The changes in Erla's statement and the longer drive were significant for the timing of the night's events.

Saevar had maintained that on the evening Geirfinnur went missing he had gone with Erla and his mother to watch a film at the cultural centre in Reykjavik. The film was about Vestmannaeyjar on the Westmann islands, a volcano that had been dormant for 5,000 years when it erupted in January 1973. A population of 5,000 people had made their home in the fishing town below, in the shadow of the sleeping giant. Early in the new year, a fissure opened up one-and-a-half kilometres long, less than half a kilometre from the startled inhabitants. A plume of bright orange lava shot 150 metres into the air, releasing huge clouds of ash. There was no option but to flee. Nature dealt the islanders a lucky card: there had been a storm the previous day so the harbour was packed with fishing boats. These became the lifeline for the islanders, used to ferry the villagers to safety. The eruption lasted for six months and destroyed hundreds of homes but miraculously, no one was hurt. It was a seminal moment for Iceland; a huge eruption which had been successfully dealt with but reminded the people just how susceptible they were to the ground beneath their feet.

It had been a powerful film, one that they would remember. What happened after the film would be contested by the police and suspects. The police believed Saevar and Erla left at around 8.40pm. This gave them plenty of time to drive around Reykjavik picking up the other passengers before heading to Keflavik where they met Geirfinnur around 10.30pm. Saevar's mother had given the police a very different set of timings. She had made a sworn statement saying she had been dropped home by Saevar and Erla at approximately 10pm. (She was sure of the time as she was diabetic and needed her insulin injection. The timing was backed up by Saevar's sister, Anna.) This would have only left a half-hour window to drive the 50 kilometres to Keflavik. Erla's new statement had them driving around the city beforehand so to reach Keflavik in time to meet Geirfinnur they would need to have raced around the city and be going well over the speed limit.

An aggressive defence lawyer would have made more of this and the statement from Saevar's mother to pull apart this timeline, but the detectives weren't worried. Erla's lawyer barely saw her and Saevar's was little better. When they did get the chance to see their clients, Orn Hoskuldsson would decide whether or not they could meet in private – normally their discussion would take place in front of a police officer. Despite these restrictions, the lawyers chose not to cause any problems. One eminent lawyer at the time, still practising and who didn't want to publicly insult his colleagues, summed up the actions of Erla and Saevar's lawyers: 'They were passive, rarely present. If they had been present, things would have gone differently.'

The police believed Erla's fanciful story about the Klubburin men who were now languishing in their cells unable to see or speak to their families. They were at least able to get some luxuries to make their time slightly more bearable. Their wives brought fruit, socks, tobacco and even beer. This didn't deal with the most pressing problem: spending virtually their whole lives in a green concrete box. They weren't used to this; they had never seen the inside of a cell or had to trudge out to wash in the basic shower or to call the guards to ask permission to use the toilet. They had been warned by the detectives that unless they confessed, they could be held like this indefinitely. Their families and comfortable existence would be gone. Their children would grow up without fathers, their reputations destroyed.

As the Klubburin suspects continued to struggle with the strictures of solitary confinement, Magnus came up with a rigid daily timetable, breaking down menial tasks like washing and eating to try to bring structure to the day and maintain his mental health. Guard Hlynur Magnusson said in spite of this, it was clear to him Magnus 'broke down mentally and physically'.

Einar was also struggling in the harsh environment. Desptie the cocktail of prescription drugs to help his mental state, Einar stopped eating, subsisting on tea, juice and the occasional biscuit. Hlynur said it was sad to watch a noted athlete, someone with such self-confidence who had spent years thinking about his physicality, collapse so quickly.

The police believed that Saevar and his gang had linked up with Einar and the Klubburin men for a smuggling operation and it was during this that Geirfinur had been killed. The police spent months trying to find evidence of Klubburin's involvement, looking at the club's finances and debts for a motive. The earlier Keflavik enquiry had already been over this ground, but found nothing. The Reykjavik team ignored this, viewing their colleagues in Keflavik as rank amateurs.

The police needed more than Erla's testimony; Orn Hoskuldsson was painfully aware of that. They called in other witnesses such as Geirfinnur's wife Gudni, who they hoped could provide some clues about the link between her husband and Klubburin. Gudni had been left in a dreadful limbo for the past two years with no concrete proof her husband was dead. (What did she explain to her son who had seen his dad leave, never to return? Did she tell him his father was dead or that he was missing?) But when the police asked about the Klubburin men she told them she had never heard Geirfinnur mention them, nor Saevar and the other suspects. Erla stuck to her story that the Klubburin men were in Keflavik when Geirfinnur was killed and Kristjan had said they were there too, although he was far more circumspect about their presence. He, Erla and Saevar had been shown photos of 16 men and after some hesitation, had independently picked out Einar and the Klubburin suspects as being in Keflavik when Geirfinnur was killed. The police focused on Magnus and Einar – they were the weak links.

In February 1976, a month after he was arrested, Einar Bollason was presented with the statements from Saevar, Erla and Kristjan implicating him in the case. Despite his weakened state Einar stuck to his guns and said their claims were 'totally baseless'. Why would these three people individually pick on him? He didn't know why Kristjan would do it, he had never met him, but he knew Erla had a grudge against him. He'd desperately wanted her to split from Saevar and he tried to get her to break off any communications between them. When this didn't work, Einar tried limiting Erla's contact with their father, whom she adored. It was for these reasons that he thought his sister had made up the whole story.

Erla had not seen her brother since she had accused him of taking part in a murder but the police thought it was about time they brought the siblings together for a joint interview. It lasted barely five minutes with both of them sticking to their stories.

The Klubburin men all had stronger alibis for the evening of 19 November than the original suspects and these had to be checked out. Einar had been at basketball training and then watched a sports movie on TV. The police even went as far as bringing him to the TV station to watch a tape of some of the sports programme to see how much of it he remembered. Magnus had been at a function and witnesses were questioned to see if they could identify him. They also had regular contact with their lawyers who were far more aggressive than the lawyers representing Saevar and his friends. Einar's lawyer complained about his treatment and Erla's constantly changing testimony. Regardless of this, and the fact that the detectives still hadn't found any evidence to back up her statement, in March Einar and the other Klubburin suspects were remanded for another month.

9

March 1976

The Reykjavik team still had no bodies, but they did have confessions. Then on 2 March there was a potentially devastating blow to the investigation. It had been a typical day for Kristjan – four separate interviews with Eggert and Sigurbjorn. By the evening, he had had enough. Sitting inside the Corner, he informed the detectives he wanted to change his previous testimony. This had happened before, adding or removing details, such as the fight that had happened that had killed Geirfinnur. Today Kristjan wanted to go much further. He wanted to retract his confession for Geirfinnur Einarsson's death entirely. He had thought it through in those lonely hours inside his cell and went through his previous admissions, one by one.

He said the previous statements he had given about the case were not true. He hadn't been in Keflavik on the night Geirfinnur went missing. He had also been lying about the Klubburin people he said were at the docks and who he claimed to have recognised from photos he had been shown. The fight he described when Geirfinnur had been hit and died had also not happened. He had constructed this story using information gleaned from the media and the rumours he had heard.

Sat across from him, a stunned Eggert and Sigurbjorn searched for some explanation as to why he had done this. When the detectives pushed him, he couldn't explain what his motivation had been, but he was fully aware of the serious offence he had committed by making up this story.

Having withdrawn his confession for Geirfinnur's murder, the worry was that it was only a matter of time before Kristjan did the same with the Gudmundur case. This could create a domino effect with the other suspects. By the time the officers left the prison it was after midnight and they shivered as they hurried to their cars. They had lost a confession, and a vital one at that.

The detectives let Kristjan stew for a few days in his cell before they returned on 5 March. They questioned him and during the next four days went over his story again and again. Kristjan tried to explan why he had constructed the story about Geirfinnur. The constant inter-rogations had frayed his nerves, particularly after the interviews where he had confessed to involvement in the death of Gudmundur Einarsson. He was on regular medi-cation and struggling to cope with life in solitary confine-ment. The confession had been a way of getting the police and prisons guards off his back.

The police weren't going to let him off that easily. The detectives planted the seed in Kristjan's mind that he had really been in Keflavik and he needed to go to the harbour to refresh his memory. For Kristjan this would be a chance to see the world outside – the changing sky, flat white clouds blocking out the light pressing down onto the land – and smell the sweet, clean air unlike the dusty concoction pumped into their cells. As spring came, thin shards of blue were appearing in the sky, the brown grass emerging from the snow covering the lava. He could feel the crunch of his feet on the hard ground, relishing the chance to walk longer than the few paces in his cell.

Kristjan had been out on these drives before, accompanied by the guard Hlynur Magnusson. Hlynur noticed on these trips, 'He was so willing to help when we were searching in the lava. He tried and tried to remember. It's like he had found a little thread and tried to remember and perhaps he believed himself that what came out when he was trying hard, were the facts.' At the beginning of the case, the confessions seemed solid, like the crust that the lava had formed over the island. But when you looked closer, cracks began to appear in the stories that quickly grew into wide fissures, through which the lava rose and spread, expanding the testimonies until they couldn't be controlled. After a few of these trips Hlynur decided, 'It was obvious those suspects had no idea where they were going; it was obvious, especially with Kristjan Vidar, as he was so wasted.'

Hlynur's doubts weren't shared by the detectives.

On 8 March, almost a week after retracting his statement, Kristjan visited Keflavik again. He was taken at night to the same deserted harbour filled with battered boats propped on wooden platforms waiting to be repaired, looking just as it did on that November night two years earlier. He had discussed this night so much with the detectives that Kristjan could shut his eyes and picture the car and the van waiting to take away the booze which was being brought to them in a little boat moored at the pier.

This visit did the trick. When Eggert and Sigurbjorn returned the next day, Kristjan wanted to offer yet another version of that doomed night in November 1974:

He said he had been picked up in the centre of Reykjavik. He could even name the street, Vatnsstigur. He sat in the back seat with Erla, with Saevar in the front and someone he didn't know driving. They made

their way out of the city towards Keflavik. Once he
was there, though, the clouds closed in; there were
some other men there, he wasn't sure how many, prob-
ably three; he couldn't remember whether he had been
taken out on a boat and what else happened there. When
it was all finished, they returned to Reykjavik but he
couldn't say who was in the car with him; he didn't
know what they intended to do there, but it was defi-
nitely illegal.

Crucially he said the name Geirfinnur meant nothing to him, that he hadn't heard any stories about how he vanished. His story was almost unrecognisable from his original testimony in January.

Kristjan had made clear throughout his evidence that his memory was like a room full of locked doors; occasionally he would find a key but then as soon as he had seen inside it would shut again. By taking him out to Keflavik the police were trying to unlock new doors, but when he opened them he would see these new images suggested by the police that he didn't recognise and this added to his confusion. He would blink, unsure whether this was a real memory or a false one suggested by his interaction with the investigators.

At the time of his arrest, Kristjan was rarely sober and taking drugs regularly to escape from the drudgery of manual work and the long grey winter that suffocates the land. He had a fragile hold on reality and his lifestyle had been so chaotic and troubled that the boundaries had started to blur. This made him vulnerable to the prodding and suggestions from Orn, Sigurbjorn and Eggert. He began to struggle with what was real and what he had imagined.

But to the detectives, Kristjan was back in the game. He was remanded for another 90 days in custody. The crisis had been averted.

While this had been taking place, another team of detectives had been focusing on the parallel investigation into Gudmundur Einarsson and the search for his body. Their big hope was Albert Klahn. He had driven Saevar, Kristjan and Tryggvi from Hafnarfjordur at the dead of night to the craggy expanse of the silent lava plains, where they said they had dumped the body. As the driver, the police hoped Albert would have been less distracted than the others and had paid more attention to where he was going.

From the first day he had been arrested back in December 1975, Albert had been put into the back of the police department's chunky American imported cars and driven out with the detectives, trying to find Gudmundur. In February 1976 he told the police he had returned to the lava with Saevar, Tryggvi and Kristjan to move Gudmundur's body to another spot where they thought it was less likely to be discovered. On this second occasion it was clear to him this wasn't a package, it was a body, but he couldn't recall where this location was. He was lost in the grey cloud that hung low over the city on many winter days, reaching down to the ocean, a slate blanket obscuring the land. The investigation team was trying to penetrate the mist that had enveloped the memories of Albert Klahn. As hard as they blew, they could never part the mist for very long.

The police would record the different places where they went in the lava fields: the aluminium plant at Straumsvik, the green ancient grazing land of Kuagerdi, the rubbish tip south of Hafnarfjordur, and countless other nameless pits and craters. The police would be hopeful when Albert would point to spots that other suspects had picked out too, but there was never any sign of a body.

Albert shied away from violence and the police thought that, like Erla, he would have been traumatised by what he saw on that freezing January night. It wasn't a surprise his mind was trying to block this out. Orn Hoskuldsson wanted to find a way to release the memories buried deep in Albert's psyche.

The police's limited techniques weren't working, so in early March the investigators got a psychologist, Geir Vilhjalmsson, to work with Albert. Maybe he could break through the barrier that was holding him back. Rather than using a conventional dialogue in an office, though, Dr Vilhjalmsson took Albert back out to the field to explore some of the locations he had visited before. The police hoped with his professional expertise the psychologist could get Albert to be more specific about where he had gone with Gudmundur's body.

From 11 March, Albert went on four separate drives with the psychologist. At first Albert was very vague, he had difficulty remembering the route he had taken and where they had parked. Then he would have moments of clarity, recalling details of roads or pits that he might have visited. These were brief slithers of light peeking out from the cracks and fissures, but still Albert's memory continued to shift and twist.

The intervention of the psychologist proved fruitless, so the police engaged a psychiatrist, Jakob Jonasson, to hypnotise Albert. Jonasson was even less successful than the psychologist; he found Albert wasn't very receptive, so the experiment stopped.

When the two experts failed to make any progress the investigation team paused and took stock. The team had tried everything in their power to get Albert to remember where he had gone, but his memory wasn't budging, it refused to give up the ghost of Gudmundur. By now he was at one with the spirits trapped beneath Iceland's dark crust.

After discussions with the psychologist, the detectives decided Albert was spent, there was no point holding him any longer. On 19 March, he was released from custody. He had been in solitary confinement for 87 days. He was free but not out of the police's grasp. He could still be called on to try and to fill in the many gaps in the case and find the body of Gudmundur Einarsson.

Tryggvi Runar had only experienced a taste of the outside and the fresh tang of the salty air once during his confinement. After his confession in January, Tryggvi had rarely been troubled by the detectives, who were struggling to deal with the multiple suspects in the Geirfinnur murder. But the police still considered Tryggvi highly dangerous. At the beginning of March, Orn Hoskuldsson had received reports that Tryggvi was getting messages out of the jail and issuing death threats to potential witnesses. It wasn't clear how this was possible as Tryggvi had no visitors apart from the police, prison guards and the doctor, but nevertheless, Orn ordered the guards to keep a close watch on him.

On 22 March Tryggvi was brought before the court when he said he had nothing to add to his previous statements and was remanded for a further 90 days. That evening he sat in his sickly green cell and wrote a long letter to Orn Hoskuldsson listing his previous crimes stretching back to the early 1970s. They consisted of thefts and fights, so many that he couldn't remember, but none that he considered particularly serious. He was trying to show the investigators that he was willing to co-operate and own up to his previous misdemeanours, and by doing this he hoped it might make the police engage with him and no longer leave him rotting in his cell.

Saevar was at the other extreme. He was never allowed such periods of inactivity and, unlike Tryggvi, he positively didn't want to co-operate with the investigators. He had also been remanded in March for a further three months and remained the police's top target with three detectives specifically assigned to him. He was the smallest of the suspects, with a skinny boy's body but he was also the most mentally robust. He was clean – he didn't take drugs or drink – and had experienced solitary confinement in the tiny cells at Sidumuli before. He claimed that he had only confessed in the first place because of the police threats. Among other things, they had told him that if he didn't he could be deported to the US on account of his American father, where he would be incarcerated and die in a grim American prison. However, the detectives couldn't pull the same trick they had used with the others, of helping them to release their trapped memories. To engage with this you had to have faith in the police, to believe that they were trying to help you. Saevar didn't trust them one iota and he was determined to oppose them whenever he could, even mounting a desperate attempt to flee.

It happened in mid February, on one of the trips out of the prison with Orn Hoskuldsson and Eggert Bjarnasson. Erla had witnessed his frustration on these trips when she had accompanied him on a few occasions – she thought as a presence to calm him down. 'Saevar was constantly trying to tell them to stop this nonsense, I don't know anything, I can't tell you anything.' On this occasion, Saevar hit Orn and sprinted off as fast as he could across the uneven lava, but he didn't get very far before he was caught.

The police weren't going to let his escape attempt go unpunished. When they got back to Sidumuli, Saevar was placed in leg irons. He remained shackled when he was taken to the toilet and other prisoners would hear him walking, the iron chains banging against the floor. When they heard this noise, the inmates would bang on their doors, knowing this was all they could do to show their support.

To the investigation team Saevar was a ruthless drug dealer intent on corrupting Icelandic society. They even had a nickname for him, the Rat. They thought the Rat was capable of murder, but getting him to co-operate was a different matter. He had confessed but he hadn't led the police to the bodies, and his inability or unwillingness to say where the bodies were buried was seen by the police as deliberately obstructive. They were sure he was holding back he was frustrating them, and they would need the prison wardens to help break his spirit.

The guards had set out to make his life as uncomfortable as possible. The order had come from the very top from the chief warden, Gunnar Gudmundsson. 'He believed these people are criminals and we must do anything to solve this and a confession squeeze out of them,' Hlynur remembered.

Early on in his custody, Saevar had been moved from his cell on the narrow, brightly lit corridor. He was put in cell 22, which was on its own in a corner next to the guards' office. It was from here that the guards monitored the inmates through a system of bells which prisoners would ring inside their cells to ask for food, toilet breaks or just simple human contact. Having Saevar next to their office meant the wardens could target him without disturbing the others.

March may be a time of year when Iceland is still subsumed by darkness most of the time, but this was not the case for Saevar. The guards tampered with the light in his cell, making it permanently bright and impossible for him to get proper sleep. He tried to cover the light, but the guards would remove whatever he used to block it out. If he did manage to sleep, they would bang on his cell door or the wall with their fists or with stones, night and day. It unnerved Saevar and kept him under constant pressure, but it was also a way for the guards to pass the long 12-hour shifts, where at night there was very little to do. Hlynur Magnusson would see his fellow guards smashing the walls of Saevar's cell, and they were bemused when he didn't join in.

Saevar's mother and sister regularly visited the jail but were never allowed to see him. They would bring clean clothes and food, which were examined to make sure his relatives weren't smuggling anything in for him. His reputation as a drugs kingpin led them to suspect even the most benign gifts: 'They wouldn't let him have oranges as they thought they had been injected with dope,' Hlynur remembered. (Strangely, in order to make sure the oranges weren't suspect, they would sometimes eat them.) The paranoia about Saevar reached such fervour that it seemed any major crime was connected to him in some way.

Warden Gudmundur Gudbjarnarson had seen this for himself when he drew the short straw for the night shift on New Year's Eve. His colleague was on edge, as some dynamite had been stolen and rumour spread that it was to be used to stage a jail break at Sidumuli. He told Gudbjamarson he was worried that 'somebody is on a revenge mission and planning to bomb the cells where the guys are'. The guard spent the night walking around the perimeter of the prison checking there wasn't a stash of dynamite being assembled next to the walls.

Gudbjarnarson was tall and gentle, though he could look after himself. He always had a problem with bullies and thought the slightly built Saevar was harshly targeted by the far bigger police and wardens. He would hear the other guards laughing and discussing what they did to keep Saevar awake. When they boasted about this in front of detective Eggertsson, Gudmundur expected a reprimand from a professional cop who knew the proper way to treat a suspect. Instead he remembered Sigurbjorn's surprising reaction, 'He said yes guys that's nice, just keep it going. He was encouraging them to keep doing it.'

There were other privations preserved solely for Saevar. Inmates were allowed books which arrived every two weeks but Saevar was deprived of anything to keep him occupied – no books, newspapers, pens or tobacco – so he could focus solely on his guilt. Hlynur said whenever he called on Saevar in his cell, 'He had nothing except light, day and night.'

Journalists were desperate to find out what was going on inside Sidumuli. They'd had leaks that Saevar and Kristjan were definitely involved in both cases and that, despite a lack of bodies or clear forensic evidence, Geirfinnur Einarsson and Gudmundur Einarsson had been murdered. Problems within the investigation also began to filter through to the press, with articles appearing suggesting widespread difficulties with the inmates. Inside the offices at Borgutun 7, Orn Hoskuldsson had tried to remain above this, keeping his distance from the media, but the pressure was building each day. He wasn't playing ball with the press and they continued to complain that few details were being released about the course of the inquiry.

After weeks of sniping from the media, at the end of March Orn Hoskuldson decided to hold a press conference to dispel some of the myths and misinformation that had sprung up about the investigation. It was also to announce that, after laying the ground work, a full judicial investigation would start in a few days' time while the police continued their work gathering more evidence. The previously taciturn Orn led the briefing. This was to be no short précis of the investigation. It was a thorough warts-and-all account of what the suspects had been telling them in the three months they had been kept in solitary confinement.

In that time there had been much speculation about how the investigation had gone from a simple one of embezzlement to a double murder case. Orn spelled out the importance of Erla to the case, how she had first revealed information about the disappearance of Gudmundur Einarsson and how the investigation into Geirfinnur emerged because of threatening and intimidating phone calls she had been receiving in January.

Orn said Erla named three people, all of whom had been arrested: Saevar, Trygvvi and Kristjan. They had been questioned extensively, alone and together. For the first time, Orn and his team set out what they believed had happened on 19 November 1974.

Erla, Saevar and Kristjan had driven to Keflavik harbour along with an unknown driver where they met Geirfinnur and the three other men who were also in custody – Magnus, Einar and Valdimar – although the police didn't name them at this point. They went out on the boat, although the police said they didn't know what it was called or who owned it. Erla, meanwhile, had crept out of the car and hidden in a deserted house nearby and she later hitched a ride back to Reykjavik.

The detectives told the eager press corps they had been told differing, conflicting accounts about what happened on the boat. Saevar and Kristjan couldn't agree on how Geirfinnur died and whether his body was thrown into the sea or buried in the lava. The police were leaning towards the lava fields.

The journalists asked about the earlier enquiry into Geirfinnur's disappearance, led by Valtyr Sigurdsson. This had produced numerous leads: the calls to Geirfinnur's home; the clay head. What had happened to all of these lines of enquiry? Orn Hoskuldsson couldn't have been any more explicit: these were not part of the current investigation. In one fell swoop the Reykjavik team belittled six months' work by Valtyr and his detectives. None of the leads the Keflavik team pursued with such vigour was now being considered seriously. It was a humbling blow for Valtyr and his detective Haukur Gudmundsson.

Though the Klubburin suspects weren't named during the briefing, it was known that they had been arrested and what became clear during the briefing was that the only evidence keeping them in prison were the statements from Saevar, Erla and Kristjan. The obvious question asked by *Morgunbladid* newspaper the next day was what if Saevar, Kristjan and Erla were lying about the Klubburin suspects to get revenge or draw attention away from their own involvement? The police had admitted this was a possibility, but Saevar, Kristjan and Erla had all told similar stories and they had not had any contact with one another since December 1975, lending credence to their accounts.

Having heard the police version of events, the lawyers for the Klubburin men struck back. Their clients had been held for 62 days in solitary confinement and they said nothing had been discovered that backed up the claims made by Saevar, Erla and Kristjan. The lawyers accused the police of failing to disclose important details about the case. Journalists began calling the prison and the detectives' offices trying to get Orn Hoskuldsson to clarify some of these issues, but he remained elusive. There was no similar outburst from the lawyers for Saevar and Erla. Their clients had effectively been tried in front of the media but their silence was deafening.

Orn Hoskuldsson may have sounded confident about the case at his press briefing, but the formal judicial enquiry had barely started when it suffered another significant setback.

The deputy prosecutor Hallvardur Einvardsson was in charge of the case. He had receding hair, thick brows, big glasses and the slow, thoughtful demeanour of an academic. He was assisted by the veteran cop, Njordur

Snaeholm, who was head of the detective department. Njordur was tall and handsome, square jawed with a thick grey streak in his neatly parted black hair. He wanted to hear from the key witnesses to confirm what they had previously told the police in their interviews.

This was a big moment for Saevar, one that he had been mulling over inside his cell for weeks. It was his chance to strike back at the police and wardens after months of cruel treatment and unrelenting pressure. As he stood inside the bland, functional courtroom with enough of his swagger still intact he said the statements he had previously given were false and he had no knowledge of Geirfinnur Einarsson. He explained how he first heard about Geirfinnur when he was away in Copenhagen in early 1975. He had gone with Erla as she was being threatened and was afraid her brother and his friends would kill her. Saevar wanted to protect her from harm and thought that by implicating her brother and the other Klubburin suspects they would be investigated for the threats to Erla.

This was a huge embarrassment for the investigation team. Saevar was the second suspect to withdraw his confession about Geirfinnur. The immediate suspicion of the detectives was the suspects must be communicating with each other, despite never being alone in the same room together.

The police weren't used to running one murder case, let alone two. The investigation team was being pulled in different directions and their limited resources were stretched. Most of their effort was focussed on the Geirfinnur case but they still wanted to find Gudmundur Einarsson.

10

May 1976

The fraught winter had given way to early summer and the mellow long days when the sun would burst through the clouds like a celestial beam, casting a silver light on the water below, rising at four in the morning and not setting until after well after ten. It wasn't hot, it never was this far north, but it was milder; the battering wind easing off and temperatures could rise to the high teens. It was the ideal time to be outside in the robust, muscular beauty of the Icelandic countryside.

On 2 May, the Reykjavik detective Njordur Snaeholm set off in a coach from the capital with 18 students from the police college. They were in good spirits. They passed around flasks of coffee, making barbed, dark jokes about the task ahead, which masked their apprehension about what they might find. They were on their way to the aquarium at Hafnarfjordur, which had come up frequently in the suspects' testimonies as a burial site for Gudmundur. Despite its name, it was more than a home for marine animals. It was a moribund place where lions, monkeys and polar bears paced around in their small enclosures, slowly going insane.

The team changed into boiler suits and long leather boots. They also wore their regulation caps, similar to the natty ones worn by the pilots in *Thunderbirds*. Some of them had long pitchforks and shovels, or poles to poke the hard, unyielding ground. They were on a mission to find Gudmundur's remains. Spreading out in one long line, they slowly made their way across the jagged, lunar landscape, covered with soft green moss and rough grass. The recruits were dots of colour as they went along, stopping to peer under rocks, delving down into fissures and hollows. They went back and forth three times but even with this many people spread out in a line they only covered a tiny section of the lava, a pinprick of the hundreds of square kilometres. All they found was rubbish and sheep bones.

Undeterred, days later they tried again. This time they sent 50 trained officers out into the petrified ocean of lava. They had some new locations suggested by Kristjan. He had told the detectives that he had taken Gudmundur's body and dumped it in a fissure so deep that it was towering over his head and formed a kind of cave. Tryggvi had rolled a large stone over the corpse, but this didn't cover it completely, so Kristjan added some rocks. The search achieved the same result as all the others: a day out for the search party, some black comedy, but no remains.

Alone in her apartment, desperate for company and affirmation, Erla too came up with new locations where she thought Gudmundur may be buried, and the police would take her out along the single lane highway to the lava fields. 'I was just doing what I was told and being co-operative, but I didn't have a clue,' Erla recalled. She believed what she had been told by the detectives: 'The police are saying that I just don't remember and the way they led me they were using some kind of techniques that were working.' Alone and isolated from her friends, Erla had begun to rely on the detectives and they convinced her she had suppressed her memories because she had been traumatised by what she had seen.

The detectives would wander from location to location with little strategy, hoping Erla would lead the way. 'We would all be walking across these rocks and asking, "Could it have been here, what do you think?" I was just saying, maybe, might. It was really pointless.' Sometimes she would persuade Orn Hoskuldsson and the detectives that this time she really had remembered where the body was. The police began digging at these locations, such as the lava pits at Krysuvík, a wild expanse of steaming volcanic vents and boiling springs framed by hills stained a multitude of blues, yellows and bright green moss. It was a futile exercise: the police would scrape away in the area for a while and find nothing. Mostly for Erla these trips were 'a big state of confusion'.

These trips contributed to Erla's diminishing ability to distinguish her real memories of 1974 from the false memories she was constructing. They were feeding Erla's fertile imagination and on 3 May she would turn the Geirfinnur enquiry on its head.

It was 8.30 in the evening when Erla was brought into the Corner. She was accompanied by Sigurbjorn Eggertsson, but this time there was a new person in the room: Hallvardur Einvardsson, the deputy prosecutor overseeing the case.

For three hours they went over Erla's story again and again, her guilt gnawing away at her, ready to burst out. When they finished the interview, it was 11.40 and Hallvardur decided Erla could harm herself if she was allowed to return home. She was a valuable witness and someone they had to protect. For her own safety it was decided she should be kept in the prison overnight. They phoned the chief warden who ordered that her cell be thoroughly searched to make sure there was nothing that she could use to harm herself with. He also assigned a female warden to keep a close eye on her. 'She will be very well cared for,' Hallvardur assured the police.

They called Jon Bjarman, the tall, bearded prison chaplain who looked like a basketball player with thick wavy hair and prominent buck teeth. Apart from the doctors he was the only outsider allowed to visit the suspects and the one person who saw them who wasn't trying to get information out of them. He was there to listen. He spent two hours in the cell with Erla trying to calm her down. Eventually at three o'clock in the morning Bjarman left, but he told the guards that if Erla needed him he was available day or night. It had been a traumatic night and Erla was given a sedative to help her sleep.

Erla's condition had unsettled the chaplain, who later phoned to check on her mental state and was reassured that she was much better. Einvardsson had checked in by phone too and was told that having taken some sleeping tablets Erla had slept that night. At lunchtime the next day she was once again taken into the interrogation room that had become so familiar. Erla was preparing to reveal a secret that would transform her role in the case from an observer to a killer.

Amid the smoky fug and coffee cups, Erla went over the Geirfinnur case once again. The setting was so vivid to them now that everyone in that room could picture the scene in Keflavik on that November night in 1974. The story began like the previous versions:

They drove the car down to the Drattarbraut, the deserted slipway with the empty warehouses casting long shadows in the sombre light over the junk strewn around the site. Within this setting were two cars and a group of men. The membership of this smuggling enterprise changed depending on who was telling the story. Erla arrived with Kristjan and Saevar, in a car driven by Magnus Leopoldsson. It was a cold starlit night, well below freezing and the roads were icy. On the drive Magnus and Saevar were talking about a man who had been causing them trouble and they needed to do something to sort it out. Magnus seemed more bothered about it; he and Einar had tried to reason with this man, but it hadn't worked. Erla hadn't picked up what they were planning to do about this man once they reached Keflavik. When they arrived, it was dim and poorly lit, exactly what they wanted as they didn't want to be seen. Saevar and Magnus got out and began talking to a man Erla didn't recognise: Geirfinnur Einarsson. She followed them out of the car.

In the murky light Saevar handed her something heavy. It was a rifle, although she couldn't say exactly what it looked like. He showed her how to hold it but it wasn't there as a scare tactic; they intended to use it. Geirfinnur was brought over and she had been so close to him she could see his face, etched with fear and horror as he realised what was about to happen to him. They had come up with a solution for this annoying, unreasonable man. Erla closed her eyes as she pulled the trigger, the rifle jolted in her hands as the bullet flew from the barrel into Geirfinnur's body. Saevar immediately took the rifle from her as they dealt with the man dying on the ground in front of them, his blood staining the snow.

It was only after the fact that Erla panicked and in the confusion she was able to sneak away and hide in a deserted house close by, where she spent the night. When she returned home the next morning Saevar was angry, he wanted to know where she had been all night. He never mentioned Geirfinnur again and refused to talk about that night. They would banish it from their minds,

*a secret they would keep from themselves. They would
pretend it never happened.*

After less than two hours, the interview ended. In that
short time, Erla had changed from a bystander to an
active participant. She confessed to being the killer. All
of the months of informal chats the interviews at the
prison, the trips to the lava fields; it had all led to this.
Erla was now one of them. For the detectives, it was this
that had brought on her trauma.

The way that her story was written down by the detectives made it seem like she was in some kind of trance,
doing Saevar's bidding. The police knew from Erla's
friends they had interviewed that she had a lively imagination and tendency to make things up. She had lied to
them before, could they believe her now?

Erla was brought before the criminal court. Her statement was read out and she confirmed that it was her
signature on the statement. In her heart Erla knew 'it
was painfully obvious we all knew nothing ever
happened. That thing of recalling what happened was
like a charade.' But what else could she say? Those were
her words on the pages, spelling out the story, confessing
that she had fired the gun at Geirfinnur. She may have
been pretending, drawn deep into 'the game' she was
playing with the police, but they had stopped playing
a long time ago. The prosecutor, Hallvardur, who had
been in the interview and brought her to the court with
Orn Hoskuldsson, now switched roles. Hallvardur
decided that what Erla had told them was so serious
that she should be held for 60 days. She was in a daze,
'I didn't understand, I thought I had done what they
wanted.'

Erla was in a parlous state, severely depressed and
suicidal. Her thinking was so impaired that she thought
by telling the police what they wanted to hear, it would

all be over. There was no forensic evidence, no bodies, just the suspects' fevered testimonies. The thing that Erla had feared the most had become a reality; she was to be taken from her beloved baby Julia. It would be a long time before she would see her again.

At 5.30 in the evening she was brought back to her cell. Erla's statement clearly contradicted Saevar and Kristjan's versions. The police would deal with that, but for now they let Erla get used to the surroundings. No matter how bad her interviews had been previously she had been allowed to leave. Now there was no escape. It didn't take long for the press to get news of her arrest. They reported that Saevar's partner had been taken into custody with information that could shed an entirely new light on Geirfinnur's disappearance.

With Erla's confession, Orn Hoskuldsson decided it was time they brought her together with Saevar and Kristjan. They waited until the evening to do this, when the suspects would be tired and waiting for the medication to help them sleep. One by one they were taken along the narrow corridor to the Corner. There Erla and Saevar would have one of their rare moments together. With the three suspects crammed into the space, having barely seen each other since they were arrested, the atmosphere was charged. Also in the room were the chief prison warden Gunnar Gudmundsson, Orn Hoskuldsson and the detectives Sigurbjorn and Eggert along with the prosecutor Hallvardur Einvardsson and the senior detective assisting him, Njordur Snaeholm. Now the main prosecutor, Hallvardur had been brought in too, participating in interviews and standing witness to mistreatment of the suspects.

Erla repeated her story about the events at Keflavik. She knew that 'it was a ridiculous story. This far into the case when they are talking about how we got rid of Geirfinnur's body, I was feeling whatever hope I had was gone... if this is how they wanted to tie loose ends I was never going to get out.'

Kristjan did the same, apparently accepting Erla's new role in the murder. Erla broke down and in tears asked Saevar what had happened the night Geirfinnur went missing. She was looking for affirmation and guidance from the man who had controlled her life for two years. Saevar had listened, incredulous at what he was hearing. He felt like the only sane person locked up in an asylum. Could no one else see through Erla's story, that it was patently nonsense? He thought the police had played on Erla and Kristjan's damaged psyches and they had been turned against him. They were prepared to lie about anything to gain the confidence and trust of the police. Saevar told Erla she was lying, she knew exactly where they were and it wasn't in Keflavik. Erla seemed to have taken on the role of the interviewer, and repeatedly shouted at him about their young child who was without her parents.

Having retracted his confession there was no way Saevar was being party to a fiction that Erla was the killer. He addressed Erla directly, asking how she had held the gun and how she had fired it. The detectives intervened trying to get him to stop, but he turned on them, bringing up the violence that they had used on him to get him to comply. Everyone in the room was convinced Saevar was guilty and that he was holding out, taunting them. The atmosphere was getting more heated as Saevar refused to agree with the fiction Erla had concocted.

Watching the lanky, long-haired, cocky rebel remain defiant was proving too much for Gunnar Gudmunsson. He couldn't bear it any longer and he lashed out at Saevar and hit him. He had clearly stepped over the line and in front of several witnesses. Although he had bravado, Saevar wasn't able to tolerate violence and was so distressed that he was brought back to his cell, but Erla's torture wasn't over. She was interviewed for another hour and a half, alone in a room with six other men, one of whom she had seen was willing to assault a prisoner if he didn't like their answers.

Erla's confession had thrown the Geirfinnur investigation into further turmoil. The woman who had drawn the Klubburin suspects into the case was now saying she was responsible for Geirfinnur's murder. Despite their struggles inside the jail, Einar, Magnus, Valdimar and Eric refused to budge. They had alibis which the detectives had spent months trying to disprove but couldn't.

The press sensed the police's uncertainty. Weeks earlier, the *Visir* newspaper felt emboldened enough to run a front-page story speculating that the four men connected to Klubburin would soon be released.

A week after Erla's confession they came before the court and were released. These men had spent 105 days in solitary confinement, and although they had access to lawyers and gifts from their families, the isolation had a profound effect on them.

When he arrived home, Einar's wife, Sigrun Ingolfsdottir, told waiting journalists: 'I was always convinced of Einar's innocence and I've tried not to be bitter. I've also tried to ignore all the gossip that's surrounded the investigation, and it's become clear these last few months which of the people we know are our real friends.' They had already faced hardship: Einar had been fired from his civil service job shortly after he was arrested and she said that 'if it hadn't been for many kind and helpful men assisting me we would've lost our house.'

The suspicions about Klubburin and smuggling, which went back to 1972, meant Magnus Leopoldsson had been the police's principal target from the beginning. On release, he moved away from running Klubburin and set up a successful property business. The other two Klubburin suspects kept their heads down and tried to get on with their lives but they found it was hard to escape being tainted by the case, although their lawyers launched a successful compensation claim against the state for false imprisonment. Eventually, years later, they were paid hundreds of thousands of pounds for their incarceration.

After the release of the men, the police issued a press release appealing for information. It said Einar and his fellow suspects would be monitored and their movements restricted, which brought condemnation from the left-wing newspaper, *Althydubladid*. The press release smacked of desperation and the newspapers saw it as a sign of weakness. *Althydubladid* pointed out Erla may have confessed to Geirfinnur's murder, but, 'Nothing is however said of where the body is or who disposed of it. Erla's story of dropping a rifle into the hands of her lover after the terrible act also seems a bit like a fairytale.'

Morgunbladid interviewed Geirfinnur Einarsson's wife, Gudni. She was adamant that she didn't recognise any of the names of the people being held and they had never come to her house. She didn't believe Geirfinnur had anything to do with them. The only rational explanation for his disappearance was that something must have happened in Klubburin a few days before he went missing.

The police had to get the case back on track. For months the police thought Magnus Leopoldsson had been the driver on the trip to Keflavik. Now he was out of custody and effectively out of the picture, the detectives had to find a new driver who had taken the three suspects to meet Geirfinnur Einarsson. Kristjan had mentioned a 'foreign looking man' during the intensive questioning he had been subjected to in the preceding weeks. The police wondered whether this man had been the driver all along. They knew exactly where to find him.

From the beginning of 1976, Gudjon Skarphedinsson had the strange feeling he was under surveillance. As an associate of Saevar's and an accomplice in the failed drugs scam, he was a marked man. Officers would call in at his apartment for a coffee and a 'friendly chat'. Chats like this, unrecorded with no notes taken or lawyer present, were common practice as officers fished for leads. He was uneasy about this but thought it was best to co-operate.

Separated from his wife and young children, Gudjon was now living with his mother in her apartment in Reykjavik, a city he had always despised. His mother had seen how his low self esteem was eating away at him. She had become so worried about his mental health that she had sent him to a doctor who found Gudjon was 'hyperactive', or manic. Gudjon admitted at times he could talk continuously all day without a break. His behaviour had become so erratic that Gudjon's brother, also a doctor, intervened and prescribed the antipsychotic drug, chlorpromazine.

He was still drifting. He had left his job as a book-keeper and for a while escaped from life in the mono-chrome urban environment by working as a deckhand on a trawler. Out in the natural world was where he felt at home and he loved the biting tang of the Atlantic. He was soon promoted to a cook.

In winter, the Atlantic could be a frightening place. This was when the brooding slate blue sea would fight to keep its precious bounty of gleaming haddock, cod and flat, brown halibut. Even though the trawler was sturdy with a steel hull, the sea was a ferocious opponent. In storms the bow would be pitched deep into the water as the boat disappeared into the ocean troughs before rising again on a wave which arced into a foaming white cloud engulfing the vessel. This could go on for hours as the boat battled its way through the waves. Gudjon wasn't scared by this, though. To him, it was an escape from the rigours and pressures of daily life on shore. But he couldn't stay at sea forever, this was only a temporary reprieve. He saw himself as lazy, easily bored and that he gave in easily to others. That made him a perfect target for the police. Days after the Klubburin men were released, the stolid detective, Eggert Bjarnasson, was despatched to bring Gudjon in for an interview.

The detectives' small offices were spread out along the narrow corridor at the team's headquarters at Borgutun 7. Holed up in these rooms for the past five months, fuelled by coffee and cigarettes, the small team had built up a picture of Geirfinnur's final night and wanted to find out what Gudjon knew. But rather than bring him here for an interview, Gudjon was taken to the more oppressive 'Corner' in Sidumuli.

They took him through the wooden main door and the clanking white barred gates, along the faceless corridor with its shiny linoleum floor, bright strip lighting and windowless cell doors. Behind these doors the suspects spent their days in a space just wide enough for a bed. They were like the animals at the moribund zoo in Hafnarfjordur, caged in tiny enclosures, with only brief respite when their keepers brought food or let them out to stretch their legs by walking to the toilet. Gudjon knew what it was like inside these cells; he had spent five nights locked up for his drugs arrest and it had spooked him. He didn't want to go back in there again.

Sat inside the interrogation room, Eggert began probing Gudjon about where he was in November 1974. Was he with Erla, Saevar and Kristjan on the night when they had driven from Reykjavik out to Keflavik? Gudjon was not threatened by Eggert, he thought he was pleasant enough, but a bit slow and no match for him intellectually. Gudjon replied in his acerbic manner that he had no idea what Eggert was talking about as he had not been there. Gudjon was willing, though, to share what he knew about the young suspects who were waiting for the next round of interviews.

Gudjon traced his relationship with Saevar from its beginnings through to December 1975 when it had fallen apart over the botched attempt to bring drugs into Iceland using Gudjon's car. When he was asked about Geirfinnur he drew a blank, he had never met him. He had heard of him of course, everyone had, and he recounted a conversation he had with Saevar in the summer of 1975. Saevar said 'he knew everything' about Geirfinnur, although he didn't say what exactly. He had said to Gudjon, 'In this country, it would be very easy to get rid of someone permanently. All that was needed was to kill them and bury them south in the lava where they would never be found.' Gudjon saw it as nothing more than Saevar shooting his mouth off, Saevar being Saevar.

Gudjon said he knew Erla less well. She had come with Saevar to Gudjon's house once in a Land Rover she had recently bought. He said he didn't know the other member of the 'gang', Kristjan, but the police didn't believe him. Before bringing him into the prison, they had moved Kristjan so he could see the swarthy man with his short dark hair and thick moustache. Kristjan got a good look at Gudjon and identified him as 'the foreigner' who he had seen in Reykjavik before they set off on that fateful drive out to Keflavik. The police didn't have enough evidence to hold Gudjon, so after a few hours he was let go. But 'the foreign looking guy' was now in the picture.

*

Erla and Saevar were still the principal focus of the police investigation. Erla's testimony put the detectives in a bind. She had confessed to shooting Geirfinnur but her earlier statements about her brother and the Klubburin men hadn't stacked up. They enlisted a psychologist to help them. He visited Erla in the week after her arrest and provided affirmation to the detectives' theory, finding her to have 'major gaps in her memory of many events that have clearly been hard for her and created emotional tension'. He went on to state she was intelligent but neurotic and demonstrated 'the need to be controlled by others, and almost masochistic behaviour'.

The police would exploit this knowledge to their own ends. By this point, Erla said, 'They knew so much already, they asked me about everything.' The detectives had gone through her relationships with her family, her mum, her friends. Erla was an open book and would always talk freely about these relationships. They were constantly trying to drive a wedge between her and Saevar by taking her back to the time of the disappearances, when after a few months with her new boyfriend she was isolated. 'I didn't want to answer how lonely I was and had no friends. I didn't want anyone talking to me about that time, that was so humiliating and they sensed that.' The police knew from the bond Erla had formed with the detective Sigurbjorn that Erla would always respond well to someone who was kind to her and treated her well. Now she was in jail they needed an insider, a warden who could befriend her.

Hlynur Magnusson was different to the other wardens – by his own admission 'rather nice'. When he went to work each morning he would wear a coat to hide his uniform. The other guards wore the black uniform with pride and would even put on their caps when they were going outside to fetch food to display their status. Hlynur would never do this – this was a job for him, not a vocation. The other guards were mostly simple men from the countryside who had second jobs as carpenters or builders; they saw the world in black and white. Hlynur preferred his lifestyle at the prison to his former life as a lonely academic. He was well paid, only worked four days a week and it was so quiet he could often get a decent sleep. He was also proud to play an important role solving the most important criminal case in Iceland's history.

When Erla was first brought into the jail, Hlynur remembered her as meek: 'She was like a terrified mouse in the corner'. Erla saw herself this way too. She remembered when she had briefly worked in a bakery and a mouse had been found in the flour and she saw it with a bright light shining on it and wanted to let it escape and run free. 'That was me in the prison – all you had to do was pick me up and let me go.' Hlynur responded to this trait in Erla. He would be the person to gain her confidence. Hlynur knew that the best way to get more information from Erla was to make her believe she was helping herself and her daughter. His orders were simple, he was told to 'bring Erla coffee or a Coke in the evening and sit there and talk to her and try to see if she would open up'.

In the minds of other guards, Erla was a black widow, a deadly, manipulative killer. (The police had fed this view with a remarkable press release issued a few days after her confession. It described how she had used a rifle on Saevar's instructions, given the gun back to him and run away and hid.) Erla felt this resentment and needed some positive affirmation; she was 'so completely vulnerable and easily abused I'd do anything you wanted if you were nice to me'.

Just as he had been instructed, Hlynur would bring Erla a drink and they would sit and chat, him on the hard stool close to her on the bed. Erla said, 'He was the

Geirfinnur Einarsson. Disappeared November 1974 in Keflavik aged 32, presumed dead but his body has never been found. (Icelandic National Archives)

Gudmundur Einarsson disappeared January 1974 aged 18 in Hafnarfjordur. Presumed dead, his body has never been found. (Icelandic National Archives)

Erla Bolladottir photographed on her release from Sidumuli prison 22 December 1976. She had spent 214 days in solitary confinement.
(Icelandic National Archives)

Kristjan Vidar Vidarsson, 25 October 1976. (Icelandic National Archives)

Saevar Marino Cieselski, 27 October 1976 after appearing in court. He had been questioned for more than six hours by the German detective Karl Schutz about the disappearance of Geirfinnur Einarsson. At this point he had spent 10 months in solitary confinement. (Icelandic National Archives)

Tryggvi Runar Leifsson photographed in March 1977 before he withdrew his confession that he had taken part in Gudmundur Einarsson's murder. He had been in solitary confinement for 15 months. (Icelandic National Archives)

Albert Klahn Skaftason in March 1977 after the prosecution had started its case for the murder of Gudmundur Einarsson. He had confessed to moving Gudmundur Einarsson's body from the lava fields to Hafnarfjordur cemetery. (Icelandic National Archives)

Gudjon Skarphedinsson in March 1977. He had been in custody in Sidumuli prison for four months. (Icelandic National Archives)

Gisli Gudjonsson when he was a
police officer in Reykjavik, 1973.
(Gisli Gudjonsson)

German detective Karl Schutz
at the end of his assignment,
February 1977, Reykjavik.
(The Icelandic National Broadcasting Service)

Karl Schutz with the Reykjavik task force of Icelandic
detectives and translators. (Icelandic National Archives)

Kristjan Vidarsson strangling a detective in a reconstruction of the murder of Geirfinnur Einarsson, January 1977, Keflavik. (Icelandic National Archives)

Police reconstruction of the night that Geirfinnur Einarsson was killed in Keflavik Harbour. The German detective Karl Schutz brought all the suspects to the scene and had them position the dummy representing Geirfinnur's body and the Volkswagen car used to transport his body. January 23, 1977. (Icelandic National Archives)

Reykjavik policeman Magnus Eggertsson (sitting against table) with Keflavik investigating magistrate, Valtyr Sigurdsson and detective Haukur Gudmundsson in November 1974, a week after the disappearance of Geirfinnur Einarsson. (Reykjavik Museum of Photography)

Erla Bolladottir listening during the Supreme Court trial, January 1980, Reykjavik. (Morgunbladid)

Kristjan Vidarsson leaving court, January 1980, Reykjavik. (Reykjavik Museum of Photography)

Saevar Ciesielski addressing judges at the end of the Supreme Court trial, January 1980. He appealed to them with a quote from Socrates. The judges reduced his life sentence to one of 17 years. (Reykjavik Museum of Photography)

Police officers at the Supreme Court trial, Reykjavik, 1980. (Reykjavik Museum of Photography)

Karl Schutz (centre) flanked by the prosecutor Halldór Thorbjörnsson and investigating magistrate Orn Hoskuldsson (far left) addressing journalists at a press conference marking the end of the investigation, 2 February 1977. In the centre of the table is the infamous clay head, Leirfinnur, which had been made of the suspect who had lured Geirfinnur to his death. (Reykjavik Museum of Photography)

Tryggvi Runar Leifsson with his daughter Kristin Tryggvadottir in Reykjavik, December 2005

(Kristin Tryggvadottir)

Professor Gisli Gudjonsson, CBE, at his home in London, March 2014. (Andy Brownstone/BBC)

Erla Bolladottir in Reykjavik old prison, March 2014.

(Andy Brownstone/BBC)

Gudjon Skarphedinsson at his home in Stadurstudur, March 2014. (Andy Brownstone/BBC)

only friendly thing – there was someone in prison that is there and listening.' They chatted about history, Rome and the beginning of civilization. Hlynur fed Erla's intelligence and desire to learn by smuggling in several volumes of Will Durant's multi-volume *The Story of Civilization*. Erla lapped it up, devouring the books, and grateful to Hlynur for allowing her mind to escape from the grey walls and to soar back to the time of Caesar and the beginnings of Christianity.

In the evenings, Hlynur would make the short walk from the guard's office to Erla's cell. They moved on from small talk and began discussing the case. He would write down her fantastic accounts of the night in November 1974 when Geirfinnur Einarsson disappeared.

Erla had very different views of the two cases she was caught up in. With Gudmundur her memory was clouded, she thought she may have indeed witnessed a murder. Geirfinnur was a different matter. She knew deep in her heart that she hadn't been there, but she was trying to please the detectives. Her imagination was running wild and each time she told her story it would change. She would name different people who had been in Keflavik and who were part of the smuggling scam and there to witness Geirfinnur's murder: there was the owner of a famous fashion shop, even a government minister cropped up at one point. Hlynur would get Erla to sign these statements and then hand them over to the police. He thought the statements were 'absolute bullshit' but the police saw it differently. There were still important elements that the police didn't know: who the driver was who brought Erla, Saevar and Kristjan to Keflavik; who else was in Keflavik with them; when and how Geirfinnur was killed, as this kept changing. And, most importantly, where the bodies were buried.

Hlynur saw in the detectives that, 'They believed everything at first, it seemed. It was like a Salvador Dali picture somehow, this case – abstract, abnormal.' Hlynur wasn't a detective but he had spoken to lots of prisoners, both innocent and guilty. He had worked at the old jail in Reykjavik, full of drunkards and petty criminals who would be fed and sheltered and even played chess with the guards. He could see Erla was caught in a vicious circle where she had to keep the police happy, and to do this she would give them more and more names. Erla's erratic testimony was a huge red flag, a warning to treat what she said with extreme caution. But the police couldn't afford to, she was too valuable to them. None of Erla's conversations were private, even those with the psychiatrist and psychologist who assessed her in April before she confessed, and prepared a report on her mental state for the police. She knew that the police and guards were listening to her conversations too. This wasn't just the paranoia of a prisoner with too much time on their hands.

She had made contact with a prisoner in an adjoining cell. They had read the same book from the prison library; they found a hollow spot in the wall and by propping a glass against the wall they could hear each other speaking. Erla said, 'We became so in tune with each other we could talk.' These snatched conversations continued for a few days until the wardens burst into her cell with noise and fury. They ordered her to strip and cover herself with a blanket while they searched her cell. 'They had a microphone in the air conditioning in my cell and they heard everything and were hoping I would say something that they could use.' When, after a few days, this hadn't happened, the wardens decided to move in anyway.

Saevar had also managed to make contact with another prisoner. He had been moved from the cell on his own to the corridor with the other inmates. He had been given a pencil and some paper by a psychologist to write down his thoughts. He started writing about the mistreatment he suffered and wanted the information to be smuggled out and published by the press. He folded the notes over a comb and slid it under the door to the cell opposite. After several days the guards discovered the clandestine communication and when they searched Saevar's cell they found letters and tobacco that his inmate pen pal had hidden in the toilet for him. As a punishment the guards removed Saevar's blanket and placed him in leg irons for the next ten days.

After the smuggled letter, the chief warden wanted to make sure there was no exchange of information between the suspects at any time. The only time Saevar got to see Erla and his friends was when he sat across the table from them in the interrogation room, when they would be accusing each other of involvement in a murder.

Hlynur strongly disagreed with this harsh treatment. He could see after a few months at the jail, that the investigation was out of control: 'This case had its own life somehow and everyone participated in it, without wanting to.' In Hlynur's view, the police had stopped asking one key question: 'If I were asked to use one word about this case it would be the word "why", the question "why?". That is the whole case.' Why would a group of young people join up with established members of Icelandic society to smuggle alcohol and then kill someone?

11

It was in the evenings when the sun's amber glow slid below the horizon that the visits to Erla's cell would happen. Time had become stretched in Sidumuli, it ceased to have the same meaning as outside. Erla was entering her third month in custody but Saevar, Kristjan and Tryggvi were facing their eighth month in solitary confinement. They had all been charged with attacking and killing Gudmundur Einarsson. Erla had confessed to shooting Geirfinnur but, as yet, hadn't been charged with killing him.

Days and evenings were all the same, just periods in between food and interrogations. For the suspects, most of the day was spent alone, staring at the blank walls and, during these endless hours, the minds of these young people would tease them, turning thoughts and fragments from the interviews into memories. Real memories stay with you, dipping in and out of your consciousness, emerging when you least expect them, triggered by an image, a smell or a sound. The memories that Erla and the others were dredging up were different, they would warp and bend so that something they were certain of one week would have morphed into a totally different recollection a short time later. These memories were infected by the discussions with the police; names would crop up like characters in a play suddenly entering the scene. They had gone over the same event, the same night, hundreds of times so it was a struggle to keep hold of that original thought from years ago of what actually happened. Originally Erla, Saevar, Kristjan and Tryggvi were certain they hadn't seen or participated in a murder, but this began to evaporate. And the prison doctor was prescribing powerful drugs to them, which further hindered their ability to distinguish between what was real and imagined.

During the time she had been in solitary confinement, Erla's mental and physical health had started to deteriorate. Her thoughts would often turn to her baby daughter, Julia. She would be given paper and pencils which she would use to write poems and draw pictures, but these would be taken away at a moment's notice.

Sleeping was always a problem – there was the drone of the air pumped into the cell which the guards never seemed able to control properly, switching between freezing and sweltering. The medication provided only a temporary reprieve.

There were no visitors allowed, but then again she wasn't sure how many of her family would make the trip to see her. Having dragged her brother Einar into the case, the rift with her relatives had deepened. But Erla did have one regular visitor to her cell, a detective who would often come at night.

'We wardens found it rather curious,' Hlynur recalled, how this detective came to interrogate Erla at night. 'Not in the interrogation room but in her cell. He was not visiting other prisoners that way.' Hlynur and the other wardens kept their mouth shut, though – the policemen were above the prison's chief warden in the hierarchy.

Inside Erla's cell there were only two places to sit, the bed and the stool which was within touching distance.

The detective would sit and talk for hours with her about how difficult it must be for her alone in the cell, that she must be lonely and needy. He assured Erla that she could always rely on him. The tone of his voice shifted and the conversation became more personal. 'I was not sure what he was doing,' Erla recalled, 'but his voice became awkward.' He promised to stay over in the cell when he had the means to.

Erla was disturbed by this new development. She liked his friendship, but she didn't like the idea of their communication going beyond a friendly chat. Erla hoped that he would forget this conversation, that it was an aberration. A few evenings later, she was lying down reading when the detective appeared in the door and sat down on the bed next to her. She could tell straight away from his manner that he wasn't there for a chat. He had a sense of purpose and she didn't like it, 'I sat up while my heart was beating rapidly, I was feeling insecure.'

The detective wanted to make sure they were undisturbed. He stood up and checked whether any guards were walking along the corridor. Sidumuli was small and at night there were only two wardens on duty. They wanted an easy time of it in the evening; they would take it in turns to sleep and most of the time they would stay in their office, unless the inmates rang their bells asking to be taken to the toilet. There were no guards near the cell so the detective decided it was time to act. Erla said, 'He slipped down his trousers and took out his penis. I was terrified.' She couldn't believe this was happening here in the prison just yards from the wardens.

The detective began putting on a condom. Erla was alone and trapped in her cell, 'I pressed myself against the wall as far from him as I could. He reached for me and told me to lie down on the bed.' She was paralyzed with fear and had no one to help her. 'I dared not ask for help but obeyed. He had my life in his hands and I didn't know where it might end if he disapproved of me.'

She did as she was told, lying there staring at the greasy walls and ceiling while he raped her. He was on top of her, putting his hand over her mouth to prevent her shouting. At one point he thought he heard a noise in the corridor and jumped up to check what it was, telling Erla to lie still. After what seemed like an eternity, he finished and put his trousers back on. Erla recalled his parting words were that 'he was taking great risks to do this for me' and she should be grateful.

After her rapist had left, Erla remained frozen on the bed, debased and trapped. She couldn't even wash herself to get rid of his smell as she was only allowed to shower once a week. She stared at the walls thinking where she might get help, but there was none. There was only one way to cope with it, Erla would have to bury it deep inside her, another secret that she would keep hidden. It would be years before she publicly talked about it and decades until she tried to bring her attacker to court, but by then it would be too late. The statute of limitations meant he would never be prosecuted.

Hlynur and the other guards had noticed that this officer often visited Erla late in the evening and they would discuss it in their office while they waited for a bell summoning them to a prisoner's cell. Afterwards, they professed ignorance, but there was an awkward detail they couldn't hide. After the attack, the morning after pill was ordered for Erla. Hlynur Magnusson said he was not aware of this. He did notice, however, the change in Erla's demeanour. It was impossible to ignore. Her mental health plummeted and there were fears that she might be suicidal. For Erla, her treatment by the authorities 'was like a rape from the beginning to end at different levels. That physical rape was symbolic of the whole thing'. Her attacker could walk out into that bright night relieved that he had got away with it, undetected. The guards would never speak up against a detective when there was no definitive proof. Her attacker could carry on without any fear of discovery. Who would believe her?

This betrayal dented Erla's already shaky confidence. She still had one 'friend' and confidante, Hlynur. He would come with drinks in the evenings when it was quiet, a gentle presence, bringing in the outside world through his discussions of ancient Rome and the noble history of Iceland. Of course, Hlynur was betraying her too, constantly feeding information back to the police. Then according to Erla his close proximity to her began to get to him too; he started to misread the signals from the vulnerable 'little mouse' he first encountered. One evening after one of their long conversations he leaned over and kissed her. Once again Erla felt that her vulnerability had been exploited and Hlynur had stepped over the line. He doesn't remember this, but it is etched on Erla's memory. 'He was the only one who wasn't the enemy, but after this everything crumbled. He was just one of them.' To Erla he was like a soldier who had become caught up in the febrile atmosphere which leads good men to do bad things.

Saevar had been subject to repeated mistreatment from the police and wardens. Hlynur's collegues had grown increasingly frustrated at their inability to break him and get him to tell them where the bodies were buried. They gathered with detectives in the prison cafeteria to discuss effective methods to get Saevar to tell them more They knew Saevar had a fear of water. Hlynur was there when they mentioned it. So too was the deputy prosecutor, Hallvardur Einvardsson, the man who was responsible for bringing a fair case against Saevar and the others. He said if Saevar ended up falling into the water to 'let the bastard drown'. It was a throwaway comment but one that the guards remembered.

In July they seized the opportunity to strike. There were three guards on duty when Saevar went to wash in the tiny bathroom. It was a small pleasure for him, as he only got to do this once a week. He would stand for a moment and let the water cascade over him, breathing in the sulphurous smell from the liquid that had travelled from deep underground caverns up through the lava and ash to the surface, still containing the heat of the lava. It was part of Iceland's geothermal network that provided hot water across the country. Washing was a brief chance for Saevar to feel connected to the land.

Saevar noticed right away the guards were on edge. He was no physical match for any of the wardens – a cocky seven-stone weakling who would crumple at the first big punch. 'When I got to the shower cubicle [the guard] asks me to wait and then he grabs the neck of my shirt and attacks me.' Saevar's head was pushed down into a sink full of water. He thrashed around, struggling to break free and breathe, the water filling his mouth. This was the moment that all of the pent-up tension among the guards was released. As he gasped for breath, Saevar's head was lifted out of the sink, and he sucked in lung fulls of air but his reprieve was short lived. His head was thrust back into the water. The second time was worse as he tried to stop himself from swallowing the water. He thought it was only a matter of time before he was going to die. The guard was shouting at him, 'Who did you bring to Keflavik? Where did you go with Gudmundur Einarsson in Hafnarfjordur?' Even if Saevar wanted to respond he couldn't. The guards' anger had been unleashed, like a volcano that had exploded and could no longer be contained. The torture only stopped when a more senior guard intervened, realising that any longer under the water and Saevar would be dead. They returned Saevar to his cell a soaking wreck. There was also an implicit threat that any time he went to the bathroom that this could happen again. One of the few remaining acts that he could carry out in peace was now tainted too.

The guards had crossed a line where torture was now acceptable. They no longer saw Saevar as a prisoner on remand but as a manipulative monster. These guards who had worked as farmers, carpenters and electricians, were not intrinsically bad men. They were simple, straightforward and scared of what Saevar represented: a darker side of Iceland that they couldn't control. They felt no shame in what they had done. When he was back on shift shortly after, Hlynur recalled the wardens being proud. 'They boasted of it. They knew he was afraid of water, they took his head and put it in the sink and tried to drown him.' Hlynur was appalled; he knew that it was wrong but said nothing. 'It is a tasteless comparison,' he conceded, but 'like Nazi Germany, I just obeyed orders.'

Gisli Gudjonsson was plunged into this febrile atmosphere that summer when he bounded into the detectives' headquarters. Short and stocky with dark blonde hair and a dimpled chin, Gisli looked a bit like Kirk Douglas and, though he wasn't a swashbuckler, he was brave. He had shown during a previous stint as a temporary uniformed police officer that he would be the first person to chase a suspect, determined to take them down no matter how big they were.

He was eager to get into the cramped space that would double as his office and interrogation room. He was not working on the Geirfinnur case but knew the officers who were. 'They were competent, good people, these investigators. I knew them, I had to work with them. I liked them, I respected them.' The detective's department wasn't big, there were only 30 officers covering the whole country, so it was easy to pick up on the frustration within the Geirfinnur inquiry. 'They were angry and frustrated that they were not getting anywhere, the general impression I perceived was that [the suspects] were not co-operating. They were being awkward.' He could see that the police, the investigating judges and the prosecutor were having problems because there were such inconsistencies in the stories. They felt, 'These people are all guilty, all we had to do was prove how they did it, find the bodies and prove they did it. I got caught in that, I accepted the police assumption that they were guilty.' This thinking had permeated all levels of the case; Gisli saw it as 'like a runaway train'.

Gisli was on a placement as part of his psychology degree, as he was interested in finding out more about offending behaviour. He had previously been a beat bobby during his university summer holidays, when the regular officers went on holiday. His police work so far had been mostly clearing the streets, breaking up fights and arresting drunks. This was the closest he got to the few nightclubs in Reykjavik, like Klubburin, which were exciting for many of his friends but which he preferred to keep at arm's length. Gisli was a serious student and had big ambitions, preferring studying and athletics to smoking and drugs.

As a student, Gisli had already made waves in Iceland. He had been fascinated by the Breidavik boys' home, where Saevar had been sent years earlier. Gisli had made the long drive out to the isolated school and worked his way through the boys' files. He also spoke to the staff to get a clearer picture of the home, which was seen by the Reykjavik social services as successfully rehabilitating delinquent children. When Gisli published his findings, they were devastating. The young student concluded that the home was far from a success story; if anything it was a breeding ground for criminals. Three quarters of the boys who went there committed crimes after they had left, often alongside other boys they had met at Breidavik. For Reykjavik social services Gisli's report was highly damaging. It was marked 'strictly confidential' and its findings buried until years later when it was leaked to the press. But it made Gisli into someone willing to challenge the status quo.

The nightmare of the Cod War was at last coming to an end for Justice Minister Olafur Johannesson. But now he had a new headache that wouldn't go away: the Gudmundur/Geirfinnur investigation. Sat at his desk, feet up, Olafur was considering how he didn't like the way the investigation was going. It was taking far too long and becoming an embarrassment to the country and to his government. His patience was wearing thin but Olafur was not one to rush anything; he liked to weigh up the options and then take a decision. He would read the most recent twist in the case in *Morgunbladid* or later in *Visir*. He was troubled by his name and that of his party being linked to the case, through the Klubburin men. Their release had been splashed all over the newspapers and questions asked again about why the police had based so much on the testimony of Erla, Saevar and Kristjan.

The political ramifications of the case were becoming more pronounced. The influence of America and the air base they ran for NATO on the island had led to suspicions among the growing leftist movement of spies in their midst and CIA moles. In the newspapers' letters pages readers speculated, 'It is highly likely that the CIA has for years had their officials here in the country to follow events and try to manipulate it to their advantage.' Head of Customs Kristjan Petursson had received training in America and this led to lurid suspicion that he worked for the CIA. When Olafur lead opposition to the US base and threatended to shut it down during the Cod Wars, the rumour went that Petursson then manufactured the allegation about links between Klubburin and Olafur's party as a way of smearing the minister.

Olafur found all this unseemly and wanted to put a stop to such speculation. A stickler for procedure, he knew that he couldn't interfere directly. He needed someone from outside with proven experience in big, complex cases to come in and rescue what had become a shambles. The investigation had become too big for Iceland's inexperienced police force. They needed a saviour and the opportunity came from an unlikely source.

A colleague of Olafur's, Peter Eggerz, was a career diplomat who had spent his life in anonymous, stuffy conference rooms, discussing the minutiae of treaties and trade deals. He had been based in the anaemic West German capital, Bonn, for years. It was a dull place but it was the ideal setting for Peter to indulge his hobby of researching the Second World War and the Holocaust. As Ambassador to Germany, Eggerz had been embroiled in the negotiations to find a solution to the increasingly fraught battle over fishing rights with the UK, Germany and other European nations.

The Cod Wars had been a regular feature at NATO meetings, especially after Iceland had threatened to pull out of the alliance. The Americans were never going to let that happen; Iceland was strategically too important, a bulwark against a possible Soviet fleet sailing south to attack Europe. The loss of the latest Cod War to Iceland was a humiliation for Britain, and a hard-fought victory for the plucky underdogs who had stood up to a much bigger, better armed navy. Inside Iceland, however, it had opened up divisions between the older generation who fully supported NATO and the post war baby boomers who wanted to re-shape their nation and forge a new, independent identity, free of American imperialism.

With the third and final Cod War now over, for Peter it was time for another important mission. He had been told by Olafur to use his extensive contacts to find someone who could get the Geirfinnur investigation back on track. Outside of one of the interminable meetings, Peter buttonholed one of his contacts at the German interior ministry, Siegfried Frohlich. He explained that Iceland needed help, an expert who could get the country out of the mess the two cases had caused. Peter was in luck, Siegfried told him, he had just the man for the job. He knew a veteran, hardened detective who had worked on major cases and was now retired. His name was Karl Schutz. 'Karl Schutz is the talent,' Frohlich told him, 'if he can't solve this issue, it is insoluble.'

12

When Karl Schutz got the phone call from Peter Eggerz, he had no particular desire to leave the mellow, calm canals of Holland, especially for the bitter chill of Iceland, a country he knew nothing about. For the last six months, Schutz had been living a blissful life. He had retired in 1975 and was on his boat pottering around on the placid canals, stopping off whenever he wished for a long lunch with a beer or a glass of wine. There were museums to visit, cafes to relax in – although he avoided the hash cafes in Amsterdam.

He'd had a glittering police career, with a highly demanding final post, running three different departments in Bonn where he was responsible for over a thousand staff, two thirds of them investigators. And yet Schutz was a cop above all else and was finding it hard to resist the challenge of taking on a case in a whole new country. But if he did, it would have to be on his terms. Schutz was a pioneer of criminal investigative techniques still used by the police today. He sent the Icelanders a book he had written about his most notable investigation where he had developed what, at the time, were novel techniques during a complex inquiry.

The crime took place in January 1969 in the small town of Lebach in the north west of Germany. In the dead of night an ammunitions depot belonging to the Parachute Regiment was raided. Four young conscripts were killed and another was seriously injured. The attackers got away with a few weapons, some ammunition and the books the soldiers were reading. The crime was shocking for a country that was relatively peaceful and yet to experience the emerging menace of terrorism. The police were baffled, wondering if it might be politically motivated. Karl Schutz was put in charge of the case, which developed into the biggest operation mounted by the German federal police with a team of over a hundred officers. Schutz was methodical and systematic, using the latest technology available at the forensics laboratory at Wiesbaden to examine the bullets and cartridge cases found at the scene.

While the police were trying to track down the killers, the case took an unexpected twist. The gang who had carried out the attack tried to blackmail a series of high profile wealthy Germans. Schutz and his special commission succeeded in tracking them down and arresting them. They were not career criminals or politically motivated activists, but three young gay men who wanted the money in order to lead a life away from the bourgeois society they despised. Two of the killers were eventually jailed for life. During the trial, it became clear the trigger for the killing and their crime spree was that they were outcasts living on the margins and had been shunned by West German society.

Schutz rose to be head of the Federal criminal police in the capital Bonn where he faced an even bigger challenge, playing a key role in the fight against a new scourge of terrorism that struck West Germany in the 1970s. The Baader-Meinhoff gang was a militant left-wing terrorist group that wanted to undermine the West German state though a campaign of bombings, assassinations, kidnappings and robberies. The group had grown out of the student protest movement of the 1960s and the younger generation who were angry with the positions former Nazis held in positions of power in West Germany. They decided the only way to strike back was with violence. They formed the Red Army Faction, training with the Palestine Liberation Organisation in Jordan.

In 1972, his team were able to capture the key figures in the movement: Andreas Baader, Ulrike Meinhoff and two of the other leaders. They had gone to check on a lock up garage in Frankfurt where they kept bomb making materials. The police had a tip-off and were waiting for them and the men surrendered. Two of the gang subsequently killed themselves while awaiting trial – one on hunger strike and Ulrike Meinhoff was found hanged in her cell.

Having tackled these major crimes, Schutz was certain he could solve a murder case in Iceland. He was known for his boundless energy – one of his favourite phrases was 'the clock is ticking'. He had earned the nickname Kommisar Kugelblitz after a popular German cartoon character – an elderly white-haired policeman who went around the world solving crimes.*

---

* Schutz's career had not been without controversy. In 1962 he had led a police operation that stormed the headquarters of the magazine, *Der Spiegel*. It was the height of the Cold War and the magazine's founder and two reporters were accused of publishing West German military secrets. The operation was a disaster from the very start. The police had staged a car chase across Hamburg trying to arrest Spiegel's publisher but it was an innocent pensioner they had wrongly identified.

This was a time when the news magazine had huge power and a vast staff, with 117 separate offices. The police occupied the building for a month scouring every one of the offices. They

In July, the news of Schutz's imminent arrival was leaked to the press, who questioned what a German expert could do 18 months after Geirfinnur disappeared. Yet when Karl Schutz arrived in August there was huge expectation from the public: here was the super cop who would lift Iceland out of its darkness.

Schutz could see the difficulties he faced from the air as he approached Keflavik airport. Stretched out in front of him was a vista of ashen lava, as far as he could see. There were wide craters and the only vegetation was thin, mustard-yellow bracken. Huddled by the ocean was Keflavik, hemmed in next to the sea where granite coloured waves rolled in, turning to a white and brown froth as they crashed on the rocks. Somewhere out there beneath the lava were the bodies of Gudmundur and Geirfinnur Einarsson. 'It would be difficult to get to the bottom of it,' Schutz thought, 'but it was not too late.'

He knew that Reykjavik would not be the same as Bonn, but when Schutz walked into the detectives' offices at Borgutun 7, he was struck by how primitive and basic it was. Where were the computers? All he could see was typewriters and carbon paper. At the German Federal Police lab in Wiesbaden they were using new forensic techniques to test blood stains and hair fibres. In Iceland forensics were always secondary to confessions.

He had a task force of ten detectives, which represented a third of the country's force. He thought they seemed diligent and committed, but their methods were old fash-

---

soon reached a dead end as they realised they would have to examine millions of documents and papers to find the evidence they needed. There was a huge backlash from the German public who felt that the state was suppressing freedom of speech. The scandal would lead to the resignation of the country's defence minister and the downfall of the West German government. Schutz escaped from this without a blemish.

ioned. There weren't the processes and systematic approach that he was used to at home. He could see immediately that getting things done here would take an awful lot longer than it did back in Germany.

Schutz's arrival meant that the investigating magistrate Orn Hoskuldsson was no longer running the show. He was now second in command to a man who, although vastly experienced, knew nothing about Icelandic law and didn't speak a word of Icelandic. Peter Eggerz had accompanied Schutz back to Iceland to become his interpreter and would be by his side throughout all of his interactions with the suspects.

Schutz wanted to go back to the beginning of the Geirfinnur case to see how much the original investigators had found out, which meant a trip to Keflavik. His first meeting was with Kristjan Petursson, the domineering head of customs at the airport. Petursson had been an active participant in the early stages of the case and had been obsessed with getting Saevar. Schutz was not impressed by what he heard. Petursson boasted that he had conducted intensive criminal investigations outside of working hours, much of it directed at Saevar. Schutz later summed up the meeting, saying Kristjan Petursson 'was polite but very slow'. He spat out 'some hypotheses that he could not substantiate', and was unable to provide 'any realistic evidence in the Geirfinnur case'. Schutz was so dismissive of the Petursson that he felt the prosecutor should have taken action against him for neglecting his actual job.

He was less harsh about Haukur Gudmundsson, the Keflavik detective who had first investigated Geirfinnur's disappearnce and his boss Valtyr Sigurdsson. Haukur had been guarded when he first met Schutz but slowly opened up and became friendly. They complained to Schutz that they had not received much help from their superiors. When they asked for more money, it fell on deaf ears and after a while they were told to focus on other cases. They were able to tell him what kind of man Geirfinnur was, and that it was impossible that he lived some kind of double life.

The Reykjavik team had built up countless potential leads. There were hundreds of pages of statements and notes they had collected that had to be translated from Icelandic. Schutz had a choice: should he build on this or start the investigation again, using his experience and ability to get whatever resources he needed? A year and a half into an enquiry, it was too late to go backwards. This was a paid assignment and Schutz decided he had two main tasks: to find the bodies and to make the conflicting statements of the suspects all match. Schutz would interview the suspects himself and use his contacts at the lab in Wiesbaden to try to get vital forensics evidence linking the suspects to Gudmundur and Geirfinnur.

Karl Schutz had chosen the best time to arrive in Iceland – the white nights when the bleached sun would not set until close to midnight. As the winter mellowed it was a time to trek and explore the inner wilderness, the Highlands, the Brennisteinsalda volcano, its sides stained red, green and blue from sulphur, iron and mosses, with fumaroles, holes where steam would rise up from the earth. From the Blue Mountain he could see five glaciers and the folded earth below a vista of dormant volcanoes, brown, green and black shadow. The temperature rarely got above 15 degrees. But the heat in Iceland didn't come from the sun, it was found beneath the earth. The country straddles two tectonic plates, the Eurasian and North American plates creating the Mid Atlantic ridge. It is mostly on the ocean floor but in Iceland it rises above sea level and can be seen on the land. This was the Reykjanes ridge where steam would creep along the cracks and faults and burst out in hissing plumes.

The summer brought a change to the glacial landscape with a bloom on the face of the lava fields

You could roam in Asbyrgi, the horseshoe shaped canyon created in Norse mythology by Odin's eight-legged horse, Slepinir, leaving its hoofmark on the world. Below the steep rocky face was a radiant green landscape and above, crystal blue skies with thin filaments of cloud stretching out like elegant fingers. Asbyrgi was the capital of the Huldufolk, the hidden elves whose queen would emerge from the rocks when the waterfall flowed. At the ocean's edge, puffins nestled in the rocks, while out beyond the black sand, seals bobbed lazily in the ocean.

Schutz's home wasn't in this rural idyll but in Reykjavik. The city looked the same as it had for decades but the young post-war generation was changing Iceland. They wanted more than to be fishermen or farmers, working with their hands. They watched the American TV piped in for the thousands of servicemen at the Keflavik air base. This new generation learned English and travelled to the US and Europe and wanted to reshape their agrarian, conservative nation.

This was Erla, Saevar and Kristjan's generation, anti-establishment and at the edges of the social movements sweeping through Europe. Saevar and Erla's links to the US meant they had seen and felt this new wave, and they scared the Icelandic establishment who wanted to preserve their island nation, to protect it from the corrupting influences of the US and the West. Icelandic state TV had only started a decade earlier but it shut down on Thursdays and during August to encourage families to come together and escape the interference of the new box in the corner of the room.

Schutz read through the investigator's reports before he arrived in Iceland but he wanted to meet the suspects himself as soon as possible. His principal focus would be on the more complicated Geirfinnur disappearance, but first he wanted to put the Gudmundur case to bed and tie up any loose ends. That meant finding the body and any forensic evidence which linked Saevar, Kristjan and Tryggvi to the killing. He would start with the most co-operative witness.

Albert Klahn had been freed in January 1976, but he was still subject to continued police interviews and journeys out to the lava. Albert was glad he didn't have to face the Corner, which still held dark memories for him. Instead, he was brought to Orn Hoskuldsson's far more comfortable office at the court. His interview also began at a reasonable hour, 10.30 in the morning. He still had to go over the same story but there was no need for a lawyer to be present, the police reassured him he was just helping with their enquiries.

Albert was always susceptible to being dominated by stronger more forceful characters and Schutz certainly fitted the bill. He had faced down terrorists who had bombed and killed at will, so Albert and his friends were a much easier target. Schutz saw no need for the physical violence of the past, but he let the threat of it linger, always in the back of the suspects' minds.

Schutz didn't need to lean on Albert; he re-assured him that he wasn't a felon but that he knew he hadn't always told the truth. Months after his first interview, Albert still wasn't clear about the events on the night Gudmundur went missing or what he had done and where he had been. Schutz watched in his quiet, thoughtful manner as Albert nervously told him he didn't know where the body of Gudmundur was buried. There had been endless attempts to jog his memory: repeated trips, endless questioning by the detectives and even a psychiatric assessment, but they had all come up with nothing. Schutz calmly told Albert he didn't believe him, that he must know where the body was.

Schutz wanted Albert to correct some details in his testimony that he had got wrong previously. First and foremost was the car he had driven to move Gudmundur's body. In all of his interviews Albert had been very clear that he drove his dad's yellow Toyota. But when the police checked, they found out his father didn't own the yellow Toyota at the time of Gudmundur's disappearance. Instead, he had a battered old Volkswagen Beetle, a common sight in Reykjavik. When the Reykjavik detectives had discovered this, they didn't worry about this detail, but Schutz saw it as a problem. Albert had been clear that he had watched events through his rearview mirror and seen Gudmundur's body placed in the boot. The Beetle had its boot in the front, however, so this couldn't have happened. What's more, his dad's Beetle was in terrible condition and they would have to convince the judges that the car could have navigated the roads in dense snow.

As they discussed this, Schutz switched from good cop to bad cop, fixing Albert with a cold stare. He warned Albert that if he found out he was hiding something he would prosecute him for complicity in the crime. As he so often had been in the past, after Albert's interview he was taken out to 'refresh' his memory. Schutz, his interpreter Peter, a detective and Albert squeezed into a white police Volvo and took the familiar route south to the Aquarium. Albert said on that January night in 1974 they had tried to get in to but had failed, so Kristjan, Tryggvi and Saevar had gone off into the lava with the body and returned about half an hour later and Albert had driven them home. So Albert couldn't tell the police where the body was buried.

After this frustrating trip Schutz had concluded the suspects were refusing to disclose where Gudmundur was hidden because it was likely Geirfinnur was buried in the same place. If he could get the Geirfinnur suspects to reveal the location of the body, Schutz believed he would find Gudmundur's remains there too.

Schutz spoke first to the most compliant of the Geirfinnur suspects, Erla, who felt more optimistic than she had for months. She was about to see Karl Schutz for the first time and she thought it could bring clarity to the investigation. 'I had this hope, about someone new, an expert from another country.' It had been months since she had seen her daughter. At her remand hearing in July 1976, when her detention was extended for another 60 days, the judge said she would have to wait to speak to Schutz in order to see her baby. So this was her opportunity to come clean and convince Schutz that, after all of the previous lies, this time she was telling the truth. She hoped he would see through the madness that had taken hold of the country and infected the minds of the investigators, that he could coolly assess the statements and see the lack of forensics and the glaring inconsistencies in the testimonies.

Schutz indeed saw the confessions as a mess of conflicting accounts. According to the numerous statements collected about Gudmundur Einarsson, he had been beaten to death, then it had changed to a stabbing, then back to a beating. His body had been dumped in a variety of locations in the lava fields. Saevar, Kristjan and Tryggvi had at various times each delivered the fatal blows. But Gudmundur's case was straightforward compared to Geirfinnur's. There, the statements varied wildly on the cause of death; first it had been an accident, then a fight and then he was shot by Erla. There was a changing cast list present, although Erla, Saevar and Kristjan were always there. The fiasco of the false imprisonment of the Klubburin men was still a sore point, as well as the smearing of politicians and prominent businessmen, all roped in through rumour and gossip. Schutz saw his primary task, though, as making sure the confessions were consistent. Erla would be integral to this as it was her testimony that had started both investigations.

Erla's first interview with Schutz was not as she had hoped. Her optimism was snuffed out before he even walked in when she was thrown a blanket and told to strip naked, the heavy-handed tactic the guards used when they searched the cells. Erla waited in the Corner in this vulnerable state for a long time, the blanket hard and itchy against her skin. She then heard footsteps and the door opened. It was Orn Hoskuldsson, and with him was a short, smart, well fed man and his well dressed shadow, Peter Eggerz. Erla was immediately struck by her new interrogator's appearance, particularly his 'beautiful white hair, really sparkly eyes, they were so bright blue. His eyes were amazing, like a child's'.

Schutz offered to shake Erla's hand but even accepting this small gesture of apparent decency was difficult for her as the blanket was heavy and stiff and she had to hold onto it tightly to stop it falling and revealing her nakedness. It was a tactic Schutz had brought with him from Germany, a way to strip away even the most basic protection and meted out to the terrorists and gangsters that Schutz specialised in.

Despite this, Erla immediately poured out her heart to Schutz. 'It was really difficult and I broke down and cried in humiliation,' she recalled, as she confessed to lying about her own brother Einar. She admitted making other false statements but her excuse was that she thought by telling the police what she thought they wanted to hear she would be released and allowed to go home.

As he listened, Erla could see Schutz had a quiet poise and confidence that was markedly different to the more jumpy Icelandic detectives. He stared at her, trying to figure out what was true and what was fantasy. The months of stories, retractions and breakdowns had blurred this for all of them, but Erla was sure Schutz would be the man to forge a new path through this fog. He never changed his expression or showed any emotion. He let her speak and say how sorry she was: 'He let me talk until I finished and I really had to get the courage to say "it's all my fault".' She felt she was to blame and her weakness had allowed her to be led by the police into a situation where there was no backing out. She told him it had all been lies, that she knew nothing about Geirfinnur or what had happened to him. She hadn't officially withdrawn her confession about Geirfinnur Einarsson's death but she had effectively taken it back.

Schutz waited until she had finished and then he replied, 'Do you think I'm an idiot? Do you think I'm here to play games with you?' Erla sunk lower into her chair. She had opened up and come clean but it was of no use. Schutz didn't believe her. He told her she had to tell the truth if she wanted to keep up their dialogue and sent her away.

Erla felt a profound sense of disappointment after meeting Schutz. He didn't want to re-examine the case, he just wanted the confessions to be consistent. After a few days languishing in her cell as the air duct pumped out dry, hot air, she decided that she wouldn't be used any longer. She was going to fight back. Erla wanted to get her point across without being bullied or cowed by the police. She still had paper and a pen so sat down at the desk on the hard stool in the early hours and wrote a letter to Orn Hoskuldsson, the man who, on paper at least, was still in charge of the investigation. When Orn opened the letter he wasn't sure what to expect, but he soon realised it wasn't good news.

'I ask you above all to take my words at face value, because they are true,' Erla wrote. 'To begin with, I raised this issue to draw attention to myself. Then I saw in my mind's eye the image of the event and I was in it. I told you about it again and again and it became increasingly trapped in my head. My existence, or presence in this night is a fabrication. A myth which started when you asked me if I had been there.'

She also apologised for implicating her brother Einar – her imagination had dreamed up a link between him and Saevar. She started to see Saevar in a new light, suspecting him of more crimes. She was wrong to mention his potential involvement in the Geirfinnur case. As for her shooting dead Geirfinnur she was adamant: 'My confession was deliberately fabricated' and she wanted to retract it. She had tried to do this with Schutz, but he was having none of it. She was willing to be punished for making up these stories, but it was time to put an end to the nonsense. She wanted to talk to Orn in person so she could repair the damage and pleaded, 'Orn, would you stoop so low as to talk to a girl who has led you astray in your work and in public, although I am hardly worthy? Your sincere and excited, Erla Bolladottir.'

A pattern of retractions had started. First Kristjan, then Saevar and now Erla had all withdrawn their confessions in Geirfinnur's death. The police suspected that the suspects must be communicating somehow, this would explain Erla's sudden retraction, so the next day, Schutz, accompanied by Orn Hoskuldsson and Eggert Bjarnasson entered Erla's cell and watched as the prison guards searched it. They were looking for any evidence of communication with Saevar to explain the withdrawl of her confession. This prompted her to write a second letter to Orn admitting what she called 'a mistake on my part'. She was now retracting her retraction. The letter shows her confused state and how, in 24 hours, she could shift from withdrawing her confession to apologising for daring to do so She wrote:

I sit here and think, I think incredible thoughts about these things and why no one talks to me. I do not know what happens and I am desperate and angry with life and think I wrote this letter (14.8) as a continuation of such thoughts. I take it back, in the hope that you forgive me and I can imagine how much this letter has angered you [...] I hope for your forgiveness and even conversation, in connection with my child who I live for.

Chief Warden Gunnar Gudmundsson had been watching these events with increasing frustration. The day after Erla wrote her begging letter, Gunnar took it upon himself to try to clear up the confusion around Erla's testimony. He wanted one of the wardens to help him, one who he thought Erla trusted. Hlynur was the natural choice, he had been specifically selected to befriend Erla, but Gunnar didn't know he had stepped over the line by kissing her. 'I could not talk to him, I had to pretend to be nice to him,' she said. Gunnar may have thought he was helping the case but he just created more problems.

Gunnar and Hlynur questioned Erla in her cell in one long interview, although Gunnar never kept note of exactly how long they were in her cell. During the interview Erla's story took a significant turn. For the first time she said she was there when they had dumped Gudmundur's body. They also discussed Geirfinnur's murder. Erla was now clear that Gudjon Skarphedinsson had been there with them that night in Keflavik.

It was exactly this kind of amateurish meddling that was the reason Karl Schutz had been brought in to run the investigation. With his arrival, the tempo of the investigation had changed, taking on a shape and structure that hadn't been there before. Each of the detectives was assigned to a particular suspect, though Saevar was so important he had three officers investigating him. Each morning there was a team meeting and Schutz would assign tasks to the detectives. The other detectives working along the corridor would hear his refrain, *'schnell, schnell'*. The trainee psychologist, Gisli Gudjonsson, could see that the German detective was well organised: 'He was very firm, a very domineering individual and he would sometimes lose his temper with people. He became very impatient when police officers were not doing what he wanted them to do.' Schutz saw his role not just as an investigator but as a teacher too, who could bring the Icelandic police force into the twentieth century.

And yet the detectives continued to blame the investigation's stalemate on the obstructiveness of the suspects. Repeatedly during his time at Borgutun 7, Gisli heard the bemoaning of the stubbornness of the suspects who were refusing to give the police what they wanted. According to Gisli, the detectives remained adamant that it was the suspects' fault as 'they were not basically doing what they should be doing, and that means opening up, helping them to find the bodies and help them to incriminate themselves more'.

Gisli couldn't have picked a more hectic time to have a placement as a detective in the police and he was really enjoying being in the thick of it. He had flirted with becoming a permanent copper like his twin brother, but in training to becoming a psychologist he had chosen a different path. He wanted to develop his skills in the UK and bring them back to Iceland to help his nation. He felt that being able to watch a complex case being run would help his studies: 'My motivation was to learn about this case to understand what makes people commit murder, what makes people confess to police.'

At the end of August, the chief superintendent called him into his office and asked if he would like to be part of a new murder squad. Gisli didn't miss a beat before saying yes. They already had their first case.

*

As Gisli approached the house on Miklabraut – the noisy, wide road that connects Reykjavik to the suburbs and the countryside beyond – he was apprehensive. He had never been to the scene of a murder before. Outside the row of houses there was no indication of the horror that lay within. When Gisli stepped into the house he was overwhelmed: 'There were blood scatters, brain scatters all over the place,' he recalled, the killer 'had been running after the victim hitting her on the head, it was an absolutely horrendous crime scene. He completely lost his temper and had gone berserk.' Lovisa Kristjansdottir, a 57-year-old housewife, had been brutally killed inside the house. She didn't live there but was a neighbour of the owner who was away on holiday. There was no forced entry so the killer must have been inside when she had surprised them.

Gisli could only imagine the terror Lovisa had gone through as the killer beat her with such force. It looked to the detectives that she had been chased around the house. It was 'extremely messy, it was overkill by someone who had completely lost control'. It was a busy residential area and with any luck there would be eyewitnesses who could have seen the killer entering or leaving the house.

Gisli was assigned to interview a witness, Asgeir Ingolfsson. Anyone who watched television knew him straight away. A former newspaper reporter, he was a regular presence on TV as a newsreader for the state broadcaster. Slim, with a square chin, dark set eyes and neatly parted hair, Asgeir had the bland, unthreatening air of a TV personality. The police knew he had previously had an affair with the house owner's daughter so they naturally wanted to speak to him so he could be eliminated from the inquiry. Gisli took Asgeir's statement about where he was at the time of the killing: 'He said he had a problem with his car and then went to the cinema,' but to Gisli, 'his alibi looked very suspicious.' Gisli felt something wasn't right.

It's hard to keep secrets in a small city like Reykjavik, where a distant relative or a friend, or a friend's friend is bound to spot you. It was the charm of the city but it could also be claustrophobic, especially for anyone who craved anonymity. When the police started knocking on the doors of the other grey and white pebbledash houses, neighbours told them they had seen Asgeir Ingolfsson's car in the area before Lovisa was killed. No longer a witness, he was now a suspect. He was taken to Sidumuli, where the detectives called on the expertise of Karl Schutz in interviewing and extracting information from suspects. Gisli was dispatched to drive Schutz to the crime scene, accompanied by Peter Eggerz and a forensic scientist from Germany who was helping with the Geirfinnur case.

For a few days Asgeir played dumb and stuck to his story of being at the cinema. Then he asked to speak to the German detective. As the youngest member of the detective team, Gisli was sent to collect Asgeir from Sidumuli and bring him to the detectives' offices in Borgutun 7. Gisli was allowed to sit in as Asgeir was interviewed. He could see how the renowned detective worked, up close.

Gisli watched, fascinated, as Asgeir started to talk. (Asgeir spoke German so he could speak directly to Schutz.) Beneath his bland, calm exterior, Asgeir revealed a dark side: during the course of his affair with the young daughter who lived in the Miklabraut house, he had noticed a valuable stamp collection stored in a glass cabinet. The delicate, thin squares in magentas, blues and greens were carefully laid out underneath crisp sheets of protective paper, keeping them from being damaged. Asgeir had formed a plan to steal them in order to make some money. He had even gone to the trouble of making a copy of his mistress' door key so he could let himself in when no one was there.

Asgeir knew the owner was away on holiday with her daughter in London, so he could enter the apartment and go about his business undisturbed. He had gone in the late morning when most people were at work, making it less likely he would be spotted. His copied key had worked perfectly and he had come prepared with a crowbar to prise open the cabinet where the stamps were stored. He also took some jewellery. It was all going exactly to plan when he heard the front door open.

Lovisa Kristjansdottir, being a good neighbour, was popping in to water the plants and make sure everything was OK in the house. She was surprised when she saw the stranger inside, but recognised Asgeir immediately. He had been caught red-handed, and it was pointless trying to pretend he was there for legitimate reasons. He decided to come clean and appealed to Lovisa: if he put everything back, would she forget about what she had seen?

Iceland was an honest country; the crime rate was so low because people were expected to stand up and admit their crimes. This was one of the reasons the police depended so heavily on confessions – guilty people were expected to confess. Asgeir had done just this but he wasn't willing to pay the price. Lovisa could never live with herself, she was a principled woman, she couldn't just let Asgeir get away with it and betray her friend's trust. She wouldn't hear of it, she would have to tell the owners. It was a decision that cost her her life.

Inside the interview room, Gisli studied Asgeir's demeanour as he calmly described how he flew into a rage, chasing Lovisa before hitting her with the crowbar. After he had finished, he washed the blood off his hands and dumped the murder weapon in a rubbish tip nearby. The police had their confession; now they needed the murder weapon and Asgeir led them straight to it.

It was Gisli's job to shovel through the detritus on the rubbish tip searching for the bloodied crowbar. It was grim work but he didn't mind. 'It was my first murder case and I was in at the deep end. I believed in justice and fairness.' As for Schutz, his celebrity status was enhanced. He had solved the brutal murder of a woman because he got the confession and this had solved this case. Gisli said it was 'a perfect confession, he confesses and tells you where the murder weapon is and we go and find it – there is perfect corroborative evidence'.

Back in his hotel room, with its chunky furniture and long windows looking out over the city bathed in warm evening sunshine, Schutz could feel pleasantly satisfied. He had only been in Iceland a month and had already wrapped up one murder. His reputation had clearly led Asgeir to seek him out and confess his crime. Schutz was like a missionary flown in from abroad to heal a bruised nation haunted by the ghosts of two young men trapped in cold, dark rocky tombs. Maybe it wouldn't be as hard as Schutz had imagined when he first arrived. The ease with which he had obtained the confession cast the Geirfinnur suspects in an even more negative light. Asgeir had done what was expected, admitting his guilt and showing the police where the evidence was. Why couldn't the others do the same?

13

September 1976

Karl Schutz wanted to show his paymasters in the Icelandic Government the professionalism and organisation he had brought to a previously chaotic inquiry. On 20 September he wrote the first of his weekly reports to Justice Minister Olafur Johannesson on the progress of the investigation.

In Germany, writing reports was a tiresome chore. Schutz would dictate them and get one of his secretaries to type it up. But in Iceland there was a pleasure in writing his regular update for the minister. It wasn't just the soft, melodic clacking of the typewriter as the keys tapped against the carbon paper, imprinting their fading ink, it was that Schutz got to write in German.

Schutz went through the Gudmundur case first. He had organised a day long search for Gudmundur involving 25 police officers and a dozen other workers. They focused on an area west of the aluminium factory at Straumsvik, which kept cropping up in the suspects' testimonies. The search had found a torn shirt and some cloth they thought might be a sheet. This could be important, he said. 'Erla Bolladottir and some of the perpetrators claim that the corpse of Gudmundur had been wrapped and hidden in a bright sheet or blanket... If necessary, it will be examined at BKA [German federal police] forensics lab Wiesbaden.'

The police showed this cloth to Gudmundur's parents to see if they recognised it, but they didn't.

He went into other details of the forensic work they had been carrying out. They had tested a button which had been sewn back onto Kristjan's coat (it was thought one had been ripped off in the fight with Gudmundur). Schutz had ordred a comparative study of the threads used to fix the button on the coat. No clue would be left untested – this was the kind of meticulous detail that was vital in cracking a murder case. He went on to list the other items that were being tested, and what he hoped the lab might find:

(a) Blood on the hem of a coat worn by Kristjan.
(b) Blood on the side wall of the car, in which the corpse of Gudmundur was transported.
(c) Blood on the floor carpet of the apartment [where Erla lived].
(d) Examination of Gudmundur's hair [to see if it matched any of the blood on the suspects' clothes].

This was just one half of the investigation. Schutz had a second section of his report for the work that was going on in the Geirfinnur case. They had seven defendants which included the Klubburin men (although officially they were out of the picture). There were numerous others under suspicion and Schutz had created a card index of 600 names of people of interest. Among them Schutz singled out Gudjon Skarphedinsson:

It is possible that he was the 'foreigner', who on 19.11.74 was at the shipyard in Keflavik and organised the use of a fishing boat to get alcohol from the sea. He was also said to have led a group of people and drove the van from Reykjavik to Keflavik and took part in the action. He is said to be known as a narcotics smuggler and friend of Saevar.

Schutz was trying to show the Justice Minister that with his expertise and access to one of the best criminal laboratories in the world, they could achieve a breakthrough. He signed off the three page report with his minimalist signature. Like Schutz, it was hard to read.

Schutz continued to assign tasks to the team of detectives in an attempt to gather more evidence and bolster the case. They were still searching for witnesses, the cars that had been driven to Keflavik and their drivers, and the boat that had been there bringing in the smuggled alcohol. Schutz was also trying to find clear links between the two missing men and the suspects.

But the extensive forensic testing at the laboratory in Wiesbaden in Germany was coming up with nothing. They tested clothing worn by Saevar, Tryggvi and Kristjan; the floormats, ashtray and door handles from Albert's car; carpets from Erla's apartment in Hamarsbraut looking for microscopic blood spots. There were none, except on a coat worn by Kristjan, and in the end they couldn't prove it was from Gudmundur. They also tested bones they found on their searches of the lava, but this too came to nothing.

Although Einar Bollasson had been released, Schutz was still looking for evidence he was linked to Geirfinnur. He sent off a hotel guest book for handwriting analysis to see if the two men had stayed there at the same time. This proved to be another dead end.

Schutz also decided to issue a public appeal for information on four issues relating to Geirfinnur's disappearance. First, if Geirfinnur had been in contact with any owners of small boats. Second which was a very vague request, if anyone knew whether Geirfinnur had revealed a secret that led to him being threatened. Third, if anyone knew if Geirfinnur had been paid to keep quiet about something. Finally, if anyone knew about the smuggling of alcohol that was supposed to have taken place. It was the kind of appeal you might expect a few days into an investigation, not two years in. It showed publicly there was still an awful lot that the police didn't know.

They were also still looking for the car that took Erla, Saevar and Kristjan to Keflavik and more importantly, the driver. For months, the suspects said it had been Magnus Leopoldsson, the Klubburin manager, but he had been freed as there was nothing to connect him, so the question remained: who was the driver?

With Schutz's arrival, the suspects were no longer being treated as one single group in Sidumuli. On 15 September Erla was transferred from Sidumuli to the old prison, the Hegningarhusid, as the detectives were worried for her safety and that she might harm herself. She would still be in solitary confinement but in a bigger, more comfortable cell. The Hegningarhusid had just one corridor, with doors separating the male section from the female. From her cell she could hear life carrying on outside the prison; people walking on the street, joking and hurrying down Skolavordustigur towards the shops and coffee bars where, over a drink, they might speculate about the 'killers' being held in prison. Her detention had been extended for another 90 days.

Tryggvi was also agitating for a move out of Sidumuli as he was often left for weeks with no investigators talking to him. The restrictions on Tryggvi had eased slightly; he was given a brief chance to stretch his legs for 15 minutes a day in the exercise yard, albeit alone. Orn Hoskuldsson had granted the inmates this small concession. There wasn't much to see in the yard but Tryggvi could feel the rays of the sun, the chafing wind.

It gave him a sense that he was still part of this island that viewed him and the other suspects with suspicion and fear, fuelled by the regular sensationalist press coverage that took the police at their word and reported every little snippet of gossip.

He would still have occasional interviews about the Gudmundur case. There were two of these in September but there was little new he could tell the detectives. He still didn't remember what had been done to the body, its transportation to the lava or its final resting place. The answer would have to come from elsewhere.

Over the summer, Schutz had ordered extensive psychological assessments of the suspects. Tryggvi had gone through two months of this in June and July with the psychiatrist Asgeir Karlsson. His report set out Tryggvi's chaotic young life drinking and taking drugs and how he had been hospitalised because of his drugs intake three times. Karlsson said it was difficult 'to get on with an accurate overview of his life because of how insecure he is and inaccurate, and he often needs to think a lot about his answers and to correct them... His judgment is poor and he has little attachment and shallow emotions, and he has some anxiety and a sense of worthlessness.'

The psychologist Gylfi Asmundsson was equally damning, concluding, 'Tryggvi Runar is neither retarded nor psychotic but is poorly diagnosed and has character defects, which occur as (psychopathy). He has been an alcoholic from the age of 16 and dependent on psychotropic drugs (drug dependence) from the age of 17.'

Tryggvi was moved to Litla Hraun – the newer jail out on the southern coast. The move from Sidumuli considerably improved his mental and physical health. He wrote to the detective Sigurbjorn who had questioned him the most. Starved of any other contact, Tryggvi felt he had struck up a bond with Sigurbjorn in their interviews just as Erla had done. It seemed like a kind of Stockholm Syndrome, where people held captive develop feeling of trust or affection towards their jailers. Tryggvi described to his 'friend' how the new jail was like a paradise compared to Sidumuli. He was in good shape physically and wrote, 'I was ready to talk to you, my dear friend. I was very grateful for what you have done for me.' He sent Sigurbjorn good wishes for his summer holidays and hoped to hear back from the detective: 'I'll write more next time so hope I get a little line from you because you were my friend. Best wishes from me, Tryggvi.'

Saevar had also been having regular psychiatric evaluations with Ingvar Kristjansson, who visited him half a dozen times. In September Ingvar published a long evaluation of Saevar's mental health. It set out his fractured, difficult upbringing with his parents splitting when he was 12 years old and him being sent away to Breidavik boarding school for 'delinquents'. He had developed anxiety and heart problems when he was 16. The psychiatrist set out his descent into serious criminality:

In 1972 there was a major change in Saevar's life when he acquired a new social circle of people who were older than him. In this company he has learned more about drugs and so he began to conduct drug trafficking and importation, hashish and LSD, in collaboration with others that will bring the money into this business. In total, he has gone on four trips abroad from autumn 1973 to January 1974 to buy drugs. Saevar will have described himself as a sensitive man with a love for animals and humans and has an aversion to violence.

They discussed the cases and Saevar told the psychiatrist about the conduct of the police and how he had been coerced to sign confessions, but these claims were casually dismissed by the final report.

This wasn't the first time his mental health had been assessed. The report referred to a separate analysis that a psychologist had conducted in the spring:

> Saevar constantly tried to 'manipulate' the psychologist and tried to avoid taking psychological tests by various means... His behaviour and reactions have all been typical of a psychopathic personality with an extremely flat emotional response... IQ 84, but the probability was that he was intelligent by nature. Profound disturbances have occurred in his personality, which were reflected among other things in shallow emotions, and disregard for anti-social behaviour.

The expert conclusion from the psychiatrist was that Saevar had no evidence of any major mental illness such as psychosis but he probably had a personality disorder: 'He seemed moderately intelligent, his orientation, concentration and memory all seemed normal. The investigation concluded that Saevar was neither an idiot nor insane.'

These assessments were incendiary and highly damaging for Saevar. Here was expert testimony which painted him as a manipulative psychopath, with no attention paid to his complaints of his treatment at the hands of the police.

These assessments were fed to the investigators, strengthening their conviction that Saevar was a deceitful monster who couldn't be trusted. It also justified his cruel treatment and enforced solitary confinement. For months this had been tolerated as a necessary evil, but for the first time during the investigation, questions began to be asked publicly about the isolation the suspects were subject to.

The most forceful voice was Kristjan's lawyer, Paul Arnor Palsson, who had become increasingly concerned about the effect solitary confinement was having on his client's mental state. Kristjan didn't hide the difficulties he was having mining his memories and, after years of drink and drugs, having to go cold turkey in prison. At the end of August, Palsson had had enough and wrote to the court to express his grievance. This was out of the ordinary, defence lawyers rarely kicked up a fuss. Sometimes they could go through a whole trial without saying anything to defend their client.

Palsson was not in this camp of passive lawyers. He accepted that the investigation into the disappearance of Gudmundur was difficult and there was the separate but overlapping investigation into Geirfinnur. He never described them as killings. Without a body or forensics to prove anything, to him they were still missing men. He pointed out that Kristjan had been a helpful witness, reporting everything he knew about the disappearances, but after eight months in solitary confinement he could see no reason to keep him in isolation any more. Kristjan was a hollowed out shell of his former self, racked with uncertainty, constantly changing his story to try to please the detectives. Palsson wanted him taken out of solitary confinement immediately.

Palsson's letter to the court revealed the disdain which the police showed to the lawyers. He had been denied access to his client despite urgent requests to see him, and had been kept in the dark about any details of the investigation. The first time he'd heard about the Geirfinnur investigation was from reading press reports, and he'd only discovered Kristjan was accused of involvement in his murder in April, months into the enquiry. Orn Hoskuldsson's team told him that he didn't need to be present when Kristjan was questioned as he was being treated as a witness rather than a suspect. Yet Kristjan was up to his neck in it, a prime suspect in both cases, and for months Palsson had heard nothing and been given no copies of any interrogation testimony. He asked for all the files on his client and that the court make sure he was present at all future interrogations that Kristjan had.

His intervention provoked a pointed response from the detectives. A day after it was delivered to the court Kristjan was interrogated in his cell for several hours. The detectives said this was at his request; he was clearly dying to get something vital off his chest. Palsson wasn't present and neither was he days later when Schutz and other detectives interrogated Kristjan all day. As to his other request, there was no question of Kristjan being taken out of solitary confinement. The detectives wanted to keep up the mental pressure on him to squeeze him until he had given them exactly what they wanted.

The investigation had clearly become like one of the tankers that ploughed through the Atlantic for a destination that was always just over the horizon. When fog began to form clouding their view, the captain told the crew to carry on, it would soon dissipate. But each day land looked as far away as ever.

Palsson was not the only one to challenge the treatment of the suspects. The prison chaplain, Father Jon Bjarman remained the one outsider who had visited Kristjan and the other suspects during their detention. The priest had lost count of the number of times he had walked up the gentle slope on Sidumuli Street and waited outside the wooden door to be allowed in to see the suspects. He had seen all of them on numerous occasions, and was the only person who wasn't feeding information back to the police. He had spent many hours listening to the hardships that Saevar and the others had to endure. Bjarman was not a troublemaker, he was unfailingly polite, but he too felt he could no longer hold his tongue.

Bjarman visited all of the prisons; not only Sidmuldi but Hegningarhusid, the dark and squat century old jail in the centre of Reykjavik, and Litla Hraun, the more modern jail in Eyrarbakki, a fishing village of a few hundred people. On his visits to these jails, Bjarman had been told by several prisoners of brutal punishments including one akin to a medieval rack where they would be chained to the floor.*

He had spoken to two inmates with very different offences who had been subjected to this same punishment. One of them had been kept in this position for four hours. In September he wrote to the Ministry of Justice about the practice. He said there had been a shift in the culture within the jail, and there had existed an 'abnormal state in Sidumuli since 23 Decemeber 1975', when Saevar and his friends were arrested. Since then, he said, 'the prisoners have been kept in constant fear'. Bjarman urged the authorities to launch an independent inquiry into the undue pressure and hardship placed on the inmates.

Such protestations from a priest and from Kristjan's lawyer, Paul Palsson, hinted at a pattern of behaviour which the Ministry of Justice couldn't easily ignore. They made a half-hearted attempt to investigate, questioning the prison guards and the police, who denied the claims. Their word was believed and the matter went away. The

---

* Even among the prison guards there was unease about this. Gudmundur Gudbjarnarson, then a gangly 20-year-old warden said, 'There wasn't a week when we didn't have to handcuff people' in this way. This had been sanctioned from the very top and was a favoured tactic of the chief warden on Saevar. Hlynur Magnusson, one of the other prison guards who still worried about their conscience, wasn't willing to sit by and let it happen. When he came on shift, he saw the man whom Saevar had passed notes with cuffed on the floor and he took immediate action: 'I freed him and that never happened again when I was on watch.'

prison journals which logged all of the interrogations and punishments meted out to the suspects were never examined. The prisoners would remain in isolation for as long as the detectives wanted.

Bjarman's complaints riled Orn Hoskuldsson, who didn't like his attitude, and after this would intermittently restrict his access to the prisoners. In the paranoia now engulfing the detectives, they thought Bjarman, a sober Lutheran minister, was a conduit for the prisoners passing messages to the outside.

14

October 1976

The Fossvogskirkjugardur was where the dead lived. According to Icelandic folklore, they were guarded by Gunnar Hinriksson, the first person to be buried there in the 1930s. Within the cemetery's gravel paths were simple white crosses, proud headstones, obelisks and bigger plots protected by low white painted walls surrounded by trees, their bark covered in green lichen. On one side, laid out in neat rows, were the simple stone graves of two hundred soldiers – British, American and Canadian – who had died in the Second World War. A cross and the insignia of the Royal Air Force was carved into the grey stone and in the soil, colourful plants grew, bringing new life. Set away from the road, Fossvogskirkjugardur was an oasis of calm. On some days you could even hear the gentle lapping of the water in nearby Fossvogur cove. The only interruption was the occasional hum of one of the small planes landing at Reykjavik airport bringing passengers from elsewhere in Iceland and Greenland.

One morning in October, the police arrived here with a digger, disturbing the otherwise tranquil setting. The foreman at the cemetery confronted the police and asked what the commotion was about. They told him they were looking for a body. He quipped that they had come to the right place as there were bodies everywhere, but they wouldn't be digging anywhere. He told them to let the dead rest in peace and sent them away. The cemetery had become the focus for an increasingly desperate search for Gudmundur's body. The police had been directed there after a bizarre set of interviews with Saevar and Albert.

During a late-night interview on 4 October, Saevar told the police about a drunken conversation he had with Kristjan in August 1974 that would once again shift the focus of the investigation:

> We went to Albert Klahn and told him of our busi-
> ness and asked him to drive us out of Hafnarfjordur
> to the lava and try to find a place where we had
> left the body of Gudmundur Einarsson. I want to
> point out that we took two big black plastic bags.
> We went in a Toyota car, which belonged to Albert
> Klahn's father. It's yellow but I don't remember
> the registration number. When we got to the lava
> near Hafnarfjordur, we drove for a while to try to
> find the place where we had buried Gudmundur's
> body. After some searching we found the place,
> close to the red gravel pits. It was not possible to
> detect that the remains had been disturbed. We
> took two bags and put the remains in them, then
> took them to the vehicle and placed them in the
> boot. We drove to Reykjavik and went straight
> home to Kristjan Vidar's at Grettisgata 82. I believe
> that was between 1900 and 2000 that this happened.
>
> We stayed at Kristjan Vidar's until 2400 or 0100.
> We drove off, that is to say, me, Kristjan Vidar and
> Albert Klahn. We took two shovels, which were in
> the basement of Grettisgata 82. We drove
> Hafnarfjadveg past the Oskjuhlid [a hill in the centre
> of Reykjavik] to the gate which is below the actual

Fossvogur Chapel west of Hafnarfjarðarvegar. We drove the car to the back gate, and we got out here.

Albert Klahn and Kristjan Vidar had the bag together. We walked in the direction of the Chapel itself, to the north. We turned west by a narrow street, then to the south, and then I remember, we passed by a light, the lamppost in the park. Then we turned west again, and then I remember that I saw many concrete crosses at the burial site, which was for French sailors who had perished here in Iceland 40 years ago. The cemetery has a lot of paths, both wide and narrow... and I remember, we were not far from these many concrete crosses, when we found a place, we thought suitable to bury the body... it was facing in the direction of Kopavogur [a suburb of Reykjavik]. I believe that we had dug about 60 to 70cm into the ground and then put the bag into the hole and shoveled over the earth. I remember we used shovels and our feet to smooth it over... we took the shovels back into the car and then drove to Kristjan's home and put the shovels down in the cellar. Albert Klahn spent some time with us and I was with Kristjan Vidar all night. I want to mention that about a month later I went back to Fossvogskirkju cemetery with Kristjan Vidar and his grandmother (who was visiting a grave). Me and Kristjan Vidar looked for the place where we had put Gudmundur Einarsson's remains, but we failed to find it.'

After Saevar told them this tale, the police asked the cemetery foreman to check the area he had described, but he came back with nothing.

Even before this latest twist from Saevar, Albert Klahn's name had started to feature more in Saevar's testimony, so in early October the police had brought him in for another round of intensive questioning. When he was interviewed on 4 October, Albert was sure Gudmundur's body was in the lava. The next day when he was interrogated for more than four hours, he changed his story, he was now certain the body was in Alftanes on the outskirts of Reykjavik. The police brought him there to the beach, but when they could find no sign of a body Albert recanted and said he was wrong about Alftanes and his recollections were very unclear. This should have been a signal for the detectives to hold off, but they had to close the Gudmundur case. As Karl Schutz liked to remind them, 'the clock is ticking'. But Albert had no idea what he was saying or doing and his inability to find the body was making him increasingly anxious. The detectives were worried about his state of mind and Orn Hoskuldsson decided to detain him in Sidumuli on a suicide watch.

The concern for his welfare didn't last long. The next morning Albert was brought to the detective's offices at Borgutun 7 for further questioning. He had come with a reason why he couldn't tell them where the body was: 'I believe that there has been a main reason, that I feared punishment.' He said he had 'tried to hide this inside me', but he could no longer keep it in: 'I feel now at this last hearing that something is in my head. I know I was involved in this and I should be able to say clearly everything, but if I try to put myself in that I find it difficult to distinguish between fantasies and reality. From childhood I have taken various drugs and narcotics. It may have contributed to obscure these issues.'

Albert's version of the trip to the cemetery was broadly similar to Saevar's but a lot vaguer about the details. He had driven his dad's yellow Toyota* to Kristjan's apartment where some black plastic bags and shovels were placed inside it. He couldn't remember where he had

---

* Albert's father had bought the car in the summer of 1974.

driven to and whether he had helped to dig up the 'bags' containing Gudmundur's corpse.

He had driven to a cemetery, where he and Kristjan had taken the bags from the boot and carried them into the cemetery grounds. He definitely saw Saevar and Kristjan dig a grave. Albert said he was not drunk or on drugs and thought it was the same for the others, that for once they had clear heads that night. There was one important difference in his account, though – he thought Tryggvi had been there.

Throughout his interviews Albert had constantly stressed to his interrogators that he only vaguely recalled these events. His memory was starting to degrade like a negative of a photo left out in the sun, where the image starts to lose its shape and focus – eventually it would be a ghostly blur. Having given this new testimony, he was taken out to the cemetery several times in the following days with different detectives, each time seeming to remember more. After several visits the police notes said his hesitation had gone. They wrote that he said, 'After having to recall this I am absolutely sure that we have gone to Fossvogskirkjur park, but in the past this has completely been wiped from my memory.'

Albert's testimony about the cemetery brought Tryggvi back into the picture after months of no contact from the police. 'It was a long nightmare,' he recalled later when reflecting on the effects of the solitary confinement, 'I began to think it was a way to destroy me both spiritually and physically… I realised I was on my way to the grave.' But in October, with this new information, the police started to take notice of him again and interrogate him in his cell, although never for much longer than an hour.

Tryvvgi was still exercising, often for hours each day, sculpting his body and writing down all of the various physical tasks he had gone through in his cell: squat thrusts, star jumps, press-ups, pull-ups. His inspiration had been a body-building book his mother had sent him and this had transformed his life inside Sidumuli. He said of its influence on him, 'I practised three times a day. This book was kind of my bible. Suddenly I began to think about caring for my body.' Tryggvi had tried to take control over his life; by getting power over his body he hoped it would improve his confidence and his mental state.

He needed a way to keep himself sane, so he had started a diary. It was filled with the details of his daily life in Sidumuli: his meals; the weather and descriptions of the guards, the police, as well as his exercise regime. This wasn't for anyone else to read, it was a way to voice the thoughts that were swirling around in his head. The writing burns with a righteous anger. On the front of his diary from October 1976 is scribbled in green pen: 'This is a diary that an innocent man is keeping in here regarding a big case that he is wrongly accused of, but the truth will always come out, even if it is late.'

On 26 October he reflected on his long time in custody: 'The time is pretty long in isolation 10½ months in a cell. Yes it is a long time in the life of one man and for that person to be innocent.'

As the case reached a particular juncture, he would be brought for corroboration interviews with the other suspects. He found it deeply frustrating being in the same room as the people who had implicated him in the first place. After one of these with Erla, when the police were again trying to get their stories to match, he wrote, 'It's not easy to lie about something that I have no knowledge of. For example, that house in Hamarsbraut. And secondly, I don't know Erla. Why would I have been at her house?'

Tryggvi could improve his body through exercise, but he couldn't hold off the drugs that he was prescribed for his moods and sleep. He wrote how this was turning him into a zombie: 'I've got so many drugs, so much medication that I can't remember my name. I wake up and I can't remember if my mother passed away or I was dreaming it.'

He was allowed to see his lawyer, Hilmar, who was urging the police to transfer Tryggvi to the old prison in the centre of town, as the food was better and the cells had better air quality and there was more room for him to exercise.

While the Gudmundur investigation was focused on the inmates in Sidumuli, the focus of the parallel Geirfinnur investigation had shifted to the Hegningarhusid in the centre of Reykjavik where Erla had been transferred in September. It was a hundred years old, but it had been built as a prison, unlike Sidumuli which was still very much a makeshift prison. Gudmundur Gudbjarnarson had worked in both jails and found the old one a better atmosphere for guards and inmates. For the wardens, there was a kitchen where they could prepare meals, whereas in Sidumuli food was brought in from outside. The inmates in the old prison, a mixture of homeless strays and more serious criminals, had one big advantage over those in Sidumuli, as Gudbjarnarson recalled: 'The cells were bigger and there were humans working there.' The well-behaved inmates got the chance to have a taste of normality by being allowed to wash dishes after meals which earned them extra coffee and a sandwich. Instead of the hated malfunctioning air conditioning at Sidumuli, the old prison cells had geothermal radiators, powered by the vast underground reservoirs trapped deep beneath the lava.

Trying to restore lost memories was also an important part of the Geirfinnur inquiry. The investigators were willing to take increasingly desperate measures to improve the recollections of the suspects. Erla had already been subject to psychiatric assessments but on 12 October the detectives went one step further, getting a doctor to give her an injection to help her recall events. This was moving into new darker, uncharted territory: giving drugs to get her to unearth memories that she had struggled to piece together for the the past ten months. Erla said that, after a long and balanced deliberation, she would tell the whole truth about Geirfinnur. This time she had one condition: first she got to see her child. Schutz agreed – although in reality this would not happen for a long while. So Erla said she was willing to write down what she knew and the paper that was normally rationed was freely granted.

Sigurbjorn and several prison guards watched as Erla was given an injection by a therapist to try to help her remember. Then, on 15 October, three days after her 'memory' injection, Erla was led along the corridor, through the clanking metal door and up the creaking wooden stairs. She walked past the old courthouse chamber, remembering when she first stood in front of the judge back in May and was told she would be remanded for months, unable to see her child.

She entered a small, stark white room, dominated by a huge wooden desk. Across from her sat Karl Schutz, immaculately turned out in a crisp white shirt, his thick white hair neatly combed. His piercing blue eyes seem friendlier than normal, but he was sceptical that she would tell the truth. Next to him was Peter Eggerz and the detective, Sigurbjorn. Although it was early afternoon there was already a sharp chill in the air, the days were getting shorter and the temperatures at night closer to freezing. Esjan, the mountains guarding the city, would be a ghostly silhouette in a few hours time.

Schutz began questioning Erla about her conflicting testimony. She wanted to see her daughter and was becoming increasingly agitated. The police believed she had received direct instructions from Saevar but she denied this and said she was certain she had not been in Keflavik. She said she had made up what had happened and had put it together from what she had read in the newspapers and presented it as facts. Much of what she said had been fantasy and her imagination. She admitted making up details but said, 'I have received information from various sources' and set out how she had done this:

> She had been staying in Copenhagen with Saevar and some others but she didn't remember who they were. There was talk about alcohol smuggling and speculation that an accident with Geirfinnur could have happened while he was transporting alcohol. Saevar said there were serious consequences for people who might not behave as they should and referred to Geirfinnur. Erla said in February the same year, when they were still in Copenhagen, Saevar read about the Geirfinnur case in Morgunbladid newspaper. A Dutch psychic claimed to know where the body was but Saevar said the body would not be found there. Saevar said men like Geirfinnur should be bound with something heavy and discarded on the sea bed. In April when they had returned to Iceland they were having a conversation with Saevar's sister and her husband. She heard them speculating the clay head the police had made was in fact of Magnus Leopoldsson. She also speculated that Magnus, Sigurbjorn Eric and Valdimar Olsen were all acquaintances of her brother, Einar and she would not be surprised if they were implicated in smuggling.

Schutz dismissed this as yet another attempt to deflect attention from the truth. She was caught twisting in the wind by Schutz, unsure what she should say to make him believe her. The atmosphere inside the cramped room became more heated. Schutz thought she was still protecting Saevar, but she was adamant, 'I'm not protecting him. I have to protect myself.' Schutz probed further, maybe she was afraid of Saevar that's why she was shielding him? A touch of her defiance returned: 'No,' she maintained, 'I'm not afraid of anyone.'

Schutz's tone shifted. He had some good news, 'We are close to finishing the case and you will soon be released.' This was what she had been waiting to hear for the past four months she had been in solitary confinement. As cigarette smoke swirled around the room, Karl Schutz sat forward, a smile softening his features. All they needed, he said, leaning in closer, was for her to tell them how she had helped dispose of Geirfinnur's body. Erla lit another cigarette, trying to compose her tiny frame and stop herself from shaking.

Now it was Schutz's turn to set out what he believed had *really* happened to Geirfinnur's body:

They had brought Geirfinnur's body from Keflavik to Kristjan's house in Grettisgata. For several days it had lain in the basement and then on a freezing November night they loaded it into Erla's Land Rover. They drove out of Reykjavik, stopping at a petrol station to buy a jerry can of petrol. They carried on out of the city to the Raudholar, the red lava hills lit by the moonlight, casting strange shadows on the deep frozen pools covered in ice. Erla drove the Land Rover along the rough tracks, over the footsteps of the walkers and the hoofmarks of riders who travelled the hills on Icelandic ponies.

The tyres crunched on the hard stone path. Erla leaned against the car, coolly smoking a cigarette as she watched Saevar and Kristjan take Geirfinnur's body from the back of her car. They knew they had to make it as hard as possible to find him, so they poured petrol over the body, lit a match and watched as the orange flames took hold and consumed his remains. They took the shovel and dug a shallow grave for what was left.

Schutz sent the detectives out of the room so it was just the two of them and his interpreter. He leaned back in his chair, watching his tale sink in and gauging Erla's reaction. He had told her in their previous encounters he couldn't decide if she was 'an innocent country girl or a hardened and devious criminal' but he seemed to have reached a conclusion.

Her denials were of no use. Schutz had told her before: 'I'm not here to play games, the government brought me here to solve this case.' He leaned over the desk, so close she could feel his breath on her. 'If you sign the report you have a chance of being released,' he told her. If she didn't co-operate, she would never leave the prison. The rage and hurt that had been building in her could be contained no longer. Erla maintained the only thing she knew about Geirfinnur was through the conversations she had heard Saevar having. 'The rest was my fabrication,' she said. 'This is the truth.' Schutz decided to end the hearing and Erla became upset; she went berserk, throwing ashtrays, coffee cups, books, anything she could get hold of, crying out in a wail of pain, 'No one believes me here!'. The police came back in the room and held her down. After she calmed down, she saw there was only one way out. The confession had already been typed up for her to sign.

Erla saw it 'as a deal, a transaction'. If she signed the statement she would be released. This was what had happened in the Gudmundur case, when she was released after implicating Saevar and his friends. She thought by signing the document her isolation would finally be over – that was what Eggert and Schutz had told her. 'I was trying to stop it, but nothing happened. I was not released and I knew I would never come out of prison.' No one there believed a word she said, most of all Karl Schutz. She was taken back to her cell in the old prison. Whatever she said or did she could see no end to her incarceration.

It had been a dramatic day but Schutz still had to write his regular progress report to the minister, Olafur Johannesson. He told the minister:

> The work of the investigation commission in the last two weeks has focused on the discovery of Gudmundur's body. The investigation had become necessary after Saevar had said that in August 1974 he had moved the corpse from the lava fields to Fossovgur with the help of Albert and Kristjan. The site had been found to be empty after opening with a few probes at other possible disturbances. Evidence will be sought in other potential sites in the cemetery this weekend.

In his reports, Schutz was keen to show how he was trying to modernise the police force: 'I have reached agreement with the president of the German Federal Police for a licence for a computer for research programmes to be made available to Iceland.' He saw trying to improve the expertise within the police as an important part of his role. He had raised this issue the previous week in a letter to the Icelandic Attorney General:

> The police have only received the education intended for general policing in Iceland. It's absolutely essential to train investigators in collecting evidence. They need more expertise in the techniques and methods used to deal with offenders. Reasonably intelligent offenders can get one over on the police and the police can't succeed in difficult interrogations.

He said the samples from the Gudmundur case had been sent to the German forensics lab and the team would hand over all the evidence in the case to the prosecutor on 19 October 1976. In reality, that would consist of just the suspects' confessions, as the lab failed to return any forensic evidence linking the suspects to the crime. After that, the investigation would focus solely on Geirfinnur, where they were already making very good progress.

15

November 1976

By November, the gloom and murk of winter had stripped Reykjavik of the little beauty it possessed. It was a time to hunker down with friends and family with some alcohol to take the edge off the long winter nights. The dour weather reflected Gudjon Skarphedinsson's bleak mood. He had retreated into himself, spending long, quiet hours in introspection. He was like a boat cut from its anchor, out in the turbulent Atlantic battered by the roiling waves, taking on water and struggling to stay afloat.

After his previous police interview in May, Gudjon's name began to feature prominently in the interviews with Saevar and Erla. After the doomed attempt to smuggle drugs in Gudjon's car, the police saw Saevar and Gudjon as having form together. Then, at the end of October, during a nine-hour interview, Saevar went through a vivid account of that night which placed Gudjon front and centre in Geirfinnur's death. In his new version of events, Gudjon, the older man, was the person very much in control. He said Gudjon had made contact with Geirfinnur and agreed they would meet in Keflavik:

When they reached the port cafe, Gudjon had given Kristjan the phone number to call Geirfinnur and summon him to the harbour. Soon after, Geirfinnur had come to the car and sat in the back seat. They drove to the harbour and on the way there they discussed the alcohol. When they got to the harbour Saevar overheard a conversation between Gudjon and Geirfinnur, where Gudjon was asked if he was not going to 'take this', but Geirfinnur had no answer. Gudjon asked, 'What nonsense is this?' Kristjan joined in the conversation and told Geirfinnur, 'Were we not ready to discuss this at the club?' Geirfinnur said he wanted nothing to do with this and he was told that he should keep quiet. Saevar said Geirfinnur had pushed Kristjan and he had punched him in the face. Geirfinnur began fighting with Kristjan and that Gudjon joined in and hit Geirfinnur in the head with a long wooden plank. Geirfinnur fell to the ground and Kristjan hit him again while he was on the ground. Saevar said it was difficult to describe this as it happened in a very short time. He and Kristjan discussed how Geirfinnur was unconscious and Saevar realised he was dead. Saevar went back to the car with Gudjon and realised that Erla was gone.

They went back to Kristjan's apartment and stored the body in the laundry room. Two days later they wrapped the body in black bags and drove it out of the city. Gudjon brought a crowbar so they could loosen some stones and hide the body under rocks. He thought it had been about 400 metres from the road and they had later discussed moving the body as they thought the bags would be spotted.

Erla too portrayed Gudjon as a dangerous man; she said she had been frightened to mention his name to the police as she was afraid of him and what he might do to her.

Karl Schutz had been listening to this testimony and was increasingly certain Gudjon was involved in the case. In his report to the Justice Minister on 5 November, Schutz said they suspected Gudjon Skarphedinsson 'had been present in the smuggling in Keflavik 19/11/74, and participated in the fight with Geirfinnur'. In the past, this suspicion alone would have prompted Gudjon to be hauled in to Sidumuli immediately, but Schutz was more systematic than this. He wanted a list of possible criminal cases Gudjon had been involved in, even if he hadn't been charged. This information could be useful during the questioning, it would help Schutz to gauge how truthful Gudjon was being. A week after sending his report to the minister, Schutz had all of the information he needed to make his move against 'the foreigner'.

On 12 November, in the quiet of the morning, Sigurbjorn and Eggert arrived at the apartment to arrest Gudjon. He was asleep and appeared bemused when they showed up, but he didn't put up any kind of struggle. They searched the apartment but found no weapons, drugs or forensic evidence to link him to the crime. But when they looked under his desk they found a small notebook. Flicking through it, they came upon two pages that seemed odd and were of immense interest to them. Gudjon had written notes about when Geirfinnur first went missing.

Gudjon was taken to the Corner where Eggert had questioned him in May. This time, Eggert and Sigurbjorn told him he was suspected of involvement in Geirfinnur Einarsson's death. The detectives used Saevar and Erla's testimony to take him back over the events of 19 November 1974. They said Gudjon had arranged the meeting with Geirfinnur. 'You spoke to Geirfinnur on the phone? You arranged a meeting with him at 9.30 in Keflavik?' the detectives asked him. Eggert accused Gudjon of being the instigator who then contacted the others. Saevar, Erla and Kristjan had told them independently that Gudjon had arranged the meeting with

Geirfinnur. (Saevar, Erla and Kristjan had done the same when they had implicated the Klubburin men, and this had been shown to be false, but Schutz and his task force didn't seem to be worried about the suspects doing the same thing again.) Gudjon listened to this, increasingly annoyed. His reply was unambiguous: 'I never had a meeting with Geirfinnur. I didn't know him at all. I never met him. I had no contact with anyone else in Keflavik. This is all a lie.' His denial couldn't have been more emphatic. Gudjon was adamant that all he knew about Geirfinnur was what he had read in the newspapers.

Gudjon repeated what he had told the detectives in May: how he had met Saevar when he had taught him at school and after that they had intermittent contact. Saevar was always the one seeking him out, asking for favours, inviting himself around to Gudjon's apartment. He definitely was not a close friend and Gudjon only knew Erla through Saevar. As for Kristjan, he had never met him and knew nothing about him.

The minutes turned into hours. The detectives believed the gang had transported Geirfinnur's body to Kristjan's apartment in Reykjavik where Gudjon had played a key role in deciding where to dump it. Gudjon was getting agitated: 'I have never been to Kristjan Vidar's home in Grettisgata. I know nothing about the conversation about moving Geirfinnur's body. I didn't take part in carrying corpses. To tell the truth, I believe that Geirfinnur was never killed. Perhaps he is abroad somewhere.'

Gudjon still had his barbed sense of humour, but there was little to laugh about. The police line of questioning was placing Gudjon front and centre in Geirfinnur's death and burial. They even accused him of going south to Selfoss, where steam rose from the town's geyser covering the woods in a hot mist, to look for potential burial spots. 'I know nothing about the burial place,' Gudjon replied. 'This is all a fabrication, as I have repeatedly said.'

After almost six hours, the detectives called an end to the interview and brought Gudjon back to the sickly green cell, number six. He was still in shock. He assumed, as his fellow inmates previously had, that the police would soon release him. It was his first taste of his new life as one of Iceland's worst criminals.

Gudjon was questioned three more times that day and his ordeal ended at 2.30 in the morning. In total he had been questioned for over 11 hours without a lawyer being present. Unlike the other suspects, though, there were no threats from the detectives of indefinite incarceration and he was remanded in custody for a comparatively lenient 20 days.

Having spent so long on the case, the team had an established playbook. In between the 'official' interviews they would get a detective to befriend Gudjon and get information from him informally in his cell. Gretar Saemaundsson was chosen for this task. He was young and slim with a friendly relaxed manner, but underneath a steely determination. Gudjon immediately liked him. 'He was a farmer's boy like me,' he recalled. 'He was the same age as me, we had a lot of things in common, we knew the same places.' They would chat about growing up on a farm, and the joys of being in the countryside out of the city. Gudjon found, 'I had forgotten sometimes that he really was policeman and more of a friend.' Gretar was no more a friend to Gudjon, though, than the young detective Sigurbjorn was to Erla. As an experienced detective Gretar's job was to help solve the case and he would feed back whatever Gudjon told him to Schutz and the task force.

The police were also being fed stories by Saevar, Kristjan and Erla. Seavar said it was Gudjon, the older, more intelligent man who was in control on the night Geirfinnur died. Erla kept mentioning Gudjon's involvement and that she was certain he was in Keflavik and had helped to move the body. Kristjan thought Gudjon was 'the foreign looking guy' who had been driving the car to Keflavik.

Gudjon could see, 'Everybody was making up stories. And the problem was to get the stories to fit together. The road to Keflavik, what happened in Keflavik and how we got back to Reykjavik? Where did we go after that?'

After that brutal first day, the pace of the interviews slowed. To Gudjon it appeared the police were running out of steam. He sensed from the detectives that 'They were about to give it up, there was no way to build a case out of it – it was a muddle, they didn't have anything.'

Gudjon was in a muddle of his own. While he was sure he wasn't in Keflavik when Geirfinur went missing, he had no clear recollection of what he was doing that night. He would get blackouts sometimes when he would drink – maybe that had happened on that night and he couldn't remember?

After three days in custody, Gudjon got to see Karl Schutz. As soon as he walked into the Corner to face his new interrogator, Gudjon could tell immediately that things would be different. 'Schutz was very tough and you better do what he wanted to, if you want to have peace. He was able to beat you up. You know these old German motherfuckers.' Gudjon had an advantage over the other suspects in that he could speak to Schutz in German. The detective thought Gudjon was the brains of the operation, with Kristjan as the brawn and Saevar the fixer with the street smarts.

Gudjon had managed to get a lawyer, Harold Blondal. Gudjon didn't think he was ideal fit – he specialised in shipping and business. But Gudjon didn't have much choice when it came to lawyers, so he had to make do with whoever would take on his case.

Schutz focused on two areas in his interview. The first was a phone call Saevar had made to Gudjon from Copenhagen in April 1975. Gudjon was at home with his kids when the phone rang. He said he didn't know who was on the other end of the line and had no choice but to accept the call. He said Saevar had started 'asking about news from Iceland. I said there was nothing new, nothing more to add'. He remembered it as a very brief call, as Gudjon was paying the bill. Schutz thought he was lying as Saevar had told them a different version. According to Saevar, he asked Gudjon if it was safe to come home and Gudjon had told him to say nothing about Geirfinnur. When this was put to him, Gudjon shot back, 'This is a pure lie.'

The second element that Schutz kept returning to was the notebook the police had found in Gudjon's apartment. Inside were detailed notes about the first days after Geirfinnur's disappearance. Why did he have newspaper cuttings only about the first few days? Gudjon's explanation was that having been questioned in May, he decided to do some homework as he knew nothing about the case. He went to the national library and went through the newspaper cuttings to make notes. It wasn't out of some morbid curiosity about the case, he claimed. 'People disappear all the time,' Gudjon told the police, 'I can't say it's my cup of tea.' Schutz's theory was the notes were to help Gudjon contruct a plausible alibi if he was questioned by the police again.

During these initial interrogations Gudjon was still trying to figure out where he was and what he was doing two years before on the night of 19 November 1974. He thought he was in his apartment with his kids doing some DIY. But lined up against him were Saevar, Erla and Kristjan, all of whom said he was in Keflavik. How would all three of them construct the same story?

'You have no alibi,' the detectives told him. 'We have your fingerprints and we have evidence and we're sure that you're not telling the truth. You should tell us the truth.' They didn't have evidence, that's why they were relying on him to tell the truth.

The police gave Gudjon some paper to write down his thoughts and he began keeping a daily journal, written in his careful, neat script. His first entry was dated 18 November 1976: 'I know nothing about this case... Sometimes I feel guilty, that I'm guilty of something but I can't remember what happened... This is taking away all my strength. I must be ill.'

The diary would be vital for Gudjon, a way of trying to make sense of the situation and the internal monologue running though his mind. In this first week he was intensely aware of the shame he had brought on his family. 'I'm a very proud man,' he recalled, 'so if I made mistakes it takes time to make up for that.' But the police told him there was a way he could instantly put right his mistakes and make his family and his daughter proud of him, by helping them solve this terrible crime. 'I was the only one who knew all about it and could tell the truth about it. I was the one. I was different, I was older.'

The police thought that exploiting Gudjon's strong attachment to his family could yield results. They wouldn't let his wife or mother see him. Instead they brought Gudjon's uncle, the imposing figure of Jon Isberg, to the jail. Isberg was the sheriff of Issafjordur, in the Westfjords. He was tall, solid and bald with thick glasses and liked wearing his official uniform.

The police thought Isberg could sway Gudjon and persuade him to open up. Isberg was only in the cell for 15 minutes, just long enough to tell his nephew he had to confess. 'This must be solved,' he insisted, 'we must have it out of the world.' Gudjon said his uncle saw the case as very straightforward. 'He talked like it was easy to see I was involved, there was no doubt in his mind about that.' The access Isberg was allowed contrasted with that allowed to Gudjon's lawyer, who was struggling to see him. The intervention didn't work; Gudjon was only annoyed by the presumption that he was guilty.

The second anniversary of Geirfinnur's disappearance on 19 November brought a flurry of press activity. The lack of progress in the case led to questions of whether the Icelandic criminal justice system was capable of dealing with such a serious and complex crime. Journalists concluded that much was still unknown about Geirfinnur, and the only certainty was that he went to meet an unknown person on the evening of 19 November 1974. Kristjan, Saevar and Erla may have played a role, but it wasn't clear exactly what they had done. It was clear from the previous two years of enquiries that the police weren't capable of handling it, which was why Schutz had been called in.

While this was happening, Gudjon's mental health was deteriorating as the doubts built within him that maybe he was involved after all. Back in his cell, laid flat out on the bed staring into space, he began to blame himself for his clouded memory. The guilt that he felt piling in him was reflected in his diary entries, like this one from 20 November:

> New humiliation, disgrace and shame. I, who lived in the belief in the two years previously that I knew nothing about the matter and now I have been involved in it... Am I insane or have I been there? I say yes to that. Much of what I have done in recent years was insanity.

By afternoon, the light had faded and ahead of him was the empty darkness and silence of the evening inside his green stone tomb. After his first few days in detention, Gudjon would frequently end up crying during his daily interviews with Gretar and the other detectives. In the evening he would always turn to his diary as a source of solace. Two days later he wrote: 'I have lived with this for two years absolutely convinced that I had nothing to do with this. But now I think things are becoming a bit clearer. If only I knew if I was involved in this.'

The next day, when he was brought again before Karl Schutz, Gudjon didn't mince his words: 'This is cursed nonsense. I was not there that night. I'm sure.' But doubts had started to creep into his testimony, as well as into his diary. 'Are you involved in Geirfinnur, or can you not remember?' Schutz asked. For the first time Gudjon voiced the suspicions that had started out as fine threads and had begun to knit together, forming thicker strands in his mind. 'I don't remember why I say no. As far as I know. I have nothing more to say. This is all odd.' The interrogations were getting to him, eating away at him and affecting his ability to sleep:

Nights are the worst. I pray desperately for sleep but it is slow in coming, and I have intrusive thoughts. Oh, my God, my God why have you forsaken me? Because my life is destroyed, reputation defied, home, children, marriage, friends, acquaintances, relatives... I'm a sick man. In reality, I am not an evil man, but hopelessly defective... I wished I had never touched cannabis. It destroyed my life... If only I knew if I had participated in this or not.

He wanted to speak to Gretar, the policeman who had become his 'friend'. He valued their time together and wanted to help the investigation because of his friendship with Gretar. Gudjon did have one other regular visitor, the prison chaplain, Jon Bjarman. Bjarman wasn't there to make him confess, he sat and listened to the confused young man and it gave Gudjon some hope.

His diary entry for 25 November was more positive: 'Today I had a good visit from Rev Jon Bjarman. We talked a lot about the case and more. He is nice, and believes in my innocence.'

Gretar had been to see him too that day. Gudjon wanted him to fill in the gaps in his memory. He asked Gretar if it was true that he had driven to Keflavik. He had no idea if he had, but already he trusted the policeman so implicitly that he was willing to believe what Gretar said. This gave the young detective huge influence over Gudjon. He told him to write down everything, but in his diary Gudjon wrote how his policeman friend's tone was negative:

> Gretar came and suggested a lot of things and indicated that I was in a bad position in regard to the case. He wants me to get used to the idea that I could be a murderer. This is too much. According to this I should admit what Saevar and Erla are saying but it must be a misunderstanding.

For Erla there was no misunderstanding, she was sure Gudjon had been at Keflavik harbour. 'I am fully confident, 100 per cent,' she stated in the interviews she had given since Gudjon had been arrested. She said they picked him up in Reykjavik and drove to Keflavik. They went to the harbour where she saw Gudjon talking with Geirfinnur. When Geirfinnur tried to walk away, Gudjon grabbed hold of him and started fighting and Kristjan Vidar went to help. When she saw this she ran away and hid.

Erla later said, 'I was scared and weak and needed to get to my baby and that's why I lied... I was lying the whole time, it was just me alone in my bed with a nightmare.' But Erla's bad dream on a dark, snowy night, had turned into a living nightmare for the other suspects, all of whom she had implicated.

Erla wasn't allowed outside in the old prison's scratchy asphalt exercise yard or to communicate with any other inmates. The old prison was in the centre of Reykjavik, yards from the majestic white stone Hallgrimskirkja which towered over the low-rise houses with their bright tin roofs and the featureless apartment blocks. It was less harsh than Sidumuli, but also less secure. On 23 November Erla was in her corner cell when she heard a noise outside her window. When she looked out she couldn't believe it; there were two figures on the roof of the jail and they were heading towards her. When they reached her window they whispered, 'We'll be here tomorrow night. What do you want – Coca Cola or maybe something else?' Erla was bemused; she had no idea who they were but grateful for the human contact.

The next night the figures returned as promised but as they got to the cell, the lights went on outside and the men were surrounded by the police. The police had been listening, ready to pounce and within moments they were inside Erla's cell. They forced her to strip and then searched her cell. She was taken to Borgutun 7 the next day and questioned about the men. She had no idea who they were, but the police had found some slips of paper with phone numbers on them. The men had come armed with a camera and tape recorder and planned to get an interview with Erla that they could sell to the newspapers. Even if they had got an interview it's unlikely it would have changed the public's perception of Erla as a malign force who was part of a criminal network.

Gretar and his bosses were convinced that Gudjon was also part of this network. The police could see he was in a delicate state – emotional and struggling to talk about the case. They got the prison doctor to visit him. He prescribed chlorpromazine which Gudjon had taken before to treat and control his depression. Gudjon said this affected his police interviews: 'I turned very carefree in what I said. And of course I was supposed to help my nation out of this mess.'

It was inevitable that one day Gudjon would be taken out of the prison for a drive with Schutz and the detectives. It was late afternoon on 28 November, dusk in an Icelandic winter when occasionally a salmon pink sky would bring a brief splash of colour before the darkness swallowed up the light. Gudjon had Schutz and his translator Peter Eggerz for company.

They followed a route the police believed the cars had taken on the fateful night from Reykjavik to Keflavik. As they made their way out of town into the jagged shadows of the lava fields, Schutz began interviewing Gudjon in the car. He probed Gudjon on why he couldn't remember such important events from the past, and invited him to remember.

Gudjon went back to 1974 and the depression he suffered, along with the death of his father, which had been a violent jolt to his mental state. His relationship with his father was complicated; for years he hadn't lived with him and when he was expelled from school he was an obvious disappointment to the sober Lutheran minister who had devoted his life to the church. Unfortunately Gudjon hadn't received any help from a psychiatrist, so his condition had not improved.

Having explained his memory blockage, Gudjon felt the haze started to clear a little. He began to entertain the notion he had been in the Volkswagen that drove to the airport. 'Saevar could have been there,' he said. 'I'm not sure if Erla was there. Kristjan I don't know personally. Therefore, I can't say whether I went on this trip. But it is quite certain that there were people in the car.' He sounded confused and made no sense but he was slowly pulling himself into the picture, entertaining the notion that he had been in Keflavik that night.

By the time they reached Keflavik it was dark. As they entered the main street, Gudjon commented, 'I suspect we have driven here.'

The car carried on toward the Hafnarbudin, the simple wooden cafe that hung out over the ocean, where Geirfinnur was headed on his last night alive. The police said Gudjon had taken over control of their direction, telling the police where to go. They drove to the harbour, deserted where the shells of boats and warehouses were creaking in the evening wind. Gudjon wanted to get out of the car to take a closer look but the police wouldn't let him.

He asked if they could go back to Grettisgata, the shabby street in East Reykjavik where Kristjan lived. When they arrived, Gudjon said he had never been there – but he had been in the house next door.

When he returned to his cell, Gudjon lay for a while, then sat down to complete his diary for the day. It had become a vital document to him; it was his attempt to find an answer to the case, to make sense of reality:

'I see no reason other than trying to help with the case the best I can. It's a pity I remember so little. Went on a pleasant drive to Keflavik... I want to solve the case immediately and receive a heavy and long sentence. I'm finished.

He said later the ride had come to nothing, he could not remember anything. He didn't know what cars they were driving on the night Geirfinnur went missing. He might have seen a fight in the harbour but he couldn't properly see it as he said it 'was dark and I am very short-sighted'. He couldn't remember seeing a body. He wasn't sure if he was involved in digging a grave for the body. He was a hesitant suspect, feeling for answers. With each passing day, he was moving closer towards admitting his involvement and his guilt.

The next day Gretar returned to interview Gudjon and his diary reflected the growing importance of the detective in moving Gudjon towards a confession:

> I had a long conversation with Gretar today. I'm trying to remember the trip to Keflavik. I'm tired after this. I wish I could remember all this. Gretar says I just need courage and we will try again tomorrow.

Gudjon would later realise the difficulty he was in: 'The case was impossible. Nobody could turn back. The police could not, the papers could not, and the judges could not. It had all gone too far.'

At the beginning of December, Gudjon was remanded in custody for another 60 days. The court was told, 'very large gaps remain in his account' but he couldn't be released as it was feared he would influence potential witnesses.

16

December 1976

On 8 December, late at night, when the streets had gone quiet and there was a low hum over the city, Gudjon sat down for an interview with Gretar. After a month of these conversations they were comfortable in each other's company. In different circumstances they would have shared a drink and a smoke inside one of the city's bars, or in summer sit outside, wishing they could be back among the fresh stillness of the countryside.

By now Gudjon had convinced himself he had taken part in Geirfinnur's murder. He had been taken out on another journey to Keflavik with the detectives Gretar Saemundsson and Eggert Bjarnason, and there was a new urgency to the case which Gudjon wrote about in his diary: 'They want it over before Christmas. I'm feeling so bad at the moment. So tired. I can't remember anything. I do not know anything. And I'm losing my mind. I'm completely worn out.'

Gudjon and Gretar were inside Sidumuli, in the Corner, and Gudjon was racked with guilt. First for the Klubburin men: Einar Bollason, Magnus Leopoldsson, Valdimar Olsen and Sigurbjorn Eriksson. He knew when they were arrested that they were innocent and it weighed heavily on him not to have had the courage to tell the police about it. He no longer saw himself as an innocent; he was caught up in the maelstrom where the police, prison guards and the public were all convinced the suspects were guilty.

Gretar wanted to go through the case systematically, covering each key aspect as he went along. Gudjon knew this was important; he had been told this was the final interrogation. He said he was going to explain, 'The truth in this case as best as I can. A few points are unclear in my memory but I might recall them later.' Gudjon began talking and he would not stop for the next five and a half hours:

> *Saevar arrived with Erla and asked Gudjon to bring him to the airport, he was late for an appointment in Keflavik. Gudjon was reluctant, but finally agreed to take them. They drove a light blue Volkswagen that Saevar had at his disposal and there were four of them heading to Keflavik. He remembered they talked about getting tough with the man they were going to meet if he did not want to negotiate with them.*
>
> *When they got to Keflavik there were a lot of people around the cinema on the main street and Saevar told them all to duck down. They drove on to a building marked 'Pipe Making Factory' and stopped there. He said the passengers got out of the car, except Erla. They went behind a building and Gudjon drove to the corner of the main street. When the passengers returned, Saevar was upset about not being able to meet the man and talked about making a phone call. They drove towards the cafe and a passenger in the back seat got out to make a call. When he returned he told them the man was coming.*
>
> *The man arrived and got in the car. He didn't say his name but Gudjon became aware this was Geirfinnur Einarsson. Saevar talked to Geirfinnur in the car and the others joined in a little in the discussions. They were*

talking about alcohol and generally fishing for information from one other. Saevar offered Geirfinnur money for getting alcohol or information about it. Gudjon said when they got to the harbour, Saevar and Geirfinnur still hadn't come to an agreement. He couldn't remember why he stopped the car, but the men all got out. Three of them ended up in a fight with Geirfinnur that led to his death. Gudjon remembered that Geirfinnur was walking away, but he caught hold of him, to stop him. He couldn't remember if he punched Geirfinnur, but he remembered grabbing him around the neck. He didn't remember the injuries but there was no blood on him after the fight. He didn't notice when the corpse was placed in the car but he remembered the words Saevar said as they drove towards Reykjavik, that he was an accomplice to murder. Gudjon had become very frightened because of what happened and didn't have the guts to look in the back of the car but there was no doubt that the body was in the vehicle.

Erla had left the car when they were in the harbour and her jacket was still in the car. He later read a statement from a driver who said she had taken a ride to Reykjavik. (Although in reality, the driver had already seen her photo in the newspaper and couldn't be sure he had given her a lift on the night in question.) *On the way to Reykjavik, the three of them discussed what should be done with the body but didn't reach an agreement. Gudjon drove out on Alftanesveg and they stopped to put the body there. They then drove to a district heating plant in Crustal, but he said his memory might be wrong about that. He didn't remember having to take the body from the car or having driven into the alleyway at the back of Grettisgata 82. Gudjon said he thought Saevar had borrowed shovels but he was not sure. He said the fourth man he had talked about in the car was Kristjan and he didn't know him before this trip.*

The interrogation ended at 5am. Gudjon had confessed to the policeman he trusted most. He admitted to being one of the killers. Gudjon was the last piece in the jigsaw – he was the driver the team had spent months trying to find. He was taken back to his cell drained, physically and emotionally.

After waiting weeks for this statement and an admission of guilt, it was a strange confession. It was full of gaps and holes and there were still many unanswered questions. For example, why would they drive the body back to Reykjavik where it could be discovered, rather than dispose of it in the wasteland of Reykjanes where the investigators believed they had already dumped Gudmundur Einarsson's body?

Gudjon recalled how Gretar didn't react much as he confessed to the crime, but he knew the task force would be happy, 'because I couldn't take it back, because it proved I was guilty of something'. Gretar's role as befriender had worked, they had their confession.

After Gretar had left, Gudjon turned to his diary to try to make sense of what he had told the detective:

> I woke up late and started talking to Gretar and we talked for a long time. It ended at supper. We started talking again after supper and talked until five o'clock in the morning. And then I confessed my part in the death of Geirfinnur Einarsson. And I gave for the third time my account of a trip to Keflavik which was rather unlucky for me of all the trips I have taken in my life.

It was like he had woken up from a dream. The weeks of being told only he could solve the case, that he must help his nation out of this crisis, had got to him. He hoped his admission would provide some relief for the public, who had been consumed with the case:

Let's hope that Geirfinnur's body will be found in the next few days and the nation can draw a deep breath and relax. It seems to me I have become immune to such things. I'm like a machine. I find it inhuman. There is nothing that affects me anymore, I have closed myself emotionally. Actually, I'm dead.

Confessing to the murder hadn't brought the release he hoped for. He concluded, 'My burden is heavy.'

At the same time the police had Gudjon's confession about Geirfinnur, the prosecutor's office took a major step forward in the Gudmundur Einarsson case. After months of imprisonment and interrogation, on 8 December, Kristjan Vidar Vidarsson, Saevar Marino Cieselski and Tryggvi Runar Leifsson were formally accused of breaking article 211 of the Icelandic penal code and charged with the murder of Gudmundur Einarsson.

The charges stated that in the early hours of 27 January 1974, the three men had attacked Gudmundur Einarsson in the basement of Hamarsbraut 11. Kristjan Vidar used a knife in the attack in which Gudmundur had been killed and his body was taken to an unknown location. Albert Klahn Skaftasson was also charged with participation in the murder on account of having provided transport to help Saevar, Kristjan and Tryggvi remove the body of Gudmundur in order to destroy evidence of the offence. This happened in January 1974 and later in the summer of 1974 when Gudmundur's remains were transferred to yet another location. This had been achieved using a car that Albert had driven and had at his disposal.

In addition to the murder charges, Tryggvi Runar was charged with separate offences of arson, rape and theft. The arson charge dated back to 1972 when he was held in Litla Hraun jail and had set fire to some old newspapers in a wood drying room. The rape was in October 1974 when he was accused of attacking an 18-year-old woman in her flat in Reykjavik. The thefts were in 1974, one from a ceramics shop, and he was also charged with stealing a wallet.

Saevar was charged with theft and, together with Erla, theft, forgery and fraud. Saevar and Kristjan were also charged with various thefts. Saevar and Gudjon were charged together for drugs offences.

The police and prosecutor still didn't have Gudmundur's body or any idea where it was. There was still no valid forensic evidence – all they had were the confessions – but they felt these were enough to secure a conviction.

In the absence of a jury in the Icelandic court system, the case was assigned to three judges who would decide the suspects' fate: Ármanns Kristinsson, Haraldur Briem Henrysson and Gunnlaugur Briem. The judges would assess the evidence and then hear testimony in open court before passing their judgement.

The day the men were charged, one of the detectives, Harold Arnason, wrote a report about a conversation he had with Kristjan where he had set out a tale that was incredible even by the standards of the Gudmundur and Geirfinnur investigations. It concerned a young man from the nearby Faroe Islands who had gone missing in September 1974 and was never found. Kristjan claimed he had killed the man with Saevar and Tryggvi. The police account doesn't give any details of how or why Kristjan said this happened. Instead, the police account focuses on his macabre story of the disposal of the man's body:

> Kristjan Vidar said that his maternal grandmother had helped to partially dismember and hide the body of a Faroese man who has been missing since

September 1974. Kristjan reported that after the death of the man, Saevar and Tryggvi came with the body to the basement and into the laundry room at Grettisgata 82. They came to the conclusion that they would need to cut the body up. Kristjan was expected to do it, Tryggvi called him a coward if he couldn't. Kristjan met his grandmother outside and he forbade her to go down into the laundry room but this only served to arouse the curiosity of the old woman. Saevar and Tryggvi went up to Kristjan's bedroom, took sleeping pills and slept until noon the next day. Then they put the body in two bags and Albert Klahn was asked to transfer it in his Toyota. Kristjan said they decided to go with the bags to the Fossvogs garden and bury them there. His grandmother was part of this discussion and was not happy with the hiding place and that led to arguments between them. Kristjan said he wasn't sure what had become of the Faroese man's remains but he is pretty sure his grandmother does.

The detective noted that Kristjan was being vague a lot of the time: 'The truth of his narrative is questionable, but personally I find it doubtful that he lies about his grandmother, who seems to him very dear, not to mention how serious the offence is.'

It was an astonishing, crazy story; clear evidence of how Kristjan's memory was being degraded and how he was creating false memories, mixing up elements from the stories he had constructed about Gudmundur and Geirfinnur. It was never followed up but the story high-lighted the disturbed state of Kristjan's mind, and showed how far the police had travelled that they would coun-tenance such a tale.

It ended up in the newspapers. *Visir* carried a front-page story with the headline, 'Remand prisoners in

Gudmundur and Geirfinnur cases: suspected of being involved in a third disappearance.' *Dagbladid* ran the same story and said the driver in the Gudmundur Einarsson case may have been involved. It didn't name Albert Klahn, but he had already been named as the man accused of helping the others dispose of Gudmundur's body.

The day after the charges were filed, there was another front-page headline, 'Geirfinnur to the prosecutor in January?' The deadline had been set by Karl Schutz, who was about to return to Germany for the Christmas holidays. He would come back in the New Year for a brief period and wanted the cases wrapped up in January and the files sent to the prosecutor.

With this deadline in mind, the police ramped up efforts to find Geirfinnur's body. Once they had his remains, the case would be complete. On 9 December, Saevar had a five-hour interrogation with the detectives when he went through details on how he had met Gerifinnur in Klubburin days before his disappearance:

> *Saevar was trying to reach the man's wallet and started talking to him. He often used to do this, to talk to the men he was intending to rob. He asked the man if they had been together on a fishing boat but the man said they hadn't and Saevar asked him his name. He was Geirfinnur from Keflavik. Saevar thought there was someone with that name who was involved in smuggling, and he asked if he would be interested in bringing in some alcohol business and Geirfinnur answered he would. Kristjan had heard their conversation. Saevar expressed his willingness to come into direct contact with the party who had the alcohol, but his real purpose was to find out where the alcohol was stored in order to steal it. Saevar suggested 50,000 to 70,000 kronor in payment for the information. Geirfinnur was pleased*

and gave him his name and address but not his phone number. Saevar said he and Erla had later gone to Gudjon's in Erla's Land Rover and told him about this.

Saevar convinced Gudjon and Kristjan to take part in the plan to meet Geirfinnur and then steal the smuggled alcohol. The next day, on 18 November, Saevar started to put his plan into action.

The electrical system in the Land Rover vehicle was defective so they intended to take a rental car. It was decided to go to Keflavik the next evening. In the afternoon he and Erla went to Geysir rental company and hired a light blue Volkswagen. Saevar paid 5,000 kronor and told the man not to make a written contract, which he agreed to. Saevar had previously leased vehicles leased in this way from this man.

After going through the details of the killing, Saevar provided the police with a final location for Geirfinnur's remains. During that same, long interrogation he went through the plans with the detectives they made after killing Geirfinnur:

He said they drove the body straight into the alley behind Kristjan's home. He and Kristjan carried the body into the basement and put it under a pile of clothing. He reminded Kristjan to make sure nothing of any kind was put on top of the body. They had a brief discussion at Kristjan's apartment about what to do with the body and Kristjan said that it wasn't possible to have it in there a long time. The next day he met Gudjon at Mokka cafe on Skolavordustigur and they discussed what should be done with the body. Gudjon mentioned several options, such as burning it, immersing it in water or burying it. Saevar explained that on 21 November 1974 he went with Erla to Grettisgata 82 in her Land Rover. Erla waited in Kristjan's apartment while they brought

Geirfinnur's body out of the laundry room and wrapped it in something, tied a string around and put it in the back of the Land Rover. In the car were two shovels that Gudjon had lent them. They drove to the Raudholar, stopping on the way at a gas station where they bought a five-litre plastic canister of petrol. They drove into the Raudholar and dug a pit no larger than the body. Then they poured petrol over it and Saevar said he lit a match and threw it onto the body. Erla was close by and watched it: the corpse burned quickly and a very bad smell came off it and then they buried it.

Immediately the police believed this account – helpfully it explained why they had failed in all of their previous efforts searching the dreary lava fields. The day after making this statement, Saevar was taken to the Raudholar by the police. When they arrived at the rocky track that lead to the hills, they asked Saevar to point out where the body was buried. Suddenly his certainty from the day before started to recede as he was confronted with the reality of his statement. He said it was late at night when he had done this, years before, and it looked very different. He pointed to several places among the mounds which looked likely burial places.

The next day Erla was brought to the crusted, red mounds. It was a place she knew well from her childhood and she pointed out a spot which was 50 metres from the site Saevar had picked out. Erla was seen as a helpful witness, so the police dug in the area, but with no success. Kristjan was the last of the trio brought there and came up with a different location from Saevar's and Erla's, but it was close enough for the police to be convinced this was indeed the place where, among the burnished earth and rocks, they would find the burnt and desiccated remains of Geirfinnur Einarsson.

With two weeks to go until Christmas, there was an intense search in the water-filled craters of the Raudholar. The police brought a bulldozer to try to get under the stones, but despite all their scrabbling and scratching at the earth, it came up with nothing.

As well as physically searching the site, Schutz thought he could use his experience of more sophisticated investigative techniques to uncover the burial location. He ordered a comparison of the aerial surveys of the area between 1974 and 1975 to see if there had been any displacement of the stones. The Raudholar had been protected since the 1950s, after the Government had plundered the rock for use in the construction of the airport. Since then, people hadn't been allowed to remove even the stray shards of ochre coloured rock that lay around the hills, so any major disturbance would be noted on the photographs. And yet the examination of these images could find no discernible difference.

Christmas 1976 would mark a year of the suspects' time in custody, and there was a flurry of press activity. Having been tight lipped for so long, the police were feeling more confident. They revealed some more damning and prejudicial leaks about the case. *Dagbladid* ran the headline, 'Geirfinnur: the final stage'. It explained why the police hadn't found the bodies, as they believed that they had been moved at least once since the prisoners had been arrested. It wasn't clear who had done this and there was no evidence that the bodies had been moved in the past year. For the police it was a convenient way of explaining why the task force, under the guidance of super cop Karl Schutz, and after a year of interrogating the suspects, had spectacularly failed to find even one of the corpses. They also continued with the fiction that Erla's confession in which she said she had shot Geirfinnur 'was essentially right'.

*

Erla dreaded the court hearings, when they would decide the length of her remand and how much longer she would be kept away from her daughter. The last time she was here in September she had been remanded for 90 days by Orn Hoskuldsson. When this happened, Erla had lost control: 'I am never going get out of here,' she told him. 'How can you do this to me?' Orn made her a promise: 'You will be out of here before this year is over.' It's not clear why he set this arbitrary deadline; the only logical explanation was that he already knew that this was when Karl Schutz wanted the case wrapped up. Yet here she was on 22 December, back in court again. This time she was brought before Hallvardur Einvardsson, the deputy prosecutor.

Erla was then taken to Orn Hoskuldsson, the investigating magistrate who had the strange dual role of running the inquiry but also being the magistrate who would decide on the length of the suspects' remand. He ordered everyone else out of the room so he could be alone with her. Erla had never taken seriously Orn's promise that he would release her before the end of the year. She saw it as another lie, a way to calm her down and control her anxiety. But as soon as they were alone Orn surprised her. 'I made you a promise,' he said, 'and I intend to keep it, I'm going to let you go.' Erla was overwhelmed and started crying, overjoyed that she would be reunited with her daughter.

What had motivated him to keep his word and release Erla at this stage, before the investigation was formally finished? Was it guilt, regret at how she had been treated by the investigators? Erla said during the months of interrogations when she still felt some empathy for them, 'I know this sounds strange but these were the only people I ever spoke to. A lot of the time they were very friendly. I was in such a desperate need for human contact they were never the monsters – just guys I knew well.

They spoke about their families. It wasn't till afterwards I wished I could see them die.'

Erla's release came with conditions: she would have to show up twice a week at the district court, stay within the jurisdiction of Reykjavik and be kept under police surveillance.

Being free was a mixed blessing for her. She no longer had to breathe in the fetid air in Sidumuli or hear Saevar clanking past in his leg irons, or fear the police and guards. But Reykjavik is a tiny place where it's impossible to be invisible. When she was outside she could tell that people now saw her as 'the scum of the earth... people would go out of their way to spit on me in public'.

Erla's release added to the anguish of the other inmates; it brought home the fact that they wouldn't be freed until the case was solved and they were found guilty. This was gnawing away at Kristjan. His bizarre admission in early December of involvement in a third murder was a warning sign that his mental health was plummeting. On Christmas Eve it all became too much for him and he slit his wrists. The guards found him before it was too late and he was transferred to the old prison, the Hegningarhusid, where they could keep a closer eye on him. The move did little to ease Kristjan's anxiety. He tried to kill himself again early in January, this time setting fire to his mattress before slashing his wrists again. He was taken to hospital and treated for his wounds, but it was a second lucky escape. When he was searched, the guards found a razor blade and a broken mirror. There would now be a round-the-clock watch on him to make sure he couldn't try for a third time.

Gudjon felt the lure of this too. Drugged up on sedatives, for weeks he too actively considered taking his life. Initially he was only sleeping three hours a night, and in those other 21 hours he wrote in his diary 'I'm always thinking about suicide' or that he ought 'to say farewell to this nonsense once and for all'. His mother would regularly bring supplies for him and inside one of the boxes he noticed there was a razor blade. He thought this was the opportunity he needed: 'I could have done it with a short cut, and no one could have done anything.'

But, never one to rush into anything, Gudjon read books on the subject of suicide; he even got a book about it from the prison chaplain, Jon Bjarman. It was his religious faith that saved him. Gudjon wasn't going to rush into this. He had his wife, children and mother to think of and he thought about the added pain and suffering he would inflict upon them. Gudjon believed in the end what stopped him was what he called 'a simple thing' – the belief that your life is 'not your property, it's not at your disposal. You are not free to get rid of it, it's given to you it's a gift. It's all wrong to think you can take it away yourself, you're not allowed.'

He would confide in Jon Bjarman, who would flash his gap-toothed smile on his regular visits to the cells in Sidumuli. He was the one person that Gudjon and the other suspects could trust. In the year they had been in custody, the chaplain had listened to all of the suspects' woes and anxieties. Bjarman also served a useful purpose for the police: he was a trustworthy figure who the suspects could confide in and hopefully that would carry through to the interrogations.

For Lutherans, Bjarman was the real deal, someone who could hear confessions and had a hotline to God to grant absolution. During the course of his visits he had become increasingly concerned about the treatment of the suspects, the deprivation they were enduring and the torture meted out to Saevar. His plea for more compassionate treatment had been ignored. This was clearly a challenge to the authority of the police and the court. But

Bjarman didn't fear them, he answered to the church and God.

The chaplain could see Gudjon was buckling under the strain. Through their conversations, Bjarman had developed strong reservations that Gudjon was guilty. He made this clear to Gudjon: 'He said you should not confess anything but after that he was not allowed to visit for a long time, maybe they had listening devices in the cell to hear what he said.' It was too late for this now anyway, Gudjon had already confessed. As the year came to a close, however, there would a dramatic intervention that would call his confession into question.

Gisli Gudjonsson had returned to his psychology studies, attending a university in Britain, and was spending his Christmas holiday in Iceland. On Christmas Eve the police called on the former detective for a favour: the detectives were short of staff, as the older officers wanted to be with their families, would he collect Gudjon's wife Rita and drive her to Sidumuli? The visit was designed to be a way to put further pressure on Gudjon to tell them everything he knew.

Gisli and Gretar sat in as the couple talked. Rita encouraged Gudjon to confess everything, but he had already, he didn't know what else to say. As she told him about the family and the world outside and gave him gifts she had brought from home, he wept. He had cried a lot in the past six weeks.

Days later, Gisli would be asked to perform a much bigger favour. As part of his studies in the summer of 1976 he had conducted research on lie detectors and had brought a polygraph machine back to Iceland. It created huge interest in the country; there was even an article about it in *Morgunbladid*. Gisli found there was no shortage of volunteers who wanted to take part, even the prison officers themselves. He tested the machine on a dozen prison inmates. 'I was getting nine out of ten detecting lies, it gave the [false] impression the test was infallible. Everybody had the belief that I was dealing with a magical test.' But the truth was that Gisli was still learning how to interpret the tests.

As part of this research, Gisli had conducted a lie detector test on Saevar. He hooked up the electrodes to Saevar's palms and temple and interviewed him about the case. This was part of Gisli's thesis and not part of the investigation. There was later intense speculation about what the test had revealed, but Gisli wouldn't release it to the police because it was inconclusive and was part of his research. The general view among the police was that it provided concrete evidence Saevar was guilty. 'It created a frenzy,' Gisli remembered, 'I got caught up in it. It was never meant to be used in the cases, I didn't have the experience. I was a student.'

Now one of the detectives remembered Gisli's earlier trip with the polygraph machine and asked him to conduct a test on Gudjon. 'They thought giving him a lie detector test might bring him to his senses and help him remember,' Gisli said. 'They thought he would be very open and bring back his memory and he might tell them where the body was.' Gisli was willing to try as he thought Gudjon would be a fascinating subject. But there was a problem, he didn't have the equipment he had brought over in the summer. He would have to improvise. He decided to record Gudjon's answers and then send the interview off to a psychologist in England for voice stress analysis.

It was lunchtime on the last day of the year when Gudjon was brought to the court offices. Outside, Reykjavik was gearing up to celebrate the New Year. In the evening, families would gather for a big meal, sharing stories, excited about the evening ahead. Then it would be out to the local bonfire, huddling as close as possible to the dancing flames to keep out the cold.

At midnight fireworks would explode and light up the tar black night.

Gudjon would only be able to hear this; he had no idea when he would ever see such a sight again. He had given his permission for the polygraph test after a visit from Gisli. He had written about this in his diary days earlier. He said Gisli Gudjonsson had asked if he was willing to have a lie detector test. 'I asked for precedents but there are none.' Gudjon wanted to discuss it with his lawyer, but he couldn't until the next day so 'I gave my consent. This relates to the police not believing in my innocence, they think I am covering up. I have no problem with this being investigated with the newest technology.'

When Gisli entered the room for the test, he recalled how Gudjon looked broken: 'It was my impression he was rather defeated, he had given up.' Gisli thought it was clear from Gudjon's quietly spoken demeanour 'He was thinking he was guilty, he had a defeatist attitude, he was passive, there was a general acceptance of his predicament, he was not fighting.' Over the next hour they went through 22 questions. When they finished, Gisli went back over them a second time. When Gisli had asked the question, 'Do you know who was behind the disappearance of Geirfinnur?' Gudjon had at first answered, 'Yes'. The second time, however, he paused and said, 'No'. Gisli was surprised – why would he admit to knowing something and then deny it? Gisli could see that there was a discrepancy, but at the time he didn't think a great deal about it.

Initially, Gudjon also felt the polygraph test had changed very little, 'I just said thank you and went out and I never heard anything else.' He felt it was strange, having a student conduct a test on him. 'Schutz was in charge,' he recalled, 'he didn't want any kids like Gisli Gudjonsson roaming around the offices.' But Schutz was away in Germany on his Christmas break. Soon, though, the test started to sow the seeds of doubt in Gudjon's mind. The entry in his diary from that day is by a man in despair:

> After a lot of crying, I feel better, but I am still miserable. The lie detector test took place today but I feel like I made some mistakes. The recent inter-rogations have affected my nerves… I'm breaking down and hardly know my name with any certainty. I wish God would take me to him. I am about to give up. Where are these bodies? How should I know? I have a headache. Feel terrible.

By now, he had developed a routine to help him cope with the solitary confinement: 'I would sleep until 12, have food then I would do my diary.' The afternoon was a similar pattern: 'Some reading and more sleep until coffee about four, then more reading and sleep until seven.' After this, he would have medicine followed by tea or coffee. 'I relaxed completely in my bed and did not move a muscle for a long time – I'd just lie down with my eyes closed.'

The lie detector test seemed to have sparked some last vestige of doubt in his mind that he was involved. When he saw his lawyer soon after, he requested the statements he had given so that he could read them again. He wanted to see exactly what he had been saying to detectives and how far he had gone. He also started to read back over his diary.

It was late, after midnight, when the city had stilled; the only sounds were the low hum of the wind and the constant ebb and flow of the water lapping at the rocks. He wrote that the situation could not get any worse and he even thought it might be getting a bit better. He wondered what it would be like to be held for hundreds of days in prison.

After weeks of compliance, Gudjon now felt increasingly uncertain that he had indeed taken part in Geirfinnur's killing. His diary is filled with these creeping doubts and his poor mental condition is clear. 'Well-meaning people say: "no problem, just tell the truth". Yes, it's now just that. This brings the old question. What is truth?' He wasn't helped by growing insomnia which darkened his mood. On 2 January, he wrote:

> I find myself involved in an incredible web of lies; I never see a clear sky. There is something really wrong about the case, particularly the fact that I can't remember anything. Amnesia seems strange to me, this has never happened to me sober, to remember nothing.

There was one thing that was becoming clearer, though. He wrote, 'I never went to Keflavik 19/11/74.'

17

At the task force's offices at Borgutun 7, Schutz had returned and was confronted with a big problem. The detectives told him about a marked change in Gudjon. The prisoner was no longer co-operating and had started to doubt his involvement. Before he left for his Christmas break, Schutz was sure that he had cracked Gudjon; something must have changed to bring about this. When he heard about the lie detector test he was furious.

Gisli Gudjonsson had returned to England and his studies when he became aware of Karl Schutz's anger. Gisli found out that after the lie detector test Gudjon had changed, 'He became very ambivalent. He became concerned that perhaps he was not remembering things correctly. He became concerned that perhaps he hadn't been involved and he was innocent.'

Gudjon had started asking for his lawyer and questioning whether he should speak to the detectives. Gisli realised that the lie detector test must have had more of an effect than he recognised at the time. Being asked the questions without any pressure or coercion had given Gudjon the space and time to pause and think, 'what did actually happen?'

Schutz demanded that Gisli disclose all of the material from the test and he went through the Icelandic Ministry of Justice to demand this. Gisli had to comply, but he only sent the questions, not the answers. They would remain in his care, locked away with his other papers for many decades. Schutz made his anger and annoyance with the test clear in his weekly update to the Justice Minister, Olafur Johannesson, on 7 January 1977. He said it had been done in an 'amateurish manner that was to hinder the progress of the investigation'. He complained that it was 'diametrically opposed to the previous successful direction of the inquiry', which was 'to convince the accused that it would be best to tell the whole truth and that his supposed "memory gaps" are not at all credible'. He made it clear that he thought the intervention was what had lead Gudjon to doubt his role in Geirfinnur's death. Schutz gave examples of the questions Gudjon had been asked, such as 'Did you go to Keflavik on 19/11/1974?' and 'Did you take part in the murder?'

Schutz told the minister it was his duty to point out the obstacles that the investigation faced. It had been expected that Gudjon would confess about the last area of doubt, the location of the body. This intervention could now compromise the progress of the whole investigation. Under the title 'Further Measures', Schutz wrote they would start to identify witnesses who would strengthen the 'facts' in the confessions. The police would spend the next few weeks going through a multitude of tasks trying to firm up the confessions: asking each of the suspects about Geirfinnur's clothing to see if their descriptions matched; interviewing witnesses who were in the harbour cafe; retracing the route from Reykjavik to Keflavik and timing it to see whether the suspects could have got there in time to meet Geirfinnur; examining the house in Keflavik where Erla said she had spent the night after running away from the harbour.

Without Gudjon's full co-operation, the whole Geirfinnur investigation could collapse. Gudjon felt the pressure on him when he wrote, 'They are going to be hard with me. They are going to break me down by not speaking to me and by banning the priest and delaying or losing my parcels. I'm getting suspicious and hateful being in isolation.'

A few days later, Gudjon was brought for another interview about the case and the police notes show his refusal to engage was hardening:

He did not know who Geirfinnur was and had never heard of him. He said he was not able to tell whether the person who entered into the vehicle in Keflavik was Geirfinnur. He said he had not heard his name mentioned. He couldn't describe the clothing of the man who came into the vehicle. He had previously reported that he was unclear about the events in the harbour and he was not clear that some devastating event had happened. The only description he had of clothing was what he had read in *Morgunbladid* already in a report about the disappearance of Geirfinnur. He remembered the talk was that Geirfinnur was dressed in a winter coat; Gudjon thought that it has been described as a grey-blue. He dared not say whether this description was made from the newspaper or if he was the person who entered into the vehicle on that occasion.

Gudjon refused to sign the statement. The detectives were getting increasingly frustrated with his intransigence. Schutz had one final ace up his sleeve. He was working towards a big last push to bring together all of the suspects for one final showdown.

*

There was a soft dusting of crunchy, frozen snow on the ground as Kristjan, Erla, Saevar and Gudjon set out from Sidumuli on a strange mission on the morning of 23 January. They were all in a fraught state: as the detectives' primary target, Saevar was still facing daily interviews and trips outside with the police; Erla had been released from prison but was living in a hostile Reykjavik where she was openly despised; Kristjan's mental health was still frazzled after his suicide attempts weeks earlier and Gudjon was also in a black space having experienced his own suicidal thoughts. The detectives accompanying them were wrapped up in thick woollen coats with Russian bearskin hats, making them look like the Politburo on a day out.

Gudjon's testimony was crucial; the police needed him back on board, engaging with them. He was the older, educated suspect who believed for a long time that he needed to help the police. They needed him to think like this again.

Schutz wanted all of the accused to stage a reconstruction of Geirfinnur's death at the slipway in Keflavik. He had set out his reasons for this in his notes: to investigate their testimonies on the ground and most importantly to work on the areas where their stories were not the same. He wrote of clear 'inconsistencies in the detailed accounts of the events', in particular the final moments of Geirfinnur Einarsson's life, and 'for that reason it was only right to stage a plausible reconstruction of the location of the vehicles, and Geirfinnur and the defendants'.

Schutz was feeling tense about this judging by his manner when he interviewed Gudjon a few days before the reconstruction. Gudjon was still questioning his involvement and tried to row back on his earlier confession. He said Schutz had lost his temper and started screaming at him, which was highly unusual. At one point, Gudjon thought he was so angry Schutz might attack him, but the detective was too professional to go this far and managed to maintain control.

Though the suspects had been out to the lava many times, and sometimes in pairs, this was the first time they had been there all together. During these previous trips the discussions had focused on possible burial locations, but today would be different. This time they would go through the parts they played on the night, in detail, marking out where they were and what they were doing.

They set off late in the morning, which would give them a few hours before the sun started to drift down into the horizon. They headed out along the Reykjavikurvegur under a flat sky, covered in thick billowy clouds which blocked out the winter sun.

In Keflavik, the police vehicles parked next to a set of shabby, mournful, dark warehouses with rusting corrugated roofs, surrounded by discarded metal and rotten wood. At the end of the slipway two seemingly abandoned trawlers were perched on wooden rests, waiting to be repaired. The police brought props with them to make the event as realistic as possible. At the harbour the police had parked a Mercedes van and a VW car. It was time to knit together the disparate versions of that night.

Saevar was first. Dressed in a black polo neck, trousers and coat and with his long slick, dark hair, he looked more like a rock star on a photo shoot than a criminal suspected of Iceland's worst ever crime spree. At the slipway, the investigators wanted Saevar to mark the exact spot where the VW had been parked. The police had brought numbered markers which they used to record these locations and a photographer who would capture the whole bizarre event.

Saevar marked the spot, pointing down towards the sea, near the trawlers. He told them that during the argument with Geirfinnur, Kristjan had put the man in a choke hold and strangled him. The police brought a stopwatch to help time how long this had taken – Saevar estimated about seven seconds. He had gone back to check on Erla but when she saw the fight she'd run off between two buildings at the harbour. When Saevar got back to Kristjan, Geirfinnur was lying on the ground on his front. Kristjan had turned him over and listened to his heart and announced: 'He is dead.' Saevar tried his pulse and couldn't find one.

Schutz wasn't content with the suspects telling them what happened, though – he wanted to see it. Kristjan stood in the spot where the fight had apparently taken place. He wasn't dressed for the winter cold, he had on a white zipped cardigan with a bright flowery shirt and dark trousers. He stood awkwardly, arms by his side his feet pointed out, like a schoolboy posing for a class photo. Behind him was the VW pulled up at an angle and markers with the numbers 2, 3, 4 and 6. The police wanted to see how he had killed Geirfinnur.

Kristjan described how Gudjon had grabbed hold of Geirfinnur and then he had also grabbed Geirfinnur from behind, pushing his knee into the man's leg, knocking him off balance. With the aid of the stopwatch, Kristjan said thought he had held onto his neck for about ten seconds. Saevar had then started hitting Geirfinnur with a stick and Kristjan said that Geirfinnur had then fallen on his side. The police had brought a dummy, hastily outfitted with a coat, trousers and boots, so the suspects could mark out the location and demonstrate how Geirfinnur was lying. This spot was also marked with a number.

Kristjan had long struggled with which of his memories were real and which were false, implanted into his psyche by the conversations he had with the detectives. These had been augmented by his repeated visits to the locations where the killings were supposed to have taken place. This move into a more tangible, physical re-enactment was bound to exacerbate this further. He was being forced to go through these motions in real life, in the present, that he had started to believe had taken place two years ago, but until this point were still shadowy impressions in his mind.

Erla's memory of the night Geirfinnur was killed had shifted so much that it was if it had been written on tracing paper. As the other suspects' stories changed, her imagination went on new flights of fancy, writing a whole different version of the night. Her idea that she had shot Geirfinnur had now long since faded away.

She said she no longer remembered how the killing happened, but she recalled seeing Geirfinnur lying on his stomach and she could see Saevar, Gudjon and Kristjan standing over him. She had run away to a distinctive red house standing on its own on a corner, a few hundred yards from the harbour. It was the same colour as the rocks at the Raudholar, a muddy red stained with iron from the earth. It had once been a fisherman's hut, but in 1974 it was used for storage and normally left unlocked.

The police used the descriptions the suspects had given to make drawings of the crime scene. Saevar's was the most detailed, with a series of trawlers on props in descending sizes. His drawing was then filled with an indistinguishable blur of dots as he tried to map the attack on Geirfinnur as he fought and struggled with Kristjan, Saevar and Gudjon. It looked like the plan for an elaborate dance sequence.

The drawings produced by Erla and Kristjan's descriptions were far more rudimentary – there was the slipway with three boats in the harbour and dots marking the positions of the various participants in relation to the car. They each put the location of the attack in a different position in the harbour, but from the detectives' point of view they were acknowledging their presence there and they had each been able to map out the setting that night.

Gudjon was reluctant to play any part in what he considered a charade. He remembered how at the time, 'The reality it all gets mixed up, that's why I think Erla was always ready to make up stories and get it away from herself. That's why I took part in that silly happening in Keflavik with Schutz.' He refused to do as Kristjan had done and physically re-enact the killing. From the outset he couldn't remember where certain people stood. He pointed out it was very dark and if he said something now, 'it could be crap'. When asked where the fight took place he refused to give a definitive answer. 'I have to think more about it,' he said, 'and I think it will be more reliable.' He was trying to placate the detectives as he now knew he didn't know what had happened that night. He couldn't describe how Geirfinnur died. He didn't check for any signs of life and didn't know who had. He couldn't remember whether the body was carried to the car or whether the car had been driven to the body.

They returned back in separate cars in the afternoon, cold and in need of food and warmth. Kristjan, Erla and Saevar had all engaged with the reconstruction, Kristjan most of all – there were countless photos taken of him standing by the cars and the macabre fake body. Gudjon was the exception, he had not delivered what they hoped. After the lie detector test in December he was still proving less co-operative.

After dinner, Gretar took him for an interview in the Corner. Gretar – the detective he thought of as his 'friend' – was the one who could still get through to him. He told Gudjon of the urgency in the investigation. 'We are pressed for time,' he said, as Schutz would be returning to Germany soon and he wanted the case wrapped up. They spent three and a half hours talking, but Gudjon no longer felt he was guilty. 'It dawned on me that this is impossible, but then the police said you have said too much, you must stick to it, don't let him off the hook.

Even if they can't make the case work and find out how it all hangs together, nevertheless he is likely to have done something.'

Gudjon knew he had said too much and there was no going back. He felt trapped in a nightmare. 'You think you have been driving somewhere in the dark. It's just a dream. And if you have been telling someone for a while where he has been, what he has done, and tell him that other people were involved, in the end you can sway him. He doesn't have his memory any more or the power to say no all the time. After a whole night you will get him to say "enough", and then you keep on.' That was exactly what the police had done with him. As soon as he said he had taken hold of Geirfinnur and held him by the neck, he was sunk. He could never take it back.

For Schutz, the reconstruction had worked out as he had wanted. The suspects had all placed themselves in the harbour on the night Geirfinnur was killed. The scene that they had talked about for over a year, originally blurry and imprecise, had become clearer in the crisp daylight with all of the props helpfully supplied by the police. The visit was all that Schutz needed to close the Geirfinnur case. He was ready to make a big statement to show the government and the jittery Icelandic public that they could rest easy, the killers had been caught.

The reporters filed in to the court offices. Karl Schutz was sat at the head of a long table. Next to him was Orn Hoskuldsson, whose leather coat, skinny tie and check shirt was a stark contrast to the crisp white shirt of Schutz and his interpreter, Peter Eggerz, in a dark suit with pocket square. Around the room sat the detectives from the task force. Behind Schutz on the wall was a two-metre long aerial photo of the lava fields dissected by the thin white line of the Reykjavikurvegur. There were other aerial photos of Keflavik and the diagrams of the harbour that had been drawn from the suspects' recollections following the reconstruction. In the centre of the table sat the infamous clay head of the mystery caller.

Schutz had called the press conference for a momentous announcement: the Geirfinnur case was at last at an end, the evidence was being passed to the state prosecutor to prepare for the suspects to be tried. When this had happened in the Gudmundur case there had been an official acknowledgement but no major press gathering like this.

Such press conferences would be expected at the end of a trial when the defendant's guilt had been decided and their case couldn't be prejudiced. However, Schutz decided to brief the media on all aspects of the case long before the trial had begun and the three judges heard the evidence.

As the journalists hunched over their notepads scribbling shorthand as fast as they could, Schutz set out the 'definitive' account of what the police believed had happened and the evidence they would be taking to court. He started by taking them back to two days before Geirfinnur disappeared.

It was 17 November 1974 and inside Klubburin it was throbbing. Geirfinnur was on a rare night out with his friends and Saevar saw him as a target for pickpocketing. But as Saevar approached him, Geirfinnur noticed him and introduced himself. Saevar said he was Magnus Leopoldsson, the manager of Klubburin. Struggling to hear themselves amid the chatter and blaring music, Saevar told Geirfinnur he was interested in buying some cheap booze, as he assumed the man from Keflavik was some kind of salesman for illicit alcohol. Geirfinnur wasn't a smuggler or even much of a drinker and was in no fit state to talk. They agreed to meet a few days later. Geirfinnur went back to his boozy night, Saevar started to hatch a plan.

On 19 November Saevar and Erla rented a car for 5,000 kronor – a cash transaction, no contract and no questions asked. They met with Kristjan and drove to Keflavik to meet Geirfinnur. At this point, Schutz revealed the identity of the mystery caller who summoned Geirfinnur to his death. During one of his drives with Saevar, Schutz said he was told, 'There was a phone call made to Geirfinnur from a cafe in Keflavik and this as we say, got the ball rolling.' It wasn't Saevar who made the call, though, it was Kristjan. He had gone into the Hafnarbudin cafe with Saevar and while Saevar bought cigarettes and chocolate for Erla, Kristjan had phoned Geirfinnur. 'Are you Geirfinnur?' he asked when the man answered. 'We are here,' he told him, 'you should come on foot and alone.' (Despite the police's certainty, neither Elin Gretarsdottir nor Gudlaug Jonssdottir, the two women who had been working in the cafe that night, were able to definitively identify Kristjan as the man who had come in to make the call.)

The cause of Geirfinnur's death had gone through a remarkable set of changes over the previous two years. First he had drowned after trying to retrieve smuggled alcohol. Then he had been shot by Erla. Finally the police had settled on him being strangled and beaten to death by Kristjan, Saevar and Gudjon. In these later versions his death had been the result of an argument that got out of hand. But now a darker version was presented. The investigators believed the suspects' intention had been to kill all along; they had told Erla from the outset she would need to hitch-hike back to Reykjavik to make space for the body.

As to the Klubburin men, who had been held for over three months in solitary confinement before being released without charge, Schutz explained that Kristjan, Erla and Saevar had decided they would implicate others if they were ever caught. The rumours about Klubburin and their use of smuggled alcohol was the perfect cover. They had met three times to coordinate their statements and to fabricate a story.

Then there was Gudjon, the fourth member of the gang that night. He was also in custody and the reporters asked why it had taken so long to arrest him. Schutz wasn't going to take the flak for this, he handed over to Orn Hoskuldsson who admitted this was a difficult one to answer. When Gudjon was interviewed in May 1976, the Klubburin men had just been released, attracting huge criticism in the media. At that time the investigators weren't quite sure exactly how Gudjon was involved in the case and they didn't want more bad publicity for arresting the wrong man.

Schutz let the voyeurs of the press into some of the work they had been carrying out in the past six months. At first, they had tried to find witnesses but he said they soon gave up. 'The biggest difficulty was that is has been a long time since the murders happened. We couldn't work that well with witnesses and suspects because their memories had faded. There were many details. In fact, solving the case was like a mosaic.'

The detectives also found that many of the friends and associates of Saevar and the rest of the gang were unstable and their testimony was of limited value. 'After two months, we turned around completely,' Schutz explained. 'We applied the same approach as in Germany. We found a few fixed points we could use between the defendants. We always had to be alert because Kristjan Vidar, Saevar and Erla tried repeatedly to mislead us, and they were often subtle… We can tell you that we have five confessions from people of whom three will most likely have caused the death of Geirfinnur.' These people weren't a 'mafia', as the press had speculated, they were middle ranking criminals who he said 'used every opportunity they could to get their hands on money. It is beyond reasonable doubt… it's safe to assume it's an open and shut case.'

There were still questions left unanswered, of course, the biggest of which was the location of bodies. 'We're not in a position to give you a fully solved case because the bodies haven't been found. Those who caused the deaths have made statements about where they are buried.' They had made many attempts to dig at various locations he explained, but the cold weather meant the ground was too hard. He said, 'It's also possible the locations might be wrong. Maybe those responsible are afraid if we find the bodies then we will know how they were killed. Or they hope a trial without a body will end more favourably for them.'

Schutz conceded the case was based '95 per cent on the confession statements but we were very careful to substantiate what they said. We came to the conclusion the confessions were widely plausible. The result also relies on the sequence of events which is almost beyond all reasonable doubt.' Having set out for two and a half hours, chapter and verse, the case and his belief in the confessions they had obtained, Schutz declared, 'You know that in a state ruled by law, no one can be found guilty except by a court, so we can't tell you that the suspects are guilty... [but] solving of this case must be considered a good result above all from the point of view that it has been a great mystery in Iceland for many years and hasn't given Icelanders any peace.'

Having listened to Schutz's version of events, the journalists wanted a comment from the Justice Minister, Olafur Johannesson, the man who had brought Schutz to Iceland. In a statement he enthused about him: 'I am extremely thankful to the men who worked on this,' he said, 'and especially Karl Schutz, the German criminal expert.' His sign-off would be picked up by the papers the next day: 'The nightmare is over.'

*

Karl Schutz's parting gift before returning to a peaceful retirement in Germany was a final report on the Reykjavik investigation of the killing of Geirfinnur Einarsson, primarily for Olafur Johannesson, who had lavished praise on him for solving 'a wicked crime'. Schutz wrote his report before leaving the brutalist hotel that had been his home for the past six months.

He reported that Saevar, Kristjan, Gudjon and Erla had deliberately tried to complicate the issue for a long time but had now largely admitted their crimes. There were many similarities in their accounts of the preparation, implementation and aftermath of the crime. Gudjon though, was still a problem. Schutz was still angry about the lie detector test, which had led to Gudjon changing his mind about his involvement and not submitting a final confession. For weeks he had avoided being formally questioned. When he did talk to the detectives he kept saying, 'I do not remember exactly.'

There was another section stamped 'CONFIDENTIAL'. This went into the motivation for the killing and the personalities of the suspects. His harshest condemnation was for the two men who had been charged with both murders, Saevar and Kristjan. Schutz said the interrogations showed the killing of Geirfinnur was not something that got out of hand but had been pre-meditated:

> Before the act was committed, the offenders (Saevar and Kristjan) had discussed killing Geirfinnur and that they should take the action together. It is the pattern of these defendants that gives rise to suspicion that they had a careless attitude towards the death of Geirfinnur. Both had murdered Gudmundur Einarsson to prove that they were capable of killing a man for a trivial reason. Saevar imagined that Geirfinnur's death could be beneficial in two ways. Even though he (Geirfinnur) had been vague about

the hiding place of the alcohol Saevar could recover 70,000 kronor and eliminate an uncomfortable witness (to the smuggling).

It wasn't clear how Saevar would find out where the alcohol was as all the suspects said Geirfinnur didn't know. During his months of interviews with these two killers, Schutz found particularly troubling signs with Kristjan and his need to physically dominate others:

> His 'combativeness' seems to be his only weapon in order to gain recognition. He uses every opportunity to show his strength and he seems to be keen on 'destroying' his opponent. For this reason you should not ignore the possibility that Kristjan might be seized by a kind of 'killing lust'.

Although Schutz believed Kristjan had dealt the final blows to Geirfinnur, he had not acted alone. Saevar had always been the boss in their relationship and he was just as culpable for the death as he knew things could turn ugly.

> Although he is well aware that it could take a dangerous turn, due to the fact that Geirfinnur, in his opinion, was not willing to tell them where the alcohol was stored. If so, he has, to some extent, deliberately failed to fulfill his duty to stop Kristjan. From this point of view, Saevar has killed Geirfinnur through Kristjan, looking at Kristjan's actions as if they were his own.

When he moved on to Gudjon, it was a different matter. He said he wasn't violent and his personality and behaviour suggested he had no intention of killing Geirfinnur, but his inaction clearly irked Schutz. He explained that

Saevar and Kristjan could have organised Geirfinnur's death:

> However, Saevar has clearly stated that Gudjon should have gained his share of the 'business'. There was clearly a deal with him. According to the results of the investigation, he was a driver on the way to Keflavík and was actively involved in the basement of the house at Grettisgata. There are no reasonable arguments that he does not look at his company's actions as if it were his own work. Anyone who goes for illegal purposes to a pitch-black harbour must be held responsible for the operation. He had done nothing to prevent the actions of his friends. It is clear his excuse 'they would have tortured me' must be considered incredible. There was almost deliberate negligence.

Then there was Erla, the person who had started it all. Schutz had never believed her when she had tried to retract her confession on their very first meeting. He felt that through the work of the detectives assigned to each suspect they had built up good character profiles for them. Erla had helped Saevar with various offences such as fraud and theft, but kept quiet about serious criminal offenses such as the Gudmundur case:

> She gave police information that led to the situation being investigated. She gave this information of her own accord. It was also her statement that brought the Geirfinnur case to a halt. With a deliberately incorrect testimony she drew innocent citizens into the matter which caused them to be subjected to many months of isolation.

This of course was the Klubburin suspects and her half-brother Einar who had spent three and a half months locked up in isolation. This was nothing compared to Saevar and his 'gang' but still enough to have damaged them. Schutz said Erla was only present at most to provide 'psychological assistance'. She hadn't gone to help Geirfinnur or to the police as she was worried about prosecution, but also felt bound to Saevar and that she had done this 'on her own initiative'.

Schutz reported that her testimony was very confusing: it changed from day to day and she had frequently lied. Her confession that she had shot Geirfinnur was thought very unreliable. Schutz didn't elaborate on how they decided when such a consummate liar was telling the truth. This was undoubtedly when it suited the police most and matched the testimonies of others.

There was a final chapter to his report, titled 'Secondary Effects'. This traced six cases that had cropped up during the investigation that needed further investigation. The principal one was Kristjan's highly dubious confession of killing a third person:

> Kristjan Vidar Vidarsson has during interrogations said that he had killed another man at Grettisgata in August/September 1974, with Saevar and Tryggvi Runar. He claims to have killed him with an iron bar. On closer inspection it might be possible to discuss Villy Petersen from Faroe Islands, who has disappeared this time, and nothing has been asked about him since. In parallel, Kristjan has given an account of his grandmother chopping up the body in the cellar and then it was transported in a cloth in Albert Klahn Skatfasson's car. Kristjan's story is very dubious, but this matter should be investigated further.

There was also Kristjan's arson and suicide attempt while he was in the old prison, the Hegningarhusid. Saevar had confessed to an attempted burglary at a chemist in Selfoss, while Saevar, Erla and Kristjan had repeatedly made false accusations about innocent Icelandic citizens who they claimed had participated in the Geirfinnur case.

Before leaving Iceland, Schutz gave a final, expansive newspaper interview reflecting on his time in the country. He mentioned some of his previous big cases and said the Icelandic officers he worked with were diligent and hardworking but they lacked the necessary specialist skills to deal with complex cases. They needed training in modern investigation methods. 'I'm not just talking about fingerprints or footprints,' he said, 'but also all possible other signs that a criminal has entered into a crime scene, including blood, sweat and even dirt, which might have come loose from the offender's shoes.'

They also didn't have the technology or equipment to properly analyse any forensic clues they did find, he said. The police had to use laboratories abroad, which Schutz warned 'can cause considerable damage in the investigation of criminal cases' as the evidence can 'suffer major delays in research and this creates undoubtedly great danger'.

He had written to the attorney general with recommendations to improve policing in Iceland and said he didn't rule out returning to Iceland again. Days after the final dramatic press conference he was gone, never to return.

PART 3

18

March–December 1977

With Schutz out of the picture, the suspects had a new sheriff in town. Gunnlaugur Briem, the lead judge in the court, was dapper in a casual way, with a round, friendly face and thick hair he wore neatly combed back, revealing a prominent forehead. The prosecution and defence would present their evidence to Briem and two other judges, who would ultimately pass judgement on the case. On 16 March, the judges already had the other case on their hands and were going through the Gudmundur evidence when the prosecutor formally charged Kristjan, Saevar and Gudjon with the murder of Geirfinnur Einarsson.

The charges stated they had attacked Geirfinnur in Keflavik harbour and inflicted such injuries upon him that he died. They moved his body that night in a car driven by Gudjon to the home of Kristjan Vidar at Grettisgata 82 in Reykjavík. On 21 November 1974, Kristjan, Saevar and Erla had taken Geirfinnur's body in a car driven by Erla from Grettisgata 82 to the Raudholar, stopping at a gas station to get a petrol canister. In the Raudholar they put Geirfinnur's remains in a shallow grave and then poured petrol on his body and burned it.

Erla was charged with participating in these acts. Kristjan Vidar was also accused of stealing Geirfinnur's wallet from his pocket, which had 5,000 kronor inside as well as various documents and a special drawing pencil. Kristjan Vidar, Saevar and Erla were also accused of making false charges in 1976 in the statements they gave to the police investigation and the criminal court of Reykjavik falsely accusing Einar Bollason, Magnus Leopoldsson, Sigurbjorn Eriksson and Valdimar Olsen of being involved in the death of Geirfinnur and smuggling offences.

At this point the judges had already spent months going through the voluminous material the Gudmundur investigation had generated and were unhappy with the conduct of the case. This was clear in a report written in January by one of the judges, Armanns Kristinsson. He delivered a withering assessment of the Gudmundur inquiry, pointing out many flaws in the police investigation:

> Nothing had been done to try to coordinate the testimony of the different parties. There had been neglect exploring significant evidence and questioning a valuable witness. There had been no discussions with other residents in Hamarsbraut 11 [Erla's apartment] or the neighbours. There had been no discussions with the landlord when the apartment had been rented, and who was the leasee... The people who had been with Erla in the early hours of 27 January 1974 and had driven to her home to Hamarsbraut 11 have not been interrogated. Only Kristjan Vidar had described Gudmundur's clothing on the night in question, the other suspects had not been asked to describe either his appearance nor his clothing. The police also need to examine whether Tryggvi Runar had

come into the apartment in Hamarsbraut 11 on the night in question. Kristjan had said that Saevar took Gudmundur's wallet, but that issue was not studied further by the police. The investigation needed to explore the medical aspects of the case in more detail, such as whether Gudmundur could have died from a single blow without excessive blood flow. They would need to scrutinise the plausibility of Kristjan's testimony about using the knife.

Under the Icelandic system the detectives worked for the court, so Sigurbjorn, Eggert and the others would now work for these judges rather than Orn Hoskuldsson and Karl Schutz. The judges wanted more control over what was happening to the suspects and to get a grip of the wayward police investigation. The first Gunnlaugur Briem had known of Erla's release in December before charges had been brought in the Geirfinnur case was when he read about it in the newspaper days later. At the end of January, Saevar had been transferred to the old prison and placed in a cell next to Kristjan's. Gunnlaugur thought it was a dumb idea and was unhappy it had been done without his prior knowledge.

Tryggvi was also in Gunnlaugur's sights. He had been sent to the Litla Hraun jail down on the south coast in November 1976, where he was able to socialise with other prisoners. His new-found freedom didn't last long. In the middle of January, he was brought back to Sidumuli and the judge Gunnlaugur Briem ordered that he be kept in total isolation. Having had a brief taste of a more relaxed environment made the solitary confinement even more punishing. Throughout all of this, his diary shows that he maintained his innocence.

The judges had questioned him about the rape he had been accused of. They said Tryggvi had a harsh, angry tone towards the woman who said he had attacked her, and they had a witness who said Tryggvi had threatened to kill him. Tryggvi denied this was the case and that there had been 'a misunderstanding with them'.

He talked about his case with the director of Sidumuli, Gunnar Gudmundsson, who continued to break the rules and have discussions with the inmates. Tryggvi wrote, 'I do not know anything, since I came nowhere near there, even though I have confessed to being in the case.' There had been early attempts to drag him into the Geirfinnur inquiry too, but it was found that he was at sea on a trawler at the time. Even the detectives couldn't twist that. During his time in isolation, Tryggvi felt great antipathy towards Saevar and the rest of the gang for dragging him into this mess, but seeing what they were going through in two murder inquiries, he felt, 'I do not envy the guys over this. I am starting to feel sorry for them, despite all of us having been through this.'

Tryggvi tried to protest his continued detention. Despite his ongoing focus on his exercise regime, in March he refused to eat because of the delays in finishing the case. Howver, he was soon persuaded to stop his nascent hunger strike. In the evening the guards would get their own back when they came around with the drugs. 'I just took them,' he wrote. 'I am not stressing about not taking them any more – it's bad enough… you just have to be completely numb and don't know anything in your head in this cell. But in the end there must be some end to this hell.'

Now that the suspects were formally charged, the 'nightmare' was over for the nation. But there would be no easing up on the suspects. The new sheriff wanted to put the squeeze on Gudjon, who was still reluctant to fully engage with the investigation. Gunnlaugur Briem ordered some shock therapy. Gudjon was also told that all of his letters to his mother would be read by the judge and there would no longer be any visits from his wife and family. Briem banned all visits from Jon Bjarman without his special permission. Later he would ban any contact with Gudjon's new lawyer, Benedikt Blondal.

While he was trying to tie up the loose ends in the Geirfinnur case, Briem wanted to achieve what neither Schutz nor Orn Hoskuldsson had, to find Gudmundur's body. That meant bringing back Albert Klahn into the inquiry. Albert had had plenty of time to think about the case and his friends languishing in a cell several paces long and just wide enough to lie down in. On 4 March, Albert was brought in for an interview at one o'clock in the afternoon. He wouldn't leave for another 13 hours.

He told the investigators his previous statements weren't true and that 'he has now decided to make a clean break and tell the whole truth of the matter'. This was a phrase the detectives were used to hearing as the suspect grasped for a reality and a truth the police would believe.

Albert's account was significantly different to his previous testimony and made him a key eyewitness to the events that unfolded on the January night in 1974 when Gudmundur was killed:

He was with Kristjan and Tryggvi and sometime between 21:00 and 22:00 they decided to go and buy LSD tablets. They all went in his dad's Volkswagen. They didn't have any money and Kristjan and Tryggvi suggested they go to some clubs and get in touch with a guy who has been stealing money or wallets. Albert took them to various places in the capital but it wasn't successful. He drove to Saevar who was in an apartment in Kopavogur in the suburbs of Reykjavik, but Saevar didn't want to lend them any money. They drove to Hafnarfjordur at a time when the discos were finished and people were milling around. He stopped near the bottom of the slope on the main road to Reykjavik and Kristjan and Tryggvi got out. When they came back they were with another man Albert didn't know, but later he found out was Gudmundur Einarsson. He described Gudmundur but couldn't remember how he was dressed. He thought Kristjan had suggested driving to Hamarsbraut 11. It was dark at the apartment when they got there. They discussed buying a bottle of liquor and soon Saevar arrived and was annoyed at their presence at the apartment but he didn't ask them to leave. Kristjan and Tryggvi tried to get Gudmundur to give them money to buy alcohol but Gudmundur was not willing to. A fight broke out between them, he said he never saw Saevar hit or kick Gudmundur. He hid behind a couch in the front room while this went on and hadn't seen Gudmundur being hit and couldn't bear to see who did it, but he believed Kristjan and Tryggvi had both been involved. He looked into the room after the fight and Gudmundur was lying motionless on his back on the floor. He hadn't seen any blood on him and hadn't seen any kind of knife used on him.

Albert drove back to Reykjavik and then came back to Hamarsbraut and knocked on the door but Saevar told him to move the car to the stairs and wait in the car. He didn't go in the house again. They drove the body to the lava and he was not aware of any blood stains in the car or on the canvas that the body was wrapped in. He didn't remember the body smelling bad either. After they dumped the body, he described how Tryggvi had grabbed him around the neck on the way back in the car and Albert thought he would suffocate until Kristjan intervened and Tryggvi released his grip. He drove Saevar back to Hamarsbraut 11 and then Kristjan to Grettisgata

82 and finally got back to his house at about four o'clock in the morning.

The judges decided to act quickly and brought Albert to the court. His lawyer wasn't present when Albert agreed with the statement he had given, stating Saevar, Kristjan and Tryggvi had killed Gudmundur.

The investigators weren't finished with him. They brought him back for a further round of questioning. This would focus on events later that year in August 1974, a time of year when the land has thawed, the moss blooms on the lava and it's warm enough to wear a shirt in the day. It was the time when the country undid a button or two, and everything went on a holiday slowdown.

Saevar had taken Albert to Kristjan's apartment in Grettisgata. Albert knew it well, he had grown up in the narrow streets of east Reykjavik and had attended Austurbaejar school, the austere Soviet-style Politburo building in the shadow of the towering white Hallgrimskirkja cathedral. A discussion took place, with Tryggvi joining in too, about moving Gudmundur's corpse from the lava. The police didn't mention the reasons; it was likely to be paranoia the body would be discovered, not helped by their copious drugs intake. They needed to move it somewhere it would never be discovered. This conversation took place as many of them did, with one of them rolling a joint to help gather their thoughts. They needed Albert for transport and he agreed to it.

In the evening they had smoked a lot and were in no fit state to find and move a cadaver. But still they headed out to the lava near Hafnarfjordur with a black plastic bag for the remains. Saevar and Tryggvi had been given this grim task and struggled to find the burial spot. Kristjan had warned Albert not to pay too much attention to where they were going and not to monitor their movements. Seven months after his death, after the frozen winter, Gudmundur's body would have been in such a state it would leave a deep scar on those who had to handle him and deal with the stench of death. But Albert had supposedly told the police he 'didn't find any smell coming up in the car from the body'.

It didn't get dark until late in the evening so they had to wait around to take the body to the cemetery at Hafnarfjordur, where they had been directed by Saevar. He told the judges the story he had previously mentioned to the police, that he'd seen the others dig a shallow grave for the body, only about 50 to 70cm deep. He said he wasn't there when the remains were actually buried. It was very late, between two and three in the morning by the time they finished, and he drove them home after this macabre evening. Albert said he had 'told the whole truth of the matter as best as he could remember', and that he was 'willing to do everything in his power to clarify the situation'.

What could he remember clearly at this point? His interrogation had lasted 13 hours, finishing at two in the morning. This was more than double the maximum limit for police interviews.

Albert was willing to take the police to the cemetery to find the body. The next day he went to Hafnarfjordur graveyard with a police officer. The cemetery was not especially peaceful, located on a busy road behind a low grey wall shielded by conifers and thick green shrubs. Albert had wandered around the simple graves with crosses or stones with their names and dates, but he couldn't find any likely burial site. When questioned that same day at the criminal court he was quite sure Gudmundur's remains had been placed in the graveyard by Kristjan, Saevar and Tryggvi.

All of these conversations had taken place without his lawyer being present.

As Albert was succumbing to police pressure and implicating himself further in the Gudmundur murder, a few kilometres away Saevar was staging a fightback against the police. A pen and pencil can be a powerful weapon, especially in testing circumstances. The prison wardens and police had realised this, and throughout his time in Sidumuli Saevar had been deprived of even this most basic tool. Perhaps the detectives didn't want him to be able to record his memories and his recollections of 1974. After all, if he wasn't able to write them down, it made it easier to manipulate and distort what had actually happened.

Now Saevar was in the more relaxed Hegninarhusid where he started typing a series of letters starting on 4 March that tore apart the case. He wrote that the statements about the events inside the Hamarsbraut apartment were 'ridiculous in every way'. Kristjan and Tryggvi only said what they had been told by the detectives, that Saevar had kicked Gudmundur to death. The keys on Saevar's typewriter spelled out this was a '100 per cent lie'. Saevar had been made to confess to the crime after Erla had lied. When they had tried to look for the body out in the lava with Kristjan, Albert and Tryggvi, nothing had been found. His conclusion was that there had been a high-level conspiracy to bring them into the jail and let them stay for so long.

He went through some of the major flaws in the Gudmundur case, which the police were trying to clear up. The first was the phone call he had supposedly made to Albert to summon him to Erla's apartment at Hamarsbraut. The phone had been disconnected as the bill hadn't been paid so this was impossible. This had been confirmed by the Icelandic Telephone company.

He said the police had played on Erla and Kristjan's psyches and they had been turned against him so they were prepared to lie about anything to gain the confidence and trust of the police.

Erla had been a key witness, implicating Saevar and the others, but when he had been brought together with her he asked why she was lying. She knew exactly where he had been in the early hours of 27 January 1974. He was with another woman in Kopavagur. He had repeatedly told the police about this and had written it down weeks into his custody, but these papers had been taken from his cell and he hadn't seen them since.

Saevar said that during some of the corroboration interviews in the summer of 1976, Erla seemed to take on the role of the interviewer, asking if he was going to tell her what had happened. She would smile, take his hand and ask what happened in Hamarsbraut. Saevar thought they were trying to soften him up so that he would confess. He recalled a specific conversation with Erla when she said: 'You who wanted to marry me at Christmas and then lied to me,' and she began to cry. She said Saevar's actions meant, 'I could not bathe the baby at Christmas or go to a Christmas dinner.' The detectives tried to play on the guilt Saevar felt, that he was keeping Erla in prison even though he claimed to love her. The pressure had been on him to confess to the murder of Gudmundur Einarsson in the interests of Erla and their child. He said the detectives had violated the law and that 'the country has committed the worst crime to us that I know of'. The people who were supposed 'to uphold the law and right in our country are guilty of a crime'.

The bulk of his statements, however, focused on the brutality he said he had faced over the 15 months he had been held in solitary confinement. In May 1976, the detectives had been pushing hard for a breakthrough in the case as the Klubburin suspects were about to be released and Orn Hoskuldsson knew this would bring intense criticism of the investigation. Saevar set out mistreatment during interviews by Orn Hoskuldsson, Sigurbjorn and Hallavadur Einvardsson. They always denied this was the case. He went through specific events: the assault on 5 May 1976 by the chief prison warden; the beating by Tryggvi that the detectives had allowed and the waterboarding incident.

The letters were Saevar's opening salvo. Several weeks later, on 29 March 1977, he was brought into the court house early in the morning. Saevar wasn't intimidated by this; he had been here before for remand hearings to be told he would be facing another 30, 60 or 90 days in custody. Today would be different though, today he would have his say.

In the presence of his lawyer, Saevar stood tall as he told the judge, 'I was not in Hamarsbraut that night.' He spelled out in detail what he had previously told the detectives, how he had been at another woman's house all night and had met Erla the next morning. He had confessed for one simple reason, 'Because I was subjected to physical violence by the police and also by the wardens.' He told the judges of an assault in his cell by the detective Sigurbjorn that had been witnessed by one of the prison wardens. He said that Sigurbjorn had threatened 'If I didn't confess to having been in Hamarsbraut 11 that night, I would get a lifetime of detention.' Sigurbjorn was also the one to make the threat that Saevar 'would get lost in an American prison, if I didn't confess in the Gudmundur and Geirfinnur cases'.

Saevar went through the attack on him by Tryggvi in June 1976. He was determined to tell the judge about all of the injustices he had suffered. He told the judges about the attempted drowning by the wardens in July 1976. There was also the psychological pressure placed on Erla. 'Erla threatened to commit suicide in July 1976 during corroboration in Sidumuli prison when the questioning lasted for eight days, for periods more than the maximum six hours at a time'. The investigators had goaded him to end his life. He said the investigating magistrate Orn

Hoskuldsson had been urging him to hang himself, and another officer had said 'Give him the rope'.

Saevar then had to listen as the court was read in full the statements he had given in December 1975 and January, September and October 1976. In these he admitted his guilt. Saevar conceded that he had signed all of these statements but asked that they should apply the same measure to the interview he had given to the detective Gisli Gudmundsson in January 1977, when he had issued a robust denial. After seven hours in the witness box the hearing adjourned.

Tryggvi too was gearing himself up to challenge his role in Gudmundur's killing. As his body had hardened and he could see his muscles growing and tightening, his mind got tougher too. After all this time in solitary confinement, staring at the sludgy green walls and the thin layer of glass that let in light, being given endless tranquilisers, there was little else the police could throw at him. He steeled himself for his appearance in court. He wrote in his diary: 'The final goal is reached, to tell the truth for justice'. It had been a long, hard 15 months. He had only confessed because he had been threatened by Orn Hoskuldsson that he would be kept for years in isolation if he didn't admit his guilt. Orn and the police have always denied this was the case. He had gained strength from the support of his brothers and his mother. 'I always thought of my family,' he wrote, 'I knew it would come to this end and now is the time to rise in the morning... Then I get to express myself.'

At just after ten o'clock in the morning he repeated what Saevar had done the previous day. He told the judges he denied attacking Gudmundur Einarsson and beating him to death. He said he never been to the apartment in Hamarsbraut, he had been shown it by the police but he didn't know the house. He said since he was first arrested at his home back in December 1975 he had suffered a lot and he was innocent. He had insomnia and had been injected so that he could rest and this would make him delirious. There were normally three people in his interrogations: Orn Hoskuldsson, Sigurbjorn Eggertsson and Eggert Bjarnason. They said that he would be convicted because the others had confessed and had identified him. He saw no alternative but to confess to his involvement in the killing.

The next day, the judges brought all the other defendants in, one by one, to undermine Tryggvi and Saevar's retractions. Albert was the only one of them who stuck to the story of Gudmundur's body being moved. None of the others said they had any recollection of this. Tryggvi thought Albert had lost his mind: 'It is weird to say these things. I do not know what has happened to the head of this fool.'

Even if the murder had happened, Tryggvi was certain the body would not have been moved. It had never made much sense, but the detectives and judges had indulged Albert and taken him to the Hafnarfjordur cemetery repeatedly to find Gudmundur's 'grave' among the hundreds of real plots.

After his court appearance, Tryggvi found the hope he had felt a few days earlier had dissipated. 'I just hope this will end soon,' he wrote. 'They have to get me out of it this matter I have no part in it.'

The newspapers reported the significant changes in Saevar and Tryggvi's statements. With the court starting to gather evidence, the suspects hoped the end was in sight. Then in May 1977 they were remanded for a further 150 days. Saevar, Kristjan, Tryggvi and Gudjon would be in solitary confinement for another five months.

Back in Germany the press were hailing the 'success' of Karl Schutz's mission in Iceland with stories of how he had 'rescued the Icelandic government', which faced having to resign.

*

Gisli Gudmundsson was not part of the task force, but that was to his advantage, he had not been infected by the presumption of guilt about the suspects, particularly Saevar. He was brought in to work on this final leg of the Gudmundur Einarsson case. An experienced detective, he had been one of the lead investigators in the brutal murder carried out by the TV announcer Asgeir Ingolfsson the previous summer. Trainee psychologist Gisli Gudjonsson had bonded with his older namesake through their work on the case, and thought he was a solid man: 'He had good values and integrity, I identified with him and saw him as an honest, upright person. He was a man who wanted to get to the truth.'

The truth. This had become a tarnished phrase during the tortured two years of the investigation. Gudmundsson brought a new eye and vigour to Gudmundur's murder, chipping away at some of the inconsistencies. He tracked down people who the other investigators had ignored or discounted. Witnesses such as the police officer who had arrested Saevar for a drugs offence in February 1974, shortly after he had had supposedly murdered Gudmundur. The officer said he hadn't seen or noticed anything about Saevar that day that was unusual. Orn Hoskuldsson and his team would see this as evidence that Saevar was indeed a cold-blooded killer, but Gisli Gudmundsson thought it might mean something else altogether.

By March 1977, all of the suspects had at some point withdrawn their statements, except Gudjon, whose account remained hazy. When Gisli Gudmundsson started interviewing Kristjan he told him his previous statements about the Gudmundur case were not true. Kristjan's version of the incident had changed over the years; for over a year he claimed he had stabbed Gudmundur with a knife he had got in Copenhagen. The detectives had spent time trying to track down the knife but their efforts were wasted as in March 1977 Kristjan said the stabbing didn't happen at all.

Other descriptions Kristjan had given about the murder were also patently false. Kristjan pondered why he had done this and thought that perhaps he wanted to take on all the blame for the case. The sounds and smells he had mentioned were 'a fantasy'; the descriptions had probably come from Erla and the police.

Gudmundsson's interviews with Saevar also revealed a significant change in his testimony about the events on 27 January 1974. Apart from the detail of the phone in Erla's apartment not working, Saevar was still insisting that he remembered being at another apartment that night, and said Albert had come there too to buy some LSD. To a dogged detective like Gudmundsson there were too many messy loose ends that needed to be cleared up.

At the beginning of March 1977, the detective wrote a report recommending he continue with his work on the Gudmundur case. He took his findings to the judge, Gunnlaugur Briem, but he was told not to pursue it. 'He was very bitter about this,' his former colleague Gisli Gudjonsson said, 'he had been stopped, he had a conscience, he was a man who wanted to get the truth.'

That summer, the court started to hear evidence about Gudmundur Einarsson's final hours. The judges heard from friends of Gudmundur, eyewitnesses, relatives of the accused and then the suspects themselves. Kristjan had provided an exhaustive account of the night to the judges. Much of this had already been set out before but he reiterated what Albert Klahn had stated – that Gudmundur's murder had happened during an argument about buying alcohol. The knife that had supposedly been used to stab Gudmundur was missing from the account. The investigators had spent many months trying to find the knife but Kristjan's lawyers told the court the story of the knife had been pulled out of thin air. 'He told the police this because he was confused by the constant questioning, both on this issue and in the Geirfinnur case and told the story to speed up the case.'

Throughout the summer, all of the suspects were brought before the judges to go through their testimony. They told the court of mistreatment by guards and police intimidation, and how their memories had been distorted so they started to believe things they knew weren't true. All of the suspects had changed their original statements, and when they presented their new version of events the court would read back earlier statements they had signed, which confirmed their guilt.

There were occasional leaks from behind the closed doors of the court, such as the news that the Raudholar may not have been the final resting place for Geirfinnur. According to the latest statements from the suspects, Geirfinnur had been buried in a rubbish dump. He had never been brought to Reykjavik but taken straight to the dump, where the body of Gudmundur Einarsson had also been deposited. This was no more believable than any of the other dozen locations that the police had searched. Gudjon acknowledged there was almost a kind of competition between the suspects to come up with new burial sites – not because they were trying to fool the police, but because they didn't have a clue.

As they entered their second summer in prison, Saevar and Tryggvi kept up the pressure on the court, maintaining that their statements were a fabrication. Outside the stale environment of Sidumuli, the Icelandic summer stretched ahead. Saevar and Tryggvi were at least allowed outside for a few minutes each day to get some vitamin D into their system, feeling the weak sun on their faces. They both had a renewed vigour to prove their innocence.

In July, Tryggvi stopped taking all of the medications offered to him. 'I am a better man since I quit. I knew that I had to take some action,' he wrote. It took immense effort to maintain his innocence, while all around him the wardens and police were certain of his guilt. He had the support of his family, particularly his brothers Omar and Hilmar who would bring food and supplies. And there was his daily exercise regime that had helped turned him into a Charles Atlas with his 'beautiful muscles'. In his final entry of his last surviving diary in November 1977, Tryggvi reflected of the journey he had taken in the past two years. Whatever problems he still faced, he reflected, 'I'm completely clean and straight'.

Tryggvi's lawyer was also asking more questions, sending a letter to the court asking why his client had been interrogated repeatedly and why there were no notes of the conversations that took place in his cell. The detective Eggert Bjarnason was called to the court to explain this: 'The conversations took place, as best I remember, often at the request of Tryggvi Runar himself, not because I wanted to speak to him.' The reason for a lack of detailed reports about these conversations, he said, was that Tryggvi had asked for the meeting so he didn't feel the need to make any lengthy record.

Saevar was pushing for recognition of his mistreatment and there was an investigation into his beating and torture. None of the wardens or police however would admit to witnessing any cruel treatment. Orn Hoskuldsson made his feelings clear on Saevar's retraction and his claim that he had been forced to confess: 'I ignore this testimony of his, as I know better, I was present when he first said it and so was his lawyer, Jon Oddsson. He was convinced 'the Rat' was guilty and there was no way he was gnawing his way out of the trap.

Undeterred, Saevar pressed on; in September he sent his letters to the court stating that all of his previous statements about the Geirfinnur killing were incorrect and based on rumours.

Gudjon had considered retracting his confession when he went before the court in the summer of 1977 to give his testimony, but he concluded, 'There was nothing to retract – you simply couldn't retract something that was nothing.' When he was called to give his evidence to the judges, his testimony remained vague, especially on the actual murder of Geirfinnur. He couldn't recall Kristjan and Saevar's role in the fight: 'I cannot describe the events that occurred there... In our past discussions Karl Schutz told me of certain aspects of the conflict that had taken place, but I have not seen these.' He remembered Geirfinnur falling to the ground but he didn't know how this happened, he didn't remember having seen any of it. He didn't know how Geirfinnur was killed and couldn't say whether this had been during the fight with the three suspects. There was clearly a lot he didn't remember.

As they had done with the other suspects, the court read back previous statements he had made. 'It was clear from the beginning that I was in a dangerous position to have confessed or denied any of these events,' he replied. He said the statements he had signed were only a basis for discussion, but not for use as a court exhibit. He had given many similar statements to the detective Gretar Saemundsson.

By December, Kristjan, Saevar and Tryggvi were facing their third Christmas in prison. This was one of the toughest times for them, and the time when their continued absence was most keenly felt by their families. There would be the presents, the family gatherings and the bonfires and fireworks they would hear as the country celebrated moving into yet another a new year.

A week before the holiday the court delivered its judgement on the cases: all six of the suspects were found guilty. Albert Klahn received the most lenient sentence, convicted of drugs offences and obstruction of the investigation and given a 15-month sentence. Erla Bolladottir was found guilty of making false charges against the Klubburin men and also obstruction of the investigation and sentenced to three years in jail. Gudjon Skarphedinsson was found guilty of killing Geirfinnur Einarsson and received a 12-year sentence. Tryggvi Runar Leifsson was found guilty of Gudmundur Einarsson's murder and separate rape and arson cases and given a 16-year sentence. The heaviest punishments were for Saevar Cieselski and Kristjan Vidarsson who were both given the maximum – life sentences for the murders of Geirfinnur and Gudmundur Einarsson.

Like the other suspects, Gudjon had not been in court to hear the verdicts. He read about the sentences in the newspaper the next day. 'I was astonished in a way. I thought the judge didn't have much to go on and didn't see what crime he had on me.' The final verdict would come from the higher Supreme Court, but they would have to wait for that case for some time.

After the torments of the past year, though, Gudjon felt he had to get on with it and tried to see the positive side. 'What matters is that you were going to live it, there is no death penalty, you're not going to hang.' Though condemned to 12 years in prison, surprisingly he had fond memories of Christmas 1977: 'It was very nice, fine food. The Salvation Army came and I never had so many socks,' he said, with his customary sardonic grin.

On 2 January 1978, Gudjon was put inside a big American car and driven away from Sidumuli to his new home. It was chafing cold, with snow covering Reykjavik, cloaking its grey monotony. He was leaving the city he despised, heading south west across the Snaefellsness peninsula, a landscape steeped in Icelandic mythology with its scarred lava fields and the brooding, dormant

Snæfellsjökull volcano blanketed by a glacier, but with the power to unleash a torrent of sulphur and ash.

His destination was Kviabryggja, an open prison of low rise buildings at the end of a single-track road, bounded by the North Atlantic and the snow-flecked lava fields. Towering over it was Kirkjufell, the church shaped mountain sitting across the limpid fjord. Kviabryggja was like a holiday camp compared to the harsh strictures of Sidumuli. There were around a dozen inmates, each with their own room in a relaxed environment.

The other suspects would not have the same pleasures. Tryggvi, Kristjan and Saevar were just desperate to get out of solitary confinement. In the public's mind they were all condemned and Saevar and Kristjan became the first people in Iceland in over a century to be convicted of a double murder.

19

In the two years since the original conviction, the suspects had been scattered to jails around the country. Gudjon was still in Kviabryggja open prison enjoying the relative freedom. Kristjan, Saevar and Tryggvi were in Litla Hraun. They were no longer in solitary confinement but between them they had spent the equivalent of almost five years in isolation. Erla and Albert Klahn had also been sentenced to prison terms but had been out of jail waiting for the final judgement from the highest court in the land, the Supreme Court. Since the first judgement in 1977, the Reykjavik Six had taken different approaches to their sentences.

Saevar was focused on proving his innocence and that the police and the judges had fitted him up. He was determined to have his moment in court. Tryggvi, who had been equally passionate about his innocence, had mellowed in Litla Hraun. 'I have personally learned something. This prison is nothing. It's more like a big rural home... I am beginning to get an understanding because life has a purpose,' he later told a journalist who interviewed him in jail.

Kristjan was also trying to use his time in prison to get his life in order and had started studying. Albert

277

Klahn tried to keep a low profile, shunning any publicity about the case, wary of the public vilification of him and his friends as deranged, dangerous killers.

Erla too felt the hostility and reproach when she was out in the streets of Reykjavik. 'I went through a lot of image issues, it was very difficult for me to be seen in public,' she recalled.

Gudjon had taken a phlegmatic view of the case. He felt his time in Kviabryggja prison wasn't so bad. 'We would lie in the bath and smoke weed, you could listen to music whenever you want.' The inmates would make hay for the surrounding farms or work on boats for the fishermen in the town nearby. 'The doors were never locked, there was never any fighting,' Gudjon recalled.

On the wood-panelled walls of the Supreme Court hung the portraits of the august men who had previously held the offices of the highest court in Iceland. The current incumbents sat in an arc facing the courtroom with the lawyers and defendants called to present their testimony at a wooden lectern only a few feet away. To the side were long white-framed windows with thick drapes; at the back of the court were half a dozen rows of hard wooden benches, as comfortable as church pews, for the witnesses and observers. The Supreme Court had the power to quash the original conviction, to extend the sentences for those who hadn't received a life sentence or to reduce the jail terms. They would have the final word, after this there would be no further appeal.

The prosecution got the first bite of the cherry. Over four days, the prosecutor Thordur Bjornsson spent 15 hours presenting the state's case. The Gudmundur case was fairly straightforward; there was Erla and Albert's testimony and the confessions. Geirfinnur's murder was much more tricky. Again he went through the key confessions of Kristjan, Saevar, Erla and Gudjon at different points throughout 1976. He believed there was no difference between Saevar, Kristjan and Gudjon; they were all jointly responsible for the murder of Geirfinnur Einarsson. He rejected all of the points the suspects' defence had made. The defence's argument that they had been mentally traumatised by their treatment didn't hold up. He read out the doctors' reports, which stated the suspects were all mentally capable. There was no forensic evidence or bodies but Icelandic law stretched back many centuries and Thordur found three convictions from the nineteenth century that occurred without a body being found, so there was legal precedent for this. He thundered that what was most galling was that four years after the first arrest there had been no repentance from any of the suspects. He told the judges, 'It's my sincere hope that you believe you can find the truth and I hope come to the same conclusion as me' – that the six were all guilty. He delivered a final warning: 'These are dangerous people,' he concluded, 'and the country is entitled to protection from them.'

The six defence lawyers were given far less time to present their cases. Kristjan Vidarsson's lawyer was first: the fresh faced, dimple chinned, Paul Palsson. He delivered a forceful denunciation of the investigation and the subsequent prosecution. The case rested on the strength of the confessions which he contended had been obtained illegally. Kristjan had been given four different kinds of anti-depressants. He said the effects of these drugs were that you could get suspects 'to confess to almost anything'. For long periods Palsson had not been allowed to see his client. Palsson contended that the state had not provided any 'legitimate proof' of guilt. 'The body has not been found. There was no clear motive.' He rejected the prosecution claim that Kristjan had killed Gudmundur Einarsson after an argument about getting money for alcohol: 'Who kills a man for this?' he asked the judges sitting impassively in front of him.

The Geirfinnur case, he said, was even more flawed. Kristjan had retracted his confession, as had all of the accused, apart from Gudjon Skarphedinsson, but his recollection was very cloudy. 'There was no evidence found out in this matter, despite comprehensive research, the most comprehensive which has been undertaken in an Icelandic criminal case,' Palsson reminded the judges.

There had been massive inconsistencies in the statements of the suspects until Karl Schutz arrived. His press conference at the conclusion of the investigation had been massively prejudicial and Palsson said he believed 'this would have had a very big impact' on the public perception of the suspects. 'The case does not contain any evidence,' he stated. 'All the prosecution had come up with is an ancient case from Iceland in the 1800s where someone had been tried without a body being found.'

Saevar's lawyer, Jon Oddsson, spent six hours setting out Saevar's defence to the court. The Gudmundur investigation had been badly run and he listed some of the evidence that had not been pursued. There were the threatening phone calls Gudmundur's mother told police her son had been receiving from an older man. Who was he and could he have been involved in the disappearance? There was Saevar's alibi for the night of the murder that he had been with another woman in Reykjavik. The detective Gisli Gudmundsson had wanted to investigate this further but he had been told by the judges not to pursue it. There was the phone not working at the apartment in Hamarsbraut, so how did they call Albert to transport the body? Important witnesses had not been interviewed, specifically Erla's neighbours, who had not been asked about the obvious disturbance as Gudmundur was beaten to death and then loaded into a car in the dead of night to be driven to a cold, rocky grave in the lava. There were other uncomfortable truths the police had glossed over: Saevar's arrests for a drugs offence by the customs chief Kristjan Petursson, a week after Gudmundur went missing. This was in the apartment where Gudmundur had supposedly been killed but Petursson didn't see any blood on the blanket, which then, miraculously two years later, investigators had managed to find but which didn't match Gudmundur's blood type anyway and had been another red herring.

Oddsson went through the assaults and torture he said Saevar had suffered. The prison chaplain Jon Bjarman had complained about this and Saevar had been denied access to his lawyer for many months. Saevar also had an alibi for the Geirfinnur case; he had been to the cinema with Erla and his mother. The police claimed that there had been enough time for Saevar and Erla to have dropped his mother home and then driven to Keflavik. This was a point picked up by Gudjon's defence who had worked out the VW they had driven to Keflavik would have needed to go at almost 100km an hour in order to have reached Keflavik in time to have rung Geirfinnur at 10:30pm, summoning him to his death. To do this with four people inside stretched credulity.

Erla's lawyer, Gudmundur Ingvi Sigurdsson, took a different tack. He presented Erla as a vulnerable young woman, controlled by Saevar. She'd had a hard childhood, rarely in the same house for long, moving 21 times in her short life. Her parents divorced when she was 16 and Saevar had huge influence over her. She was afraid of him, he had been violent towards her and she repeatedly tried to get away from him, but he would always find her and play on her compassion and persuade her to let him back into her life. Sigurdsson pointed to the evidence from the psychiatric assessment, that Erla was vulnerable to being influenced by others. There was great uncertainty in the case, he emphasised, and asked, 'Is there sufficient proof that these young people are responsible for the disappearance of Gudmundur and Geirfinnur?' He said

Erla wanted to live for her child, but a shadow hovered over her life: a prison sentence that would make everything even worse for her.

Tryggvi's defence was emphatic: he was not at Hamarsbraut on the night of 26 January and there had been no fight between him and Gudmundur. Initially there had been some doubt about the identity of the third man who had been with Kristjan and Saevar when Gudmundur was killed. Tryggvi's lawyer, Hilmar, argued that Erla didn't know Tryggvi and the first time she gave a clear description of a man that matched his description was in March 1977, over a year after her first statement. She had drawn a picture of the third man involved in the Gudmundur attack but it was not in the police file – was it Tryggvi or was she guilty of falsely accusing someone, as she had done with the Klubburin men? Unfortunately, he said, Tryggvi didn't have the same means to defend himself as the Klubburin suspects. His lawyer said that Tryggvi had been mistreated, and had his mouth taped over. 'It is amazing something like that should be possible in an Icelandic prison,' his lawyer told the court. He went through the many inconsistencies about where Gudmundur's body was said to have been buried. It had been in Alftanes where the lava flows down to a peaceful beach and months later it was in Fossvogur cemetery, but crucially it was in neither of these places and still hadn't been found.

Tryggvi confessed because Orn Hoskuldsson said all of the other suspects had done so and he warned that if Tryggvi didn't, he could be held for two years in solitary confinement. Tryggvi couldn't see another way out so he confessed in the hope that the truth would be revealed later. In spite of this, he had been held in solitary confinement for 655 days. During this time, he was a model prisoner and had turned his life around. He had engaged in education and was training as a welder and had married on Christmas Day. On his release he planned to become a new member of society. 'I believe I have shown that my client is not guilty of the crime he has been accused of,' Hilmar concluded.

Albert's defence was short – if there was no crime then of course he couldn't have been there, but it wasn't that simple. His lawyer didn't seek to disprove the case but he appealed to the judges' sympathy, saying it had a hugely detrimental effect on Albert's life.

Gudjon was the one suspect who stood out in the Geirfinnur case, the only one who had not retracted his confession. His lawyer, Benedikt Blondal, repeated some of the deficiencies in the case highlighted by others: statements taken late at night; the impossibility of getting to Keflavik in the time the police stated; lawyers being unable to see the documents the police had. He also raised the spectre of a missing suspect: 'I think we probably haven't yet found all those who participated,' he told the court. He presented Gudjon as being duped and under Saevar's spell. 'It was more likely that Saevar would be the mentor and Gudjon the student,' he said.

Gudjon was the only one of the suspects who admitted he had been present when Geirfinnur died. He said he had tried to lead him away but Geirfinnur misunderstood what he was trying to do, reacted badly and then the fight began. Gudjon's account 'is not a confession', Benedikt said, but 'a record of an accident. This is not intentional.' Gudjon was willing to stand up and let the court decide. He had already been punished, he had been well-behaved, and Benedikt demanded the lowest sentence possible under the law.

The suspects also had their chance to finally have their say, four years after they had been arrested. Gudjon didn't want to return to the court as it meant being held in Sidumuli rather than returning to Kviabryggja. 'If you leave that cell for a few days or weeks then it's not good to come back – after I went to west Iceland I couldn't come back to Sidumuli as I couldn't keep my cool anymore.'

Kristjan had been in the court listening, waiting for his chance to say his piece. The thick-set man with a moustache and collar length hair in a suit and open necked shirt who stood at the witness stand was unrecognisable from the pasty looking young boy in his original mug shot. Kristjan made a simple heartfelt plea: 'I want to declare that I am innocent of the charges.' He had falsely accused the Klubburin men because, he said, 'I was forced to mention the names as the police were threatening me.' He didn't know anything about them and they had never done anything. He hoped that having listened to all of the evidence and the years of prejudicial coverage 'the Supreme Court will be fair in these cases'.

Erla Bolladottir didn't look very different from the elfin little girl in big glasses who had been arrested in 1975. She had sat at the front of the court listening to the days of prosecution evidence and then the far shorter defence testimony. Now she stood on the witness stand, her arms stretched out in her white jumper, to address the five judges. One of them would have trouble seeing her properly as he was hidden behind voluminous legal documents. She carried on regardless: 'This issue has had a profound effect on me. I was a very different person than I am today, She said throughout the time in custody 'we tried to tell the truth but we were not believed'. She recounted the threats she had faced during her interrogations, she said the police didn't want to listen, they were deaf to what the suspects were telling them. 'I sincerely hope the truth is revealed,' she told the judges, before leaving with hope, 'I trust the system to be just.'

Saevar Cieselski still looked like a rock star, now more haggard, but still the front man in his dark velvet corduroy jacket with his long, straight black hair. Saevar had been fighting the prosecution for years and this was his final chance to get justice. Whatever the outcome, he would make sure the judges and the public knew what had gone on inside Sidumuli in those dark years when he had been forced to confess at all costs. 'I want to have the opportunity to object to the prosecution,' he told the packed court. 'I have never known the men that I'm blamed for their disappearance. Their names are as far away to me now as they were at the beginning.' Few people outside of the prison knew what the suspects had endured inside the makeshift jail but Saevar would make sure everyone knew the hardship they had suffered. He had spent two years in solitary confinement without reading or writing material or tobacco, making do with two woollen blankets. 'I don't know the reason for this feeling towards me, I haven't got any explanation.'

He said he had been banned from talking to his lawyer for two months and there was no one listening to his complaints. He had an alibi for the night Gudmundur disappeared but the police said Albert and Kristjan had given statements that put him in the apartment and that he had killed Gudmundur. He had confessed because, 'I had become exhausted – because of fatigue and the interrogations and I gave up.'

As for Geirfinnur Einarsson, the first he knew of it was when the police came to his cell saying he had gone to Keflavik with Erla's brother, Einar. He said his mother was threatened and he feared for Erla's life, so he had given statements about the Klubburin men so they would be arrested and 'so that Erla would not be murdered'. When Erla and Kristjan gave statements that he had been in Keflavik, he realised it had gone too far and withdrew his confession.

He refuted the prosecution claims that he tried to influence witnesses and that his friends had intimidated the woman he claimed to have been with on the night

Gudmundur disappeared. He called it 'disgusting' that the prosecutor made this claim. 'I've lost all my friends and acquaintances, I've lost them all because of these cases,' he stated as he wound to an impassioned conclusion. He told the judges if the Supreme Court found him guilty, to quote Socrates, 'I to die and you to live, which of these two is the better journey only God knows.'

A month later, the judges came back with their decision. The lawyers crowded into the Supreme Court, their long black gowns over their suits. They began scouring through the 380-page ruling, which went through the whole case in detail. The judges had listened to the pleas of the suspects and the reasoned arguments of their lawyers, but they weren't convinced by them. The convictions were upheld. The court did reduce the length of the sentences: Saevar's was reduced from life imprisonment to 17 years and Kristjan's was also cut to 16 years. Tryggvi's was reduced to 13 years and Gudjon to 10 years. Albert would have to serve 12 months and Erla's sentence remained at three years. It meant Erla and Albert would now have to go to jail to serve out their sentences with time taken off for their spell in jail on remand. The reduced sentences didn't matter, the damage was done. The Reykjavik Six would forever be guilty of Iceland's worst murder case.

Epilogue

Saevar Cieselski left prison in 1984, nine years after his arrest, but the case, and his 741 days in solitary confinement, left a deep wound that wouldn't heal. Throughout his time in prison, Saevar had been working out how to get the case re-opened. He would need new evidence and would do all he could to get it. Being the most notorious prisoner in a tiny country meant that rehabilitation was tough. On release, he found it difficult to get a job. Who wanted to employ a double murderer? He faced the same difficulties finding somewhere to live, but he did meet a new love.

He had two sons, Hafthor and Sigurdor. Sigurdor looked more like his dad; taller than Saevar but lean with dark hair and deep set eyes. Hafthor had the more Icelandic blond colourings and was less angular. Saevar didn't talk to his sons about his time in jail, he wanted to shield them from it, but it was impossible to in such a small country. Hafthor remembers as a young boy being told by his mother about the great injustice his father had suffered.

Saevar initially tried moving to the United States for a new life, living in Colorado, working as a carpenter but he returned to Iceland after a year. He didn't want to hide in the shadows, he wanted to bring the case back to the Supreme Court, but in order to do so he would need fresh evidence. He made his first attempt in 1997, but the prosecutor turned him down. He tried again a few years later after several witnesses came forward highlighting his torture and mistreatment.

Working on his case was a defence mechanism for him, a way of coping with life outside. There was another reason too: 'He wanted to marry my mother,' Hafthor said, 'but he didn't want to do it until he had cleansed his reputation officially. He didn't want this dirt on his name; it would affect his family, so he wanted to cleanse his name out of this ridiculous case, just so we could move on.'

Saevar always tackled life with intensity and his struggles with authority left him frustrated and angry. This lead to the breakdown of his relationship and he started drinking, something he had avoided all through the drugs heyday of the 1970s. In 1999 he got a final rejection: his case would not be going back to the Supreme Court. After this he went on a downward spiral. His son Hafthor would still see him regularly, 'There were a lot of moments that should have brought him down to the floor but he kept standing up again.'

Saevar moved to Denmark and ended up on the streets, the once-beautiful young man, still with his trademark long hair, now a battered-looking alcoholic. In 2009 a bloated, dishevelled Saevar was shown on Icelandic TV berating the press who had maligned him, 'Why did you attack me like that when I was a boy?' He died in 2011 outside on a freezing street in Copenhagen and was buried at the cathedral in Reykjavik. The case had eaten away at him and destroyed his life. His death gave his family new impetus to clear his name and those of the other suspects. It was helped by a strange turn of events.

Kristin Tryggvadottir had never told any of her family the secret that she had found hidden in the basement of her house when she was a teenager. She had kept it locked away for twenty years. Tryggvi Runar's daughter had lived with the case for as long as she could remember. As a small child at school, she said, 'One teacher called me the daughter of a murderer. I didn't know what she was talking about but I probably did. It stings but you get used to it.'

On Sundays, she would take the long bus ride with her mother the 50km from Reykjavik down to Eyrarbakki in the south to Litla Hraun jail at the end of a single track road. 'This was another home for me, at least on Sundays,' she recalled. 'It was probably not the typical way to grow up, but it was our life and we made the best of it.' Tryggvi would try to make his prison cell look as much like a home as was possible with pictures on the wall and his football trophies on display. 'When I came, we didn't see bars on the windows, he put black plastic bags over them and pulled the curtains so I could not see.'

Kristin would play outside with the other inmates' children, feed the horses and they would have dinner with ice cream. When Tryggvi was released, just before Christmas in 1981, he felt like a new man. He had spent almost two years in solitary confinement. The world had changed in the years he had been in jail: Iceland had won the Cod Wars; it had a new prime minister; there was colour TV.

In prison, Tryggvi had trained to be a welder and he was determined to find work and put the past behind him. He was interviewed shortly before he left jail and reflected on how the previous 10 years had been wasted. He said when he had been arrested for the Gudmundur murder, 'I was searching for something, some sort of lifestyle, but I didn't wake up until I hit a brick wall.' He was optimistic, 'I am clean and determined to make a future for myself,' he declared.

Tryggvi wanted a normal family life, but Kristin could see the case still lingered for her father. 'He was worried people would recognise him. He didn't want to go out. I didn't talk about it with kids at school.' She was used to keeping secrets about her dad; she didn't tell her friends about him, because everyone would know his name. Tryggvi never discussed the case much, but Kristin could see the effect on him was profound. 'He had demons in him, a lot of anger even though he was trying to leave this behind him. It was really hard for him.' He would try and shed this through exercise or sometimes drinking.

By her teenage years, Kristin was feeling hard done by. 'I thought it was really unfair that I didn't have a normal family and a normal dad and we got into fights... so I thought maybe he's guilty, maybe he did this. But somehow I knew that this was not a possibility that he could do something like that.'

Down in the basement, Kristin found his diaries from prison. There were dozens of them and 'as a curious teenager I started reading them. I took two or three at a time up to my room, kept them under my mattress and I didn't tell anybody about them.' She knew that it was wrong, she was reading her dad's innermost thoughts, staring into his soul, but she couldn't help herself. A few years later, Tryggvi cleared out the basement and got rid of the diaries. He didn't notice three were missing. Kristin kept them secret, looking at them every now and then, scared that if the police found out about their existence they would be taken away from her.

Tryggvi Runar tried to put the demons of the past behind him. He had two daughters and a son, and grand-children, one of whom bears his name. In 2009, he was diagnosed with cancer and as his condition worsened, Kristin decided it was time to tell him about the diaries. 'The first thing he asked was, "Did you read all of them?".

And I told him, yes, I did. I think he was just happy that I did.' It was a relief after all those years of secrecy but Kristin was unsure what to do with them now. 'He said, "You will know what to do with them when the time is right".' Tryggvi died later that year.

That time came in the autumn of 2011 following Saevar's death, when a TV reporter named Helga Arnardottir was doing some research into the Gudmundur/Geirfinnur cases and came to see Kristin and her mother. As they sat chatting, Kristin remembered her father's words, and brought out the diaries which, until then, her mother didn't know still existed. As soon as she looked at them Helga thought they were significant and she knew just the man who should look at them, someone who had left Iceland a long time ago, for England.

Days later Kristin and Helga were in the living room of a large, welcoming house in south London, home to Professor Gisli Gudjonsson. The former young Icelandic detective had become a renowned forensic psychologist, noted for his pioneering work identifying false memory syndrome. His research had revealed how suspects might be induced into making confessions for crimes they hadn't committed. He had identified a range of psychological factors such as compliance, personality disorders and suggestibility which made people make false confessions. In his long career he had worked on many miscarriages of justice, including the Guildford Four and Birmingham Six and even produced the Gudjonsson Suggestibility Scales (GSS), used around the world when false confessions are suspected.

Gisli had always been reluctant to get involved in the Geirfinnur and Gudmundur cases. Saevar had approached him in the late 1990s when he was trying to appeal his conviction. At the time, Gisli was too busy and he felt there was a clear conflict of interest because he was a detective at the time that the six were arrested. But more than a decade had passed since then, and he now felt less conflicted. He decided he would look at the diaries with an open mind, if Helga brought them to him. He took them away to his study, prepared to put the thoughts of the past out of his mind. 'Even though as a young detective, I had had the view and assumed these people were guilty, I was prepared to look at the diaries with an open mind because a long time had passed and I didn't know about the case and I promised myself I would be objective.'

Kristin waited anxiously as Gisli went through the diaries for several hours, poring over the entries where Tryggvi would go through his daily routine and his constant fight to prove his innocence. When Gisli emerged he concluded, 'I was absolutely convinced that these three diaries were of significance to the case. They were actually convincing to me. These diaries looked like genuinely somebody expressing his views at the time.' The diaries on their own didn't mean Tryggvi was innocent, but there was enough in them that Gisli felt needed further investigation. 'It certainly raised in my mind the possibility that these were miscarriages of justice.'

In October 2011, Gisli did an interview for Icelandic TV stating this. Kristin knew that with Gisli on board this couldn't be brushed aside.

Inside Iceland's Ministry of Justice, they were listening. The fate of the six had been plaguing the thoughts of the interior minister, Ogmundur Jonasson who remembered growing up with the case. 'This has been with us all this time since the late 1970s. This was very much part of our lives... everybody knew about this.' A week after Gisli's interview, the minister announced the formation of a commission to investigate how the cases had been handled. This would be the first step to clearing the suspect's names. Gisli Gudjonsson was asked to be one of the committee members. Thirty-five years after first coming across the case as a young detective, he would be delving back into the past.

The committee assembled a huge cache of evidence. They read through all of the police reports and prison diaries which showed what was happening to each of the suspects. What emerged was a consistently negative and harsh view of the six young suspects. What was particularly shocking to the seasoned psychologist was the extent of the interrogations and the length of the solitary confinement: 'I was absolutely horrified because I've worked on miscarriages of justice in many different countries…. I'd never come across any case where there had been such intense interrogation, so many interrogations and such lengthy solitary confinement.' He interviewed the four surviving suspects – Gudjon, Erla, Albert and Kristjan – and concluded 'the effect of the solitary confinement was absolutely crucial to the way they were reacting'. Examining the case files over 18 months, it became clear to him that Gudjon, Erla and Albert were the most susceptible to making false confessions. 'They were kind of yes people – wanting to help the police… if they have a good relationship with the police officer who is interviewing them and they trust that police officer, that makes them vulnerable.'

Gudjonsson's own role in the affair didn't go unnoticed. He knew the police officers who had investigated the case, he liked and trusted them – he had been one at the time. 'What shocked me was what had actually happened to these individuals; that I had been there but oblivious to what was going on really – you know that I was naïve, I was idealistic. How did I fail to notice what was going on and the enormity of it all?'

He went through the diaries kept by Tryggvi Runar and the committee also discovered the existence of Gudjon's diary. This was even more revealing to Gisli than Tryggvi Runar's writing. 'I never ever worked on a case where I've seen such detailed, informative diaries of everyday living. I'm absolutely convinced these diaries were not written so they could be used as a defence later on. They were used to kill time.' Gudjon's diary also charted in forensic detail how his memory had been distorted. 'It tells you how an intelligent individual who knows he is innocent at the beginning gradually began to think that he is wrong and that he had been involved in a murder of which he has absolutely no memory.'

Having gone through all of the records and files, the committee found glaring problems with the investigation. 'Nobody could provide any solitary, tangible evidence to support their confessions,' Gisli Gudjonsson found, 'You would have thought, two bodies – out of these individuals somebody could say, "You know, I know exactly where their bodies are".' He had seen this before in previous miscarriages of justice, where the people convicted had no knowledge of what had happened, and he thought this was the case with the Reykjavik Six: 'They were just trying to appease the police; they were trying to be cooperative because they knew if they were not cooperative they would be given more solitary confinement.'

In March 2013, the working group issued a report almost 500 pages long, concluding the confessions were unreliable and the case should go back to the Icelandic Supreme Court. Gudjonsson had looked at all of the evidence and felt that the lengthy solitary confinement had led five of the suspects to suffer from false memory syndrome. 'It completely damaged the confidence in their own memory, so the impact is actually to disturb the whole memory process. You are getting people to distrust their own memories. Some of these people had alibis, had good alibis, but the alibis were kind of ignored.'

After two years of investigations there were no bodies, no forensic evidence, no real eyewitnesses, and all the investigators had were the confessions. These admissions had been extracted from the six young suspects during periods of solitary confinement that Gisli Gudjonsson said has only one contemporary comparison. 'I have not seen a case where the time in isolation has been for so long. The only thing I can think of is Guantanamo Bay.'

This working group had established that the investigation had been appallingly run and that the suspects had been subject to mistreatment and torture, but it didn't have the power to send the case back to the Supreme Court to quash the convictions. A second, specific committee was convened for this and again spent several more years deciding whether this should happen. In 2017, it recommended the cases related to the murders should be re-examined by the country's highest court. The one exception was Erla. She hadn't been convicted of any part in the killings but of making false accusations against the Klubburin men. The court had not accepted the mitigation of the mental torture she had endured. This was a massive blow to her and for days after she shut herself away, shunning the many calls from journalists. She vowed to fight on and to get her lawyer to appeal the decision, although the chances of success are slim.

Among the younger generation of Icelanders, the Gudmundur/Geirfinnur cases are an aberration, an embarrassment for a country lauded for its commitment to human rights. But for some of the generation who lived through the 1970s, who read the newspaper headlines and saw the photos of Saevar, Kristjan, Tryggvi and Erla being escorted into court, doubt remains about the innocence of the Reykjavik Six.

The one constant throughout the 40 years has been the silence of the majority of the investigators. Privately, they tell friends they are still convinced of the guilt of the young people they locked in solitary confinement and questioned hundreds of times, going over the same ground again and again. But none of the key Reykjavik detectives has spoken publicly about the case since. They all carried on as detectives and many prospered. Sigurbjorn Eggertsson ended up as the second highest-ranking police officer in Iceland. When the investigators were called to give evidence to a committee in 2016, three officers attended but said they couldn't remember why the most important case in Iceland's history had started.

One group of investigators has been willing to talk: the Keflavik team who first investigated Geirfinnur Einarsson's disappearance. The detective Haukur Gudmundsson wrote a book about the case and now believes the police got it wrong. His old boss, the investigating magistrate Valtyr Sigurdsson who went on to become Iceland's state prosecutor and still practices law, doesn't share this view. Sigurdsson's face is more weathered but has retained some of the boyish good looks from his youth. He admitted that the investigators 'broke every rule, but when we did, it was a development of the criminal courts – it's like saying to doctor you should have used other methods on a patient 40 years ago'. Having read about the torture, solitary confinement and distortion of the suspects' memories, he is still convinced that they got the right people. He wasn't convinced about Erla's insistence that she gave her first statements as she was desperate to be reunited with her daughter. 'She had a young child, a lot of people have young kids – to my mind I just find it unthinkable how you can say the police made up the story.' He has visited Gudjon, his former schoolmate, and the two old men chatted amicably but avoided talking about the case. It was probably for the best, as Valtyr said when he saw Gudjon discussing his conviction on Icelandic TV he thought of him as 'the guiltiest man you've ever seen, his answers didn't make sense'.

Kristjan and Albert continue to shun any publicity about their ordeal. Kristjan spent 682 days in solitary confinement, over 17,000 hours in isolation. He served the longest time in jail, being released in 1987. He married and had two children but his life has been turbulent ever since. He was the one suspect who didn't ask for his case to be brought back to the Supreme Court.

Albert Klahn has never talked about the case publicly since his release in 1981. He spent the least time in solitary confinement – 88 days – but it had a profound effect on him. He is married with children and leads a quiet life in Reykjavik, working as a carpenter and doing charity work in his spare time. Gisli Gudjonsson is one of the few people who Albert has spoken to about the Gudmundur inquiry. Even now it haunts him. 'The sad thing is after almost 40 years, Albert Klahn doesn't know what happened. He doesn't know whether he is guilty or innocent. Can you imagine? After 40 years, you're living in the dread that perhaps you were involved and you can't remember anything.'

Gudjon Skarphedinsson knows how that feels. He was the last suspect to be arrested and spent 412 days in solitary confinement. When he left prison in 1981 he was scared. 'I didn't want to be released. I was afraid but I had no reason to be afraid of anything, so I just went to Copenhagen, which we have always done for 500 years. When everything has gone to pieces, we go to Denmark.' He made a new life there, marrying and getting ordained as a Lutheran minister. He returned to Iceland in 1996, after 15 years abroad, to oversee a parish in Stadurstudur, as far away from civilization as it's possible to get. The village is a smattering of houses and farms stretched across a wide, flat plain between slate black mountains and the foaming ocean. Across the Snaefellsness plain you can see the church for miles, its red roof and spire bold splashes of colour against the thin white covering of snow. It is Gudjon's sanctuary, where he delivers services to the few hundred farmers in his parish under a curved roof painted a deep blue filled with golden stars. When he first arrived, there had been fierce opposition to a convicted murderer taking over the spiritual guidance of the locals. There were several votes to topple Gudjon but he took it all in his stride. As the tide of public opinion turned in the Six's favour he still found opposition among his friends with one convinced he was guilty. 'He wouldn't give it up, he was completely sure of it.'

Stadurstudur was a chance for Gudjon to return to his country roots. Inside his house, though, in a box, lay a brown folder, dust gathering on its spine. Gudjon hasn't looked at the lined yellow pages for decades. It sits on the table in front of him, waiting to be opened but he doesn't like reading it. 'Very soon it reminds me of something I don't want to remember or want to think about.' The man inside this diary is one he doesn't recognise, or doesn't want to. It's a painful reminder that he still has doubts. 'The case never came to an end, it was never cleared up and sometimes it appears to you that it really could have happened.'

In 2015 he retired and left his rural hideout to return to Reykjavik. Gudjon is not looking for redemption, he said the case had made him tough. 'I don't care what people say,' he claims. His memory hasn't mended. So, it remains, the nagging thought that maybe he is a killer. 'It's just one of those things that haunts you, that suddenly appears in your dreams, something from your younger days that you did wrong in your life and you can't do anything about.' Since he has been back in Iceland, Gudjon has never revisited the moribund slipway in Keflavik where he was supposed to have killed Geirfinnur, nor the lava fields where the man's remains may be. But the drives that he took all those years ago to the

Straumsvik aluminium plant; the zoo at Hafnarfjordur and the countless craters and crevasses in the lava fields, still penetrate his thoughts and make him feel like a guilty man. 'Sometimes I still think he is there in those places I was talking about in 1976. I still feel like he is there, that we buried him there. I sometimes wake up or start thinking like that, I think I always will.'

Erla didn't have the same doubts about the Geirfinnur case but when it came to Gudmundur it was a different matter. 'I was never sure with Gudmundur and that's how Albert is still – he knows it didn't happen, but then I knew it didn't happen… it sort of gradually became clear.'

After years of trying to get the police to look at the case again, to investigate who did kill Gudmundur and Geirfinnur, Erla never thought it would happen, but then out of the blue, it did. In June 2016, more than 40 years after Gudmundur Einarsson went missing on a freezing January night, the police arrested two men for his murder. They had received a tip off and it was significant enough that they searched the home of one of the men's partners looking for evidence.

A new witness had come forward who told the police she had been in a VW car driving out of Hafnarfjordur with two men when they had hit Gudmundur by mistake. They put him in the backseat of the car and drove to Reykjavik. The woman remembered Gudmundur saying he was grateful they were taking him home. She saw blood coming out of his ear and it was clear he was hurt badly. The witness got out and wasn't sure if Gudmundur was still alive and never knew what finally happened to him.

With no forensic evidence and only one witness with a recollection 40 years old, the police were unlikely to secure a conviction and, a few months after the arrests, the case was dropped.

After her release, Erla didn't talk to any of the other Reykjavik Six, there was too much pain and bitterness. Slowly over the years that changed. Erla got in touch with Saevar – after all, they had a daughter together who was growing up. When Saevar moved to Denmark on his slow inexorable decline, Erla would visit him and talk to his social worker, though they couldn't stop him sleeping out on the streets, where he spent much of his final years.

Erla has slowly rebuilt her life in Iceland. Released from jail in 1981, for years she felt weighed down by her role. 'I always thought I was guilty of all of it, I always felt solely responsible for everything that had happened. I was the first one who lied and incriminated innocent people, people I loved.'

Having examined the case in detail, Gisli Gudjonsson can see how even now there is a reluctance among the older Icelandic generation to see Erla as a victim. 'Erla has been blamed for a lot – she is seen as this awful person who is a liar who set it off and implicated all of these people. I don't think people have sufficiently looked at her and her circumstances and seen that she was in a no-win situation.'

Cut adrift from most of her family and reviled by the public, Erla felt compelled to leave Iceland as she was 'persona non grata for years'. She lived in Hawaii with her sister and then moved to South Africa, where she married and adopted a daughter before returning to Iceland. The turning point for her was an Icelandic television documentary in 1997 which first questioned the validity of the convictions. This was the time when Saevar was trying to get the case heard again in the Supreme Court, which ultimately failed. The programme caused a huge stir in the country, setting out for the first time some of the glaring inconsistencies in the investigation. 'I sensed people saw me differently after that. I had people coming up to me saying I was a hero.'

Erla went to university and now works as a manager at an adult education centre helping immigrants to settle in Iceland. The young mother has turned into a grandmother with long blonde hair and funky clothing. She still has her throaty laugh and spiky sense of humour, but behind her thin, steel rimmed glasses there is sadness in her eyes. When she talks she tugs at her jumper nervously, pulling the sleeves over her hands like children do when they are anxious. She has created a new life, and her anger towards the police and judges who subjected her to months of interrogations has subsided. 'It's over now, I don't need to see them punished, these guys are decent people but incredibly misguided with a dark agenda serving their own interests and ruining lives. It doesn't mean I don't have moments when the ghosts get out of the room all of a sudden and I'm pissed at all of them.'

Her case was the only one not put forward to the Supreme Court to consider whether it should be quashed. She is trying to get this decision overturned as she wants her name cleared officially. 'I would like the Supreme Court to recognise there is nothing to substantiate any of these stories that are supposed to have happened and conclude that as far as the judicial system is concerned we are innocent.'

It may be a long time before the Supreme Court hears the case and decides whether the convictions should be quashed. This will be the final vindication that they are innocent. Erla said it's no longer about her, it's important this happens for the future generations of her family. 'This case is going to go down in history for a long time. They will say, "That was my great-grandmother and she was innocent." If that doesn't happen there will be a generation that doesn't know the circumstances. I have grandchildren and want them to know Gran was innocent, that their grandma isn't a killer.'

Final Thoughts

The lunchtime crowd thinned out, leaving only a smattering of loud international students and earnest hipsters
when a small blonde woman stepped into the restaurant
on Skolavordustigur in March 2014. Erla Bolladottir was
in her late fifties, dressed in black leggings and a baggy
jumper, her hair cut in a short bob. She glanced around
to see if anyone recognised her, but they were all too
pre-occupied to know that among them was a woman
who had been at the centre of Iceland's most gruesome
and complex murder case.

We sat and drank coffee, chatting about her daughters.
She was open and forthcoming as she had been when I
had talked to her on the phone back in England. Her
story was complex and layered and there were many
parts I didn't understand yet. I knew I would need
patience to tease out all the small but important details.

Across the road from the cafe stood the old prison,
the Hegningarhusid. In the years since she was incarcerated there, awaiting trial Erla had been to the old prison
many times, teaching Icelandic to the foreign prisoners.
We entered, and walked past a long row of cramped,
ageing cells. As we climbed the creaking wooden stairs
to the first floor, Erla looked tense. She was being drawn
back to the time when this jail was her home, where she
lived a miserable, solitary existence. We made our way

into a small, stark white room, dominated by a huge wooden desk. 'This is how it was,' she said, her voice starting to crack. Instinctively I reached across to touch her elbow, checking that she was fine to carry on.

'It's OK until you start asking me what it's like. Then I'm emotional. I've cried a lot in here, and had a nervous breakdown in here. I started throwing things... I could not handle what was going on.'

During my first visit to Iceland, Erla took me to her old home in Hafnarfjordur where Gudmundur was supposed to have been killed; the mournful lava fields where the police believed his body was dumped; the Raudholar where she was accused of watching as Saevar and Kristjan burned and buried the remains of Geirfinnur Einarsson. Even after all these years it was difficult for her to visit these locations. As we stood looking at the frosty red craters she reflected on how tough it had been for her 'living in this community with all the hatred towards us, the need for authorities to acknowledge what they did has only gotten stronger and it doesn't get any better.'

In the four decades since Erla had been convicted, the case kept resurfacing like a bloated corpse that refuses to be weighed down. The solution wasn't in this barren landscape, in the treacherous network of crevasses and fissures – some of them 30 metres deep, enough to swallow a man whole. The answer lay in the minds of the Reykjavik Six and the police and investigators who had placed them in solitary confinement and questioned them repeatedly. What had happened inside the prison and during the police interrogations that would make them confess to two murders they couldn't remember and didn't commit?

My journey to the Reykjavik Confessions began in spring 2014 with the forensic psychologist, Gisli Gudjonsson.

He was being interviewed for a programme about memory and had told a colleague of mine, Helen, about a strange series of events in Iceland that happened 40 years ago, a story little known outside the island nation. Six people had been convicted of two murders they didn't remember. There were no bodies, no forensic evidence, just their confessions. It was unlike any story I had come across before.

The BBC commissioned a long, in-depth online piece and a radio documentary telling the story in detail and I became an integral part of the project. It was a complex and difficult case to understand, and I had the job of writing this story and helping our readers make sense of it. (One of my editors warned me, 'This has to be the best thing you have ever written.') It wasn't just about the facts; I had to get into the minds of some of the key characters, to find out why they would confess to two murders they hadn't committed. I began having phone conversations with Erla, Gisli, Gudjon, and the children of Saevar and Tryggvi, feeling my way into the story.

Weeks later, I arrived in Iceland to investigate with my colleagues, Helen and Andy. Stepping out into that dark winter night the snow was stinging as the flinty wind that forced it under my coat hood and into the soft folds of my scarf. This was the Iceland I had experienced before, raw and uncompromising. I hurried into the warmth of the hire car. The snow began to settle as the car drove along the deserted highway 41 that cuts through the Reykjanes peninsula and the vast petrified ocean that held a secret which continued to haunt Iceland.

A few days later, when Erla took us into these lava fields near her old home in Hafnarfjordur, and we clambered over the cracked, blackened earth where the spring moss was starting to bloom, stretching out to the horizon, I began to realise the frustration of the suspects trying to pinpoint a location they didn't know, and of the police, who could never hope to find a body in such a vast monotonous landscape without help. This was where they all became lost, wandering both literally and metaphorically as the police grasped for any tangible evidence.

Erla was also our guide at the Raudholar where the police believed she had watched Geirfinnur's remains being burned and buried under the hard, red rock. It was important to see the Raudholar, a place I would return to again, to realise the impossibility of digging a grave in freezing temperatures and how the burned remains were never discovered in a place that is always filled with visitors.

Perhaps the biggest challenge was finding witnesses, 40 years after the event, who had been in Sidumuli jail at the time and could provide some insight into what went on. The former prison guard, Gudmundur Gudbjarnarson, was one of these. I had barely arrived at my ugly concrete hotel with its smeared windows when my mobile phone vibrated. It was a text message from an Icelandic number I didn't recognise.

'Is this Simon Cox?' the message asked.

'Who wants to know?' I warily replied.

'I want to meet, to talk about the case,' came the neutral reply.

Almost immediately the mystery texter pinged a follow-up message: 'It's something I haven't told anyone before.'

I'd never gotten a break like this so quickly. When I met Gudmundur a few days later, he wanted to talk about the torture Saevar had experienced and the mistreatment of the other suspects. And he wasn't the only guard who wanted to express his anger at the suspects' treatment. Hlynur Magnusson told me a similar tale when I drove out to the lonely Westfjords where he lived at the end of a steep valley looking over a silvery inlet. Their memories would help me piece together the scattered fragments of the story, even if at times they couldn't remember, or it was too painful or shameful to recall particular events.

I needed to see the documents and diaries that recorded the scrambled memories of the suspects to track how they had been distorted by the repeated interviews and in some cases, years of isolation. I needed to see these tangible remnants from the case, to read through some of the entries and see what effect they still had on the suspects.

One of the most important of these was the brown plastic folder that had been stored away by Gudjon for years in his remote house on a wind blasted plain in Stadurstudur, an hour's drive from the nearest hamlet. It contained the yellowed lined pages of the diary he had written inside Sidumuli prison, painfully charting his time in solitary confinement. Gudjon was clearly uncomfortable looking through the pages and pages of neatly written entries that charted the corrupting of his memory. 'It reminds me of something I don't want to remember or want to think about. This is not a diary about great things happening... There is some desperation and moments of collapse,' he said.

Tryggvi's surviving diaries, kept secret for so long by his daughter, Kristin, were also important to see. Their discovery had propelled the case forward and brought in Gisli Gudjonsson. Gisli too had kept the lie detector test he had conducted on Gudjon – the test that had first given him doubts over his guilt and that Karl Schutz had wanted to get his hands on.

Much of the interaction between the police and suspects was not recorded at all and on the occasions when it was, it would be the briefest precis of the interviews. There was one exception to this, a series of photos that had truly shocked me. I wasn't sure what I would find in the neat automated stacks of the Icelandic National Archive, stored inside a cavernous former cattleshed.

Inside one of the many boxes from the investigations was an astonishing set of black and white photos from 23 January 1977: Karl Schutz's infamous reconstruction in Keflavik. Seeing Kristjan re-enact his purported crimes was jaw dropping. As I went through the images of him posing next to the makeshift dummy of Geirfinnur's body and then holding one of the detectives around the neck in the way he had supposedly strangled Geirfinnur, I could almost see how his memory had been polluted and tainted. This had occurred after a year of interrogations, interviews with the other suspects and visits out to the lava fields, the Raudholar and Keflavik. How could anyone retain a clear sense of their past in such circumstances? All of the suspects had attempted to find a narrative that the detectives would believe, and had turned their fantasies into realty. These became so deeply embedded that even now Albert has doubts about whether or not he took part in the disposal of Gudmundur Einarsson's body, which is why he didn't want to talk to me about it. Gudjon still has doubts too, particularly at night, when he worries that he knows where Geirfinnur Einarsson is buried. Although their prison sentences ended decades ago but what happened to them inside Sidumuli has blighted their lives.

After the online article was published and the documentary aired, I knew the story well but there were still so many unanswered questions about the case. I knew this story was bigger than just an article. I continued wading through the hundreds and hundreds of pages of official documents about the case that recorded the relentless interviews and pressure placed on the young suspects. I spoke to as many people as possible who were there at the time and were willing to share their experiences. I contacted the original investigators, who continued to rebuff my approaches and refused to meet or communicate. Perhaps to admit they were wrong after so long was obviously too much for them, though I heard through third parties that they were still convinced they got the right people.

The evidence, however, does not support this. Whenever I tell people about the Reykjavik Confessions they always ask me 'Are they guilty?' Most people in Iceland, certainly the younger generations, don't doubt the innocence of the Reykjavik Six, while among the older generation there are those who still consider them guilty. They can't or don't want to believe that the police could have gotten it so wrong. It seems, though, that Erla, Saevar and their friends were condemned not for a crime they committed, but for existing on the fringes of main-stream society. Their confessions have long been deemed unreliable, and no evidence of a crime has ever been found. Who knows what the six of them could have done if their lives hadn't been wrecked by their convictions?

At the time of writing, the case is far from complete. The Supreme Court has not decided yet whether to quash the convictions of the five suspects whose cases have been referred to them. The book, for the first time, brings together all of the disparate strands, hearing from witnesses who have never spoken publicly before and laying out how an investigation went out of control and damaged six young people's lives. I hope it serves as a cautionary tale for those who support the use of solitary confinement.

There are so many people to thank who have helped me on this long journey. The two who stand out are Erla and Gisli. Erla was always generous with her time, willing to answer questions and to open up about what is still a very painful wound. Gisli has answered more emails and questions than I can dare to count, and I am deeply indebted to him for his invaluable insight. I also want to thank him for telling my colleague, Helen Grady, about the story in the first place, and starting me on this three-year journey to understand the Reykjavik Confessions. I want to thank Helen for her support and Andy Brownstone who came and filmed some of the haunting landscapes which were so integral to this. Gudjon was the only other surviving suspect willing to give up lots of his time to go back over the minutiae of his isolation in prison and his life before and since the case, over many cups of tea and cake. Saevar's friend Sigurdor Staffsson has an encyclopaedic knowledge of the case that he was willing to share and was always on hand to answer questions. Even in ill health, Hlynur, the former prison guard, was willing to talk or answer messages and Gudmundur – the mystery texter – wanted to tell me of his concerns when he was a prison guard at Sidumuli. Tryggvi's daughter, Kristin, also generously gave her time and energy. I hope the conclusion of the Supreme Court case will bring them all some peace and closure.

Simon Cox
London, November 2017